Schumpeterian Economics

Schumpeterian Economics

EDITED BY

Helmut Frisch

PRAEGER

PRAEGER SPECIAL STUDIES • PRAEGER SCIENTIFIC

Published in 1981 by Praeger Publishers
CBS Educational and Professional Publishing
A Division of CBS, Inc.
1 St Anne's Road, Eastbourne, East Sussex BN21 3UN, UK
and 521 Fifth Avenue, New York, New York 10017, USA

British Library Cataloguing in Publication Data

Schumpeterian economics.
1. Schumpeter, Joseph Alois
2. Economics—History
I. Frisch, Helmut
330.15'7 HB107.S/

ISBN 0-03-062766-4

Photoset by Paston Press, Norwich
Printed and bound in Great Britain by
Biddles Ltd, Guildford and King's Lynn

Print Number: 987654321

List of Contributors

Martin Bronfenbrenner, Kenan Professor of Economics, Duke University, Durham, NC 27706, USA.

Bruno S. Frey, Institut für Empirische Wirtschaftsforschung der Universität Zürich, Forchstrasse 145, CH-8032-Zürich, Switzerland.

Helmut Frisch, Institut für Volkswirtschaftslehre und Wirtschaftspolitik der Technischen, Universität Wien, Karlsplatz 13, A-1040-Wien, Austria.

Herbert Giersch, Institut für Weltwirtschaft an der Universität Kiel, Postfach 4309, D-2300-Kiel 1, Germany.

Arnold Heertje, University of Amsterdam, 17 Laegiskampweg, Naarden, Netherlands.

Eduard März, Schottenring 23, A-1010-Wein, Austria.

Mark Perlman Managing Editor, Journal of Economic Literature, PO Box 7320, Oakland Station, Pittsburgh, Penn 15213, USA.

Kurt W. Rothschild, Institut für Volkswirtschaftslehre, Johannes Kepler Universität Linz, A-4045-Linz-Auhof, Austria.

Paul Samuelson, Department of Economics, Massachusetts Institute of Technology, Cambridge, MA 02139, USA.

Wolfgang Stolper, Department of Economics, University of Michigan, Ann Arbor, Michigan 48109, USA.

Erich Streissler, Institut für Wirtschaftswissenschaften, Universität Wien, Dr Karl Lueger Ring 1, A-1010-Wien, Austria.

CONTENTS

PREFACE

THIS collection of essays is the outcome of a symposium on the scientific work of the great Austrian economist Joseph A. Schumpeter, held at the Austrian Academy of Sciences in November 1980. The symposium was sponsored by the Österreichische Länderbank on the occasion of its centennial celebration as a tribute to all those engaged in economic research. The publication of this book was made possible by a generous contribution from Insinger, Willems & Cie., private bankers in Amsterdam.

The reader may well ask, why is Schumpeter so popular among bankers? This should not be difficult to answer, as Schumpeter, although stressing the role of entrepreneurs in the economic process, had always held the view that successful entrepreneurs must be backed by bankers who will finance the innovation process and bear the risk. Schumpeter makes credit creation through a *complaisant* banking system even part of his definition of the capitalist system: 'Capitalism is that form of private property economy in which innovations are carried out by means of borrowed money, which in general though not by logical necessity, implies credit creation.' (*Business Cycles*, Vol. I p. 223)

The present volume complements a book edited by Arnold Heertje called *Schumpeter's Vision* which is concerned with the prospect of capitalism 40 years after the publication of *Capitalism, Socialism and Democracy*. The initiative to commission *Schumpeter's Vision* came from Insinger, Willems & Cie., who celebrated their bicentenary in 1979. Compared with Professor Heertje's book, this volume has a wider spectrum. It is an attempt by ten distinguished economists from different countries to assess Schumpeter's contribution to economic theory.

In the 1960s and 1970s Schumpeter's work was overshadowed by Keynes and the Keynesians. With the crisis of the mixed economy since the 1970s and the failures of the Keynesian policy programmes and remedies, it is reasonable to expect a revival of interest in Schumpeter's work and his style of analysis.

I would like to express my thanks to the Österreichische Länderbank for the sponsorship of the symposium and Insinger, Willems & Cie. for making possible the publication of this book, which I hope will contribute to deepening our understanding of Schumpeter's work and the economic and social developments of our time.

HELMUT FRISCH

INTRODUCTION

HELMUT FRISCH

J. A. Schumpeter, enfant terrible *from Vienna*

'MOST of the creations of the intellect or fancy', wrote Schumpeter, 'pass away for good after a time that varies between an after-dinner hour and a generation'. (*CSD*, p. 3.) Only intellectual achievements which last longer than one generation, he believed, may be called 'great'. Judged by this standard the works of J. A. Schumpeter, without a doubt, belong to the great intellectual achievements in the social sciences in our century.

Joseph Alois Schumpeter was born in 1883 in Triesch, Moravia, as the son of the owner of a textile factory. In the same year, Karl Marx died (whose work Schumpeter admired), and John Maynard Keynes was born. Schumpeter attended the *Theresianum* (an élite academic high school) in Vienna and then studied law and economics at the University of Vienna. At the early age of 26 and with the support of his teacher Eugen von Böhm-Bawerk he became a professor at the University of Czernowitz (in Bukowina), a cultural outpost of the Austro-Hungarian monarchy. From 1911 to the end of the First World War he taught as a professor at the University of Graz. In 1919 he temporarily left university life and stepped out onto the somewhat more slippery floors of politics: in the spring of 1919 he accepted an appointment as a Minister of Finance in the cabinet of State Chancellor Karl Renner. After only seven months, however, he slipped and resigned, without having achieved much success. He then became the president of the Biederman Bank, a small but very prestigious private bank. Unfortunately, in 1924 the bank collapsed, and Schumpeter not only lost his fortune but ended up in debt. From this rather unpleasant situation he was rescued by an appointment at the University of Bonn in 1925 where he remained as professor until 1932. From 1932 until his death in 1950 he taught economics at Harvard University, and was, together with John Maynard Keynes, the most well-known although not the most influential economist of his generation.

The first four chapters in this collection are organized around Schumpeter's two classic books, *Theory of Economic Development* and the two volume *Business Cycles*; they are from Paul A. Samuelson, Wolfgang Stolper, Herbert Giersch and Erich Streissler.

In the subsequent four chapters by Arnold Heertje, Martin Bronfenbrenner, Kurt W. Rothschild and Bruno Frey the focus is on problems raised by Schumpeter in his *Capitalism, Socialism and Democracy*. Mark Perlman's chapter deals with Schumpeter's *History of Economic Analysis* and the final chapter by Eduard März provides an assessment of Schumpeter's role as Minister of Finance in Austria.

Paul A. Samuelson concentrates on an evaluation of Schumpeter's zero interest rate doctrine. Schumpeter's theory argues that in a stationary economy (that is, a circular flow equilibrium) the rate of interest would be zero. The positive rate of interest in the non-stationary economy is the result of entrepreneurial innovations set out in Schumpeter's *Theory of Economic Development*. Samuelson who discusses Schumpeter's model in the framework of the Ramsey–Solow one-sector model finds it logically consistent but highly implausible, from an economic point of view.

Schumpeter's steady-state solution holds only under two conditions: (1) the absence of innovations; and (2) a zero rate of interest. The first point leads directly into the centre of capital theory, i.e. whether investment opportunities would quickly be exhausted in the absence of technical progress and innovations. Schumpeter's assumption that there may be no investment opportunities in a stationary state is probably related to his concept of the 'static economic agent' (*Statischer Wirt*), who repeats indefinitely his method of production once he has chosen it. As soon as we assume that a 'rational' economic agent (not an entrepreneur) exists, as in the neo-classical theory. the viewpoints of E. von Böhm-Bawerk, I. Fisher, G. Cassel and P. A. Samuelson seem more appropriate. According to this viewpoint a practically unlimited set of investment opportunities would exist, also without innovations. Investment depends then only upon the level of the interest rate. At a zero interest rate, excess demand for capital goods would develop which would in turn raise the interest rate above zero.

The second condition of Schumpeter's steady state is the absence of a positive time preference. Economic agents evaluate present and future income absolutely equal, i.e. the marginal rate of substitution of present for future income is one. Because in Schumpeter's stationary economy the economic agents always expect the same income stream it is not irrational to evaluate present and future income equally. But Samuelson argues that this is an assumption of Schumpeter and not a conclusion. Only a Robinson Crusoe who lives forever will not have a subjective time preference. Since we think of dying, we expect that people attach more weight to their present situation than to the needs of their remote heirs. Empirically, we always introduce the element of subjective time preference into the model.

P. A. Samuelson's detailed chapter is concerned with the 'extreme' version of Schumpeter's stationary economy. A less extreme version, as G. Haberler (1951) set out, could admit a positive (though probably low) rate of interest in a stationary economy. Not much is achieved with this change, since Schumpeter needs the stationary economy only as a logical contrast to his theory of economic development in which he uses a 'disequilibrium' approach.

The following chapter by *W. Stolper* contributes a careful and critical analysis of Schumpeter's 'disequilibrium approach' applied in his *Theory of Economic Development* and his *Business Cycles*. Schumpeter's central task is to explain how the economic equilibrium is disrupted. To upset the equilibrium, to destroy it, requires more than routine; it requires a particular sociological type of genius, 'entrepreneurs' who break through the stability of equilibrium with 'innovations', i.e. with new methods of production and/or new goods. To quote W. Stolper '. . . the importance and achievement of entrepreneurial action is to disrupt the equilibrium'. The innovation process will initiate a movement away from equilibrium, a cyclical upswing with high temporary profits (in other words, pioneer profits) for innovating firms. In the course of the boom phase the mills of imitative competitors will erode the transient pioneer profit. 'Innovation' to quote Stolper again, 'is the "*creative* destruction" of the existing equilibrium through a change in the production function, brought about by the "entrepreneurs" and financed typically by credit creation.'

This brings us to the second essential point of Schumpeter's vision of the capitalist development: money creation. Schumpeter's entrepreneurial innovations are financed by credit creations and not by savings. The social function of money (credit) creation is to permit entrepreneurs to take resources out of the income stream before they have put resources into it. The *complaisant* money-creating banking system is needed to break into the equilibrium stream. Schumpeter emphasizes that this system of financing innovations if of an inflationary nature. But this kind of credit is self-correcting. Once the innovation yields output and sales and hence an income stream to the innovating firm, the credit can be repaid. If for any model Milton Friedman's dictum applies: 'money matters', then of course for Schumpeter's model. Schumpeter makes money creation even part of his definition of the capitalist system: was Schumpeter therefore a 'monetarist'? By no means, answers Stolper. Schumpeter's objection to monetarism is that it ignores structural changes in the economy. Or to put it differently, the monetarists assume that it makes no difference how the additional money enters the economy. The same objection holds against the Keynesians; in this respect monetarists are no different from the Keynesians. In a somewhat charitable interpretation, Schumpeter's innovation process may be the common sense of the more recent insistence on the 'supply side economics'.

H. Giersch describes the West German process of reconstruction and rapid economic growth after the Second World War as a Schumpeterian process of economic development. The beginning of this development was characterized by:

1. A considerable destruction of the capital stock.
2. An influx of refugees.
3. The pressure on real wages through excess supply of labour, reducing real wages below the marginal product of labour.
4. An undervalued deutsch mark ensuring the low wage rate and high marginal productivity of capital in the exposed sector of the economy.

These were the initial conditions for a rapid economic growth in West Germany. The core of this process was the production and supply of 'Schumpeter goods'. The latter are defined by Giersch as 'new goods with a still secret production function'. The reconstruction and growth of the capital stock did not follow the neo-classical scheme of an increase in the capital stock in the sense of more of the same (von Böhm-Bawerk, Solow), but it was 'Schumpeter-capital', an increase in productive capacity through a changed structure because of a changed production function. The burst of innovations underlying this growth process can be explained by the new technology and knowledge imported from abroad and embodied in modern investment goods as a by-product of international trade, especially with the USA. However, the pivotal question for the Schumpeter process is, where did the wave of new entrepreneurs come from? Professor Giersch offers a sociological answer. First, from among the refugees from East Germany, Czechoslovakia and Poland, second, from among the former officers of the German military, many of whom had learned 'entrepreneurship' (leadership and ability to improvise) during the Second World War. In addition many of them faced post-war legal and social barriers to entering many of the traditional, prestigious professions. By becoming successful entrepreneurs some of them were able to gain their desired social status.

E. Streissler considers Schumpeter's economic thoughts in the context of the social and economic developments of the Habsburg monarchy at the turn of the century. In this civil service and rentier society, merchants and manufacturers hardly played an important social or economic role. Schumpeter's celebration of creative entrepreneurs and their significance for economic growth ran completely counter to all the traditional Austrian preconceptions. 'It was absolutely shocking in a conservative civil service state to praise anyone for creating disorder and to suggest that creation of unrest could have a useful social function.' (E. Streissler)

Although the glorification of the entrepreneur ran counter to the social values in Schumpeter's Vienna, it did not run counter to the academic tradition in economics. Streissler maintains that Schumpeter's elitist theory of the economic leadership of the entrepreneur was completely developed by Friedrich von Wieser. Streissler only accepts two ideas as being new and Schumpeter's own: (1) the concept that the inflationary effect of a credit expansion stimulates economic growth and (2) the idea that credit creation is a necessary prerequisite for innovation.

The idea that inflation (even temporarily) stimulates growth opposed the orthodox theory in Austria (von Böhm-Bawerk). Streissler explains this by Schumpeter's origin. The son of an entrepreneur asserts that inflation caused by a commercial credit expansion helps entrepreneurs, who in turn help society through their investments which accelerate economic growth.

The second idea was counterfactual in Old Austria. The major banks were mainly engaged in reorganizing enterprises and financing the expansion of firms to obtain the benefits of economies of scale. The Austrian banks therefore financed capital deepening of existing firms rather than innovations by newcomers.

In general Schumpeter's model of economic development cannot be considered as a theoretical description of the historical development in Austria at the turn of the century. If there is any historical equivalent to Schumpeter's model it might have been the capitalist development in England, to quote Streissler, 'of what he thought was happening in England and what he thought did *not* happen in Austria.'

Let us turn to the second group of papers, concerned with problems raised in Schumpeter's *Capitalism, Socialism and Democracy*. As is well known, Schumpeter based his forecast of capitalism's early demise on three points, which are summarized by M. Bronfenbrenner and K. W. Rothschild thus:

1. Erosion of the entrepreneurial function.
2. Destruction of the protective strata of petty bourgeois and farmers.
3. Encouragement of a rational and critical attitude which eventually turns against the capitalist system.

P. A. Samuelson (1981) draws a useful analogy from medicine. If we consider capitalism as a patient what is the outlook? Some of the doctors state that the patient will inevitably die but they cannot agree in the diagnosis. One school believes that the patient is dying of malignant cancer (erosion of the entrepreneurial function). Schumpeter's argument is that innovation (i.e. the application and implementation of 'new combinations') will be reduced more to the level of a routine. The economic leadership called entrepreneurship will become less relevant as technical progress tends to become depersonalized and automatized. In Schumpeter's own words: 'Since capitalist enterprise, by its very achievements, tends to automatize progress we conclude that it tends to make itself superfluous—to break to pieces under the pressure of its own success' (*CSD*, p. 134).

Here *A. Heertje* enters and disputes the diagnosis of malignant cancer (A. Heertje, 'Schumpeter's model of the decay of capitalism'). His analysis is based on two lines. First, he redefines Schumpeter's notion of the 'entrepreneur', and second he confronts Schumpeter's vision with the actual developments of the Western economies after the Second World War. Following Kirzner, he assumes that the entrepreneurial component of economic action is the missing link between invention and innovation. It is a particular alertness to information, the awareness for new opportunities and the response to possibilities offered by the market system. He then argues that certain stages of the application and execution of new ideas can be routinized, but the property of being alert to marketable applications is an individual characteristic not atp to being automatized. In this sense entrepreneurship never was and never will be a matter of routine. Heertje concludes that Schumpeter's diagnosis based on cancer was wrong and will remain wrong.

The second school, too, admits that the patient is dying but gives another diagnosis, namely a psychosomatic ailment. Not cancer but neurosis is the patient's problem. Filled with self-hate, he will lose his will to survive (point (3) above, the critical attitude). *M. Bronfenbrenner* in his essay 'Schumpeter's contribution to the study of comparative economic systems' develops this argument. Capitalism earns the active opposition of the class of intellectuals by displacing them from positions of social status. 'If you're so smart, why aren't you rich?' Primarily from the disaffection of the intellectuals, Schumpeter and Bronfenbrenner believe, arises the legislative overactivity which spoils the system and causes entrepreneurial capitalism to stagnate and decline.

There exists, however, a third diagnosis implicit in Schumpeter's *Capitalism, Socialism and Democracy* which was recently developed by T. Scitovsky (1980) with direct reference to Schumpeter. According to this diagnosis the patient is dying because of calcification. It is the regulatory activities of the government prompted by concerns over health, production, safety, income equality, etc. together with monopoly pricing which deprives the capitalist system of the flexibility and adaptability and leads to calcification. Given these millstones around its neck, capitalism lives only in the oxygen tent of government deficit spending and other forms of inflationary financing.

Schumpeter not only predicted the decay of capitalism, he expected simultaneously a movement towards socialism which one may approve of or not. As *K. W. Rothschild* notes in his 'Schumpeter and socialism', socialism in

Schumpeter's sense is a textbook model, a system in which control over production and investment is exercised by a central authority, and economic affairs belong to the public rather than to the private sphere. Although part III of *Capitalism, Socialism and Democracy* is labelled 'Can socialism work?' Schumpeter reveals very little about how such a socialist system functions. Bronfenbrenner says in this context: 'When Schumpeter tells us that socialism works he include in "working" anything from Utopia to the mere avoidance of breakdown. Thus, a Post Office "works" in his sense as long as (eventual) mail delivery continues between postal strikes.'

Because of his narrow definition of capitalism as the unfettered capitalism and because of his old-fashioned socialism, he was not able to give a thorough analysis of the grey area in-between, for example the bureaucratic capitalism, the Labourite capitalism (in Sweden, Norway, Austria, or the UK under the Labour government) and he did not expect the mixed economy, whose evolution he correctly perceived, to be a well-functioning method of running the Western economics. Finally, both Bronfenbrenner and Rothschild find Schumpeter's disregard for the *tertium quid*, meaning the non-socialist alternatives to capitalism, more than strange. Fascism was at its zenith while Schumpeter was writing *Capitalism, Socialism and Democracy* but he ignored its ideology almost completely in the volume. Schumpeter was so fascinated by the idea that capitalism was headed for a rendezvous with socialism that he considered fascism as eventually equivalent to socialism, or as a temporary station on 'the road that leads from capitalism to orthodox socialism.'

B. Frey in his chapter, 'Schumpeter, political economist', examines Schumpeter's model of democracy. Schumpeter's famous definition of democracy reads: 'That institutional arrangement for arriving at political decisions in which individuals acquire the power to decide by means of a competitive struggle for the people's vote.' This definition implies first that democracy is considered as a mechanism for arriving at social outcomes: it is not defined in terms of the outcome (for example, realizing the 'common good'). Second, the definition implies that democracy is closely related to economic competition. The political leaders conducting the competitive struggle are the equivalent of the entrepreneurs. Third, the favourable outcome of the competitive struggle for votes is only a side product as it is the case in the competitive struggle in the market economy. From this analysis Schumpeter drew two conclusions which have been elaborated and stressed in modern public choice analysis.

1. The competitive struggle for votes forces the politicians to adopt a short-run outlook because voters judge their performance by the immediate effect.
2. The competition for votes forces the parties to advance positions which closely resemble each other.

Although Schumpeter's *Capitalism, Socialism and Democracy* contains the essentials of what constitute today's public choice theory, B. Frey notes with astonishment that it has been developed to a large extent independently of Schumpeter. He is convinced that many hidden treasures are waiting to be discovered. His advice is to re-read Schumpeter and introduce some of his ideas into modern political economy.

M. Perlman's chapter deals with Schumpeter as a historian of economic thought. He notes that Schumpeter sought to distinguish between the history of economic thinking and the history of scientific economic analysis. While Perlman thinks that this effort had much going for it from a pedagogical standpoint, it was not in the end successful. The chapter contains a reader's guide to Schumpeter's monumental *History of Economic Analysis* (published posthumoursly in 1954). It is organized around Schumpeter's preferred subdivisions of the field: (1) an era of philosophical dominance until 1790 (thus making Adam Smith, no favourite of Schumpeter's, the tail end of a tradition rather than an innovator); (2) the classical era, 1790–1870; (3) the period of various schools and emergent sub-disciplines; and (4) finally the modern era when the effort was to discover the principles of a dynamic theory of general equilibrium.

The third part of Perlman's chapter is an interesting comparison of Schumpeter's approach with that of Wesley C. Mitchell, the other eminent and sophisticated scholar in the history of economic thought. The two men were competitors in several areas (e.g. business cycles). Mitchell was more Anglo-American history oriented; Schumpeter was by far the greater intellectual panorama painter. Mitchell thought that economic thinking reflected time-tied events; Schumpeter thought that what was dominant were underlying universal truths.

Perlman ends with a report of the principal reviews of the *History of Economic Analysis*. Most were laudatory yet full of basic or essential reservations.

In 1919 Schumpeter had held for little more than half a year the position of Austrian Minister of Finance. 'It can safely be stated', says *E. März* in his essay, 'that the young professor of economics was excellently prepared for assuming this position.' However, the *intermezzo* of this great economist in the domain of politics was not very successful. E. März analyses Schumpeter's reform programme to stabilize the desperate financial plight of the Austrian state in 1919. Schumpeter's programme was a conservative, 'monetarist' one based on five points. First, a great capital levy, mainly designed to eliminate the war debt; second, stabilization of the exchange rate of the Austrian crown; third, the foundation of the new Central Bank independent of the government; fourth, a stronger reliance upon indirect taxation; fifth, the development of conditions to increase the 'credit worthiness' of the Austrian industry. A key role in his appointment to the cabinet but also in his early political downfall was played by the prominent leader of the Austrian Socialist Party, Otto Bauer, whom he had known as a student at the University of Vienna.

Schumpeter had received Bauer's sympathy with his public advocacy of a capital levy. During his short term in office a certain animosity developed between the two politicians, caused mainly by the question of the Anschluss with Germany: Bauer strongly favoured it, Schumpeter opposed it. The actual occasion for his political downfall was the sale of the majority of the stocks of Alpine Montangesellschaft, the largest Austrian enterprise, to a Milanese banking house backed by Fiat. Bauer and the other socialist leaders accused Schumpeter of having supported the sale in order to prevent the nationalization of Alpine Montangesellschaft. Be that as it may, Schumpeter found no sympathy for his plan to reform the government budget situation. He had lost the support of the socialists but he had also lost the support of the conservative party by his rigorous conception of the capital levy and his occasional flirtation with a few socialist ideas. His early resignation was, to quote E. März, 'the logical result of his total political isolation'.

Joseph A. Schumpeter was throughout his life an *enfant terrible*, a totally 'impossible' man as Streissler says in his essay. For the sake of argument he was often ready to take extrème positions. Whenever he saw a chance to irritate those around him, he frequently seized it. Attitudinizing and an open delight in provocation had always been elements of his work. It is therefore not surprising that a large number of anecdotes about such a personality are in circulation. Perhaps it might be useful to conclude this introduction with two of them, which may characterize him better than any long description.

In 1918 he became a member of the Socialization Commission of the German socialist government in Berlin. He was asked, why he—by no means a socialist—the admirer of entrepreneurial capitalism, had accepted this appointment. He replied: 'If there has to be a suicide, a doctor really ought to be present.' In his later years, at Harvard University he liked to tease his students with the following story: 'As a youth I had set myself three goals in life: to become the best lover in Vienna, the finest horseback rider in Austria and the greatest economist in the world.' He then liked to add: 'Unfortunately, I was able to accomplish only two of them'. However, he never said which two.

REFERENCES

Haberler, G. (1951) Schumpeter's theory of interest. *Review of Economics and Statistics*, **33**, 1951, pp. 122–8.

Samuelson, P. A. (1981) Schumpeter's Capitalism, Socialism and Democracy, in *Schumpeter's Vision: Capitalism, Socialism and Democracy after 40 years*. Heertje, A. (Ed.) London and New York: Praeger.

Schumpeter, J. A. (1912) *Theory of Economic Development*. Cambridge, MA: Harvard University Press.

Schumpeter, J. A. (1939) *Business Cycles: A Theoretical, Historical and Statistical Analysis of the Capitalist Process*. 2 Volumes. New York: McGraw-Hill.

Schumpeter, J. A. (1942) *Capitalism, Socialism and Democracy*. (3rd enlarged Edition 1950. 5th Edition 1976 with a new introduction) London: Allen & Unwin.

Schumpeter, J. A. (1954) *The History of Economic Analysis*. Schumpeter, E. B. (ed.) New York: Oxford University Press.

Scitovsky, T. (1980) Can capitalism survive? An old question in a new setting. Richard Ely Lecture, *American Economic Review*, **70** (May), pp. 1–9.

Chapter One

Schumpeter as an Economic Theorist

PAUL A. SAMUELSON

SCHUMPETER was a universalist in economics. Mention a field in the subject of political economy, and you will find his name already established there: economic theory, macroeconomic business cycles, methodology, econometrics, Marxian economics, economic history, *Dogmengeschichte*—the list is only countably finite.

In a discipline that is undergoing dynamic development and being swept by gales of creative destruction, it is lucky if a scholar of age 67 is even remembered or curtsied to. Yet, at the time of his death, a citation index shows that Joseph Schumpeter was the scholar most often cited in the whole field of economics. As he himself might put it, 'This is a remarkable performance.' It is one that ought to have brought him satisfaction and fulfilment. But his was an enterpreneurial nature whose appetite for scientific achievement grew by what it fed upon.

The Wagnerian hero does not strive to be a Jack-of-all-trades and Schumpeter, I venture to suspect, would have traded his Popeship for a Keynesian revolution. Moreover, often we want what it is that we are not. A beautiful woman wishes to be clever, a sage to be an Olympic athlete. Norbert Wiener would trade ten mathematical theorems and three lemmas for one biological discovery. I have retold Schumpeter's story about his three wishes in life—to be the greatest lover in Austria, the best horseman in Europe, and the greatest economist in the world—and his regret of having failed to fulfil the second wish. It is not a joke that Joseph Schumpeter aspired to scholarly greatness, however lighthearted his tone and amusing his stories. As with Sigmund Freud and Abraham Lincoln, from the time of puberty there was a little clock in Schumpeter's breast ticking with the impulse for scholarly fame. Before I knew of Robert J. Merton's sociology of scientists, before I had myself articulatred that the coin we scholars work for is our own applause, the example of my old Harvard teacher taught me this not-really-dirty little secret about the motives that run scientists.

Yes, Schumpeter may have envied a Keynes. Or a Ricardo, who changed the course of one of intellectual history's rivers. But we know that Schumpeter also had a certain condescension and contempt towards the economist who comprised his scientific birthright for a mess of populist pottage. And it is sad that Schumpeter's great 1942 *Capitalism, Socialism and Democracy* did not have greater worth in its author's own eyes.

I suspect that, in Schumpeter's heart of hearts, the scholar he admired most was the economic theorist, Ragnar Frisch. To have innovated in the many corridors of pure theory as Frisch had done—and then himself to surpass such magnificent performance by creating his own Newtonian *Principia*—that might have brought fulfilment to Joseph Schumpeter's insatiable soul.

Nihil Nisi?

As the centenary of Joseph Schumpeter's birth looms close, we are in a orgy of discussions of him and his works. To prepare for this symposium, to contribute a chapter to Professor Heertje's symposium volume, *Schumpeter's Vision Capitalism, Socialism and Democracy after 40 Years*, and to clarify my own thinking on the economic future at century's end for the Mexico City World Economic Congress, I have found myself preoccupied with Schumpeter's thought and person. It is a pleasant orgy, and a rewarding one. But it is boring to say the same thing twice and to have to engage in elegant variation merely to avoid exact repetition.

Already I have written much on Schumpeter. For his sixtieth *Festschrift* in the 1943 *Review of Economics and Statistics*, I wrote to clarify the logic and taxonomy of statics and dynamics. At the same time I both defended the *logic* of the *possibility* of zero interest rate in the stationary state and, as much as was meet in a scholar's own *Festschrift*, queried the importance of Schumpeter's dogma on that point. Shortly after Schumpeter's death in January 1950, I contributed a chapter to Seymour Harris's 1951 memorial volume, *Joseph Schumpeter: Social Scientist*, and returned there to the subject of his own interest theory.

I was honoured to have my memoir on 'Schumpeter as a teacher and economic theorist' appear along with the excellent essays by Arthur Smithies, Gottfried Haberler, Wolfgang Stolper, Paul Sweezy, Herbert von Beckerath, Arthur Marget, Erich Schneider, and others. As I re-read my words, I feel they catch much of what that remarkable man was. Still a problem of decorum does arise, a delicate question of whether and how to apply the doctrine of *de morituri nihil nisi bonum*. Should one's pen write of a beloved teacher that he was a 'showman' (or, a bit of a poseur)? What warts—beloved warts—should be airbrushed out of the photograph?

Within the family one speaks freely of Mama's engaging foibles, Brother's accident-proneness, Aunt Sophie's tone-deafness. But that does not mean that you should sell your Grandfather for a wisecrack. For a reserved and dignified scholar like Frank Taussig, the eulogist encounters few problems. With an engaging extrovert like Schumpeter, who loved to *épater* the bourgeoisie, aristocracy, priesthood, proletariat and the universal set, how acute the problem has to be for biographers. As Paul Sweezy used to say, 'You hate to hear outsiders criticize Schumpie; but within the inner circle, you find much to criticize.'

Moses Outside the Promised Land

There is an element of anticlimax in my assignment for today—to talk about Schumpeter as an economic theorist. Since Schumpeter's most theoretical work was his first German book of 1908—*Das Wesen und Hauptinhault der theoretischen Nationalökonomie*—my inadequate mastery of German disqualifies me for the assigned task. Also, though much of the world regarded Schumpeter as the very essence of an economic theorist, he regarded himself as in a sense a theorist *manqué*. When singing the praises of more exact methods in our beloved science of economics, Schumpeter claimed he was entitled to do so with a better right since his own work was primarily not in the airy heights of mathematical theory. He would have loved to team up, later in life with someone like Nicholas Georgescu-Roegen, to write a profound treatise on modern economic theory. After that he could toss off his mathematical logic, complete his sociology, and in well-earned old age write his novel.

If it was not given to Moses to enter into the Promised Land, it is understandable that he should have tended to exhalt the promise of that fair country. So with Schumpeter. His schemata of three interacting cycles—the intermediate Juglar wave, superimposed on the shorter Kitchen cycle and the longer Kondratieff cycle—seemed less commanded by the facts of economic history than by Schumpeter's fascination with the mysteries of harmonic analysis. If a Ragnar Frisch came up with a new inflection-point technique for identifying cyclical phases, Schumpeter's admiration for Newtonian dynamics made him a favourable consumer to buy his theories. Chamberlin and Robinson, through their geometrical novelties, gained Schumpeter's support for their new theories of imperfect competition. Leon

Walras's comprehensive equations of general equilibrium represented the pinnacle of economics for Schumpeter. Böhm-Bawerk's tortured numerical examples tended to be put to a discount, perhaps because they were the sort of thing Schumpeter himself could so easily do. My own early work in *revealed preference*, Schumpeter if anything overvalued, because it brought into economics some of the elegance and economy of the most exact sciences and of mathematical logic itself.

Eclectic Methodologist

Young Schumpeter was a stormy petrel. He did not mind giving offence. He was not a good Austrian, in that he whored after mathematical economics, praised American and English economics, and questioned some of the established verities of Böhm-Bawerk. All this is in character.

One might then expect Schumpeter to take an extreme position in the debate between the German Historical School and the theorists of Austria and England. Perhaps to thumb his nose at his teachers, Schumpeter might have been expected to embrace Marxism; or to speak up for empiricism; or to denounce all grubbing in the facts. But it was not so. From the beginning his methodology took the eclectic road of good sense. In his view, inductive facts need to interact with simplifying theories whose logical implications are rigorously deduced with the help of advanced mathematics; probability techniques must be applied to interpret that which is ephemeral and singular in the empirical data from that which is persistent. Ricardo and Menger have merit. But so do Schmoller and List. Even Karl Marx, especially for his *chutzpah* in attempting to devise a dynamic theory for all aspects of the social universe, deserves praise.

Before there was a Vienna Circle, Schumpeter and Pareto embraced a separation of positivist science from normative aspiration. Before Tom Kuhn entered kindergarten, Schumpeter emphasized: It takes a theory to kill a theory; no dirty single fact can do so and, given our need to have a systematic way of thinking about complicated reality, our present theories will hold their place even in the face of cascades of *ad hoc* discordant observations.

At the same time that Schumpeter hailed the new, he warned against the Whig historians' propensity to criticize the historic great because they did not wear present-day beards and cravats and did not know all we have since learned. Each generation is entitled to its own mistakes, which if made by a Newton or Ricardo can be of interest in their own right. (I would add that this does not absolve us from the responsibility of naming as mistakes that which is mistaken.)

This core of good sense—unlike Schumpeter, I can never identify good sense with *common sense*—sometimes got concealed under Schumpeter's patronizing affectation of omniscience. It is not quite the case that Schumpeter's posthumous *History of Economic Doctrines* (1954) contains the lines, 'I shall not weary the reader with discussions of the 83 economists whose views dominated Rome from 100 B.C. to 53 A.D., for the reason that she or he will know much more about them than I do.' But somewhat similar passages do occur, and experience shows that readers will make an error if they think that Schumpeter is dropping names of authorities he has not tackled. The erudition he parades was erudition—*his* erudition.

PREVIEW

Since I was Schumpeter's student and friend for the last fifth of his life, I shall begin by recording some of my memories from his lectures and oral discourses. My account accords him less than full credit since what is memorable in a scholar is what is unexpected. The countless doctrines that he early appreciated at their correct worth are lost to memory, and one hardly remembers his judgements on people that merely agree with the conventional wisdom.

Then, in the last part of this paper, I stop chattering about theorists and Schumpeter's theoretical views. I actually do some economic theorizing, applying standard modern tools to Schumpeter's own paradigm of the interest rate. Although what I do here seems never to have been done in its entirety, it does not really have to be done. I show in the end that my extended analysis, using the standard neoclassical model of Solow, leads precisely to the conclusions and emphases arrived at briefly by Gottfried Haberler, Schumpeter's affable younger colleague. My elaborate Ramsey dynamics only corroborate what Haberler's (1951) simple Fisherine diagram showed. Nonetheless, as we approach the Schumpeter centennial year, a little excess of attention to his analysis can be forgiven.

Personal Likes

I can recall some of the theorists Schumpeter especially admired. He adored his brilliant young colleague Wassily Leontief. He had great respect for Leontief's teacher at Berlin, L. von Bortkiewicz, honouring his Herculean labours in trying to keep clean the Augean stables of economics, but regretting that more of von Bortkiewicz's energies did not go into creative innovations all his own. On the other hand, the corrosive common-sensical criticisms of an Edwin Cannan, Schumpeter rather underrated, being turned off by Cannan's antipathy to anything fancy and by his overconclusive simplifications. Knut Wicksell, Schumpeter beatified. But Wicksell's more highly publicized rival, Gustav Cassel, Schumpeter despised as a plagiarist, saying: 'Cassel is 10 per cent Walras and 90 per cent water.' He did faint-praise Cassel's textbook, as exactly what was needed on the Continent at the time. (I think Cassel, for all his personal faults, pretensions, and over-simplifications is now underrated as an original analyst.)

Before the world took much notice of American economists, Schumpeter singled out J. B. Clark for attention and respect. He found Irving Fisher amusing for his solemn do-goodism and health faddisms, but that never diminished his reverence for Fisher's theoretical innovations in value theory and interest determination. Schumpeter studied carefully the works of Carver, Fetter (who took him to his first and probably only football game), Walker, H. L. Moore, Allyn Young, Davenport, and Wesley Mitchell. Frank Taussig was an uncle figure with whom Joseph Schumpeter did not joke. As widowers, each twice bereft, they shared Taussig's massive Scott Road house in the 1932–37 years before Schumpeter married the economic historian Elizabeth (Boody) Firuski.

Frank Knight, Jacob Viner, Henry Schultz, J. M. Clark—leaders of American economics when I began my studies—Schumpeter went for whole lecture hours without much discussing. (In the autumn of 1935 I apparently became something of a joke because I so often talked about Frank Knight, whose intellect dominated the Chicago barnyard where I began my studies.) Harold Hotelling, Frisch, Tinbergen,[1] R. G. D. Allen, Hicks, Bowley, Divisia, Amoroso, Barone, Georgescu-Roegen, A. P. Lerner, Chamberlin, R. F. Kahn, Joan Robinson, von Stackelberg, Zeuthen, Lange, and Wald were mathematical economists whom Schumpeter applauded. The new and exciting *Review of Economic Studies* he recommended to his Ec 11 classes. He spoke of the brilliant Pierro Sraffa, whom he had met when the latter was young, leading me to draw the false inference that Sraffa was a bit of a lazy dilettante because of his inherited wealth.

Although Schumpeter recognized that the 1924–33 'cost controversy' was mostly a catching-up of the Marshallians to 1838 Cournot, Schumpeter

---

[1] I have commented elsewhere on Schumpeter's rapturous amazement that business cycles—his Kondratieffs and Juglars—might be produced by Frisch and Tinbergen using imaginary numbers involving $\sqrt{(-1)} = \mathrm{i}$. He could understand sin t as a cycle; and that $\mathrm{d}^2y/\mathrm{d}t^2 = -y$ had the oscillatory solution $y(t) = y(0)\cos t + y'(0)\sin t$. But that its solution could be generated by the oscillations of $ae^{it} + be^{-it}$ smacked to him of delicious black magic. Had he understood why $(\mathrm{e}^{it} - \mathrm{e}^{-it})/2\mathrm{i}$ can be short for sin t, the mysticism would have vanished, as it would if he had realized that the complex number $5 + 3\mathrm{i}$ can be regarded as a way to depict the coordinates (5, 3) of a vector that obeys certain natural laws of addition and multiplication: then only real numbers would be needed to handle the real numbers of pig-iron and price data.

overvalued the lasting importance of that controversy. It is I think indicative of a certain uneasiness in his own handling of the tools of mathematical economics that, to his final hour, Schumpeter believed he could justify against the criticism of Viner's draftsman, Y. K. Wong, Viner's contention that the long-run cost curve should go through the *bottoms* of the U-shaped short-run curves. Schumpeter conceded that Wong (and, later, Harrod) were correct in the *two-dimensional* picture of the envelope. But in three dimensions—output, unit cost, planned scale of plant(?)—Schumpeter professed he could find normative significance in bottom-of-the-U points. I cannot reproduce his argument because I have always found it hard to formulate and remember false arguments.[2]

Aside from this erroneous identification of the minimum-unit-cost point with efficiency optimization, I can recall another Napoleonic claim of Schumpeter that I should have written down in my lecture notes because I could never reconstruct the steps of his alleged syllogism. After correctly informing his Harvard Ec 11 students that truly joint costs can never be allocated meaningfully between joint products, Schumpeter went on to say: 'Nevertheless, when recently I sat down with [some forgotten expert] over drinks, I showed how it could be done by means of an infinite series . . . [? in which the costs that wool does not bear are initially attributed to mutton, after which . . ., and so on until all costs are in the end fully and uniquely allocated]. . . .' I hope St Peter confronted Joseph with the case, $TC = \min[\text{mutton}, \text{wool}/2]$, and asked for its meaningful series-expansion imputation into $f(\text{mutton}) + g(\text{wool})$.

Alfred Marshall's *Principle of Economics* was the admitted classic of the 1890–1930 period. It was typical of Schumpeter's love for theory that he rejected Marshall's view that the reader could skip the footnotes and appendixes. If time were short, Schumpeter advised, read them and skip the *text*!

Schumpeter's older Harvard colleague, Edwin Bidwell Wilson, mathematical physicist and last student of J. Willard Gibbs, devoted part of his 1936–37 seminar to Marshall's Mathematical Appendix. I was then struck by how patchy these notes are and how hard it was for us economists to answer Wilson's proper questions about them. I came to realize that

[2] Schumpeter's own Bonn student, Erich Schneider, had provided, in the same 1931 volume of the *Zeitschrift für Nationalökonomie* that carried Viner's famous cost article, a graph involving *total* cost curves demonstrating the envelope tangencies that Wong properly insisted on. I may retell the story that, as late as 1935, Viner insisted to his Chicago class: 'Although Wong is mathematically right, I can draw the envelope curve through the bottoms of the U's.' My cheeky rebuke as a nineteen year old was, 'Yes Professor Viner, you can, with a *thick* pencil!' As a twenty-five year old, I realized that I might better have added: 'Or, of course, if your U-shaped short-run curves are V-shaped, with *cornered* minima, and provided the economies of plant enlargement aren't too rapid.'

Marshall, despite his reputation as a synthesizer, was in fact primarily a *miniaturist* who lacked the energy and will to shape a coherent masterwork in analytical economics. It went against the grain to admit that Schumpeter was right in elevating Leon Walras above Marshall and the rest as the Newton of economics who discovered the system of the world in his paradigm of general equilibrium. All the more credit is due the youthful Schumpeter, since after 1900 the moon of Pareto was serving to eclipse the sun of Walras. All hats off to Pareto, but as Lagrange lamented in eulogizing Newton, there is alas only one system of the economic world to discover and Walras had already done that when Pareto was still a schoolboy.

Marshall, having managed to bury Jevons, kept Francis Edgeworth in the shade for four decades. Schumpeter accorded Edgeworth his due. 'If you don't write books, and merely squander your genius in articles, you won't command your true value in the markets of scholarship,' Schumpeter used to say. He therefore rejoiced when the Royal Economic Society brought out Edgeworth's collected papers in three large books. The cases of Einstein and Frank Ramsey (the latter's three immortal contributions to economics appeared in separate articles) suggest that Schumpeter's emphasis on books can be refuted—at least by a genius. Still, Edgeworth's own important innovations in statistics—which, despite their obscurity of exposition, anticipated much of R. A. Fisher's maximum likelihood and went beyond Karl Pearson's large-sample asymptotics—were never part of one unified book and have failed to receive the credit they deserve. In any case Schumpeter practised what he preached. He was usually engaged on an ambitious book. And, although he published articles every year, he resisted temptation to make small contributions to economic science.

Maturity and Youth

Schumpeter stayed alive as a theorist. That means he improved in his understanding, sloughing off old skins or covering them up with new. That also means that he is sometimes a bit inconsistent in his expositions of any one date. I was struck in reading his last years' work on welfare economics: in some places he betrays clear understanding of Pareto optimality; in other places he accepts L. Robbins' view that economists have virtually nought to say in this domain; in no one place does he provide a unified grasp of the subject's final status. All this is merely to say that Schumpeter was human. Even Pareto, who innovated in replacing one cardinal measure of utility by any numberings of the indifference contours that preserve ordinal rankings, often forgot about his own innovations and reverted back in his definitions of complementarity to operations on the cardinal utility he had already thrown out into the trash.

Progression in Schumpeter's thought offers special problems. Schumpeter had respect for the past. To tamper with Smith's 1776 text in the light of 1913 scientific findings he would have considered foolish. Schumpeter's own youthful classics are part of the past. What right does J. A. S. have in 1934 to second-guess the thought of J. A. S. of 1912? For better or worse, a classic should be left to stand. Besides, Mertonian study of the sociology of science suggests that you will retain a higher ranking in the history of a scholarly discipline if you stand your ground. Never complain and never explain. Newton's warts are part of his picture and to use an airbrush to shade them out is to distort the portrait and rob it of interest.

For the rest of this survey of Schumpeter as a theorist, I am going to stop talking about him as a connoisseur of theory and patron of theorists. I am going to discuss in a theoretical way one of Schumpeter's own most famous—you might say, most notorious—theories. I refer to Schumpeter's paradigm of a zero rate of interest in equilibrium when innovational development is ruled out. If this view is correct, it is only as a result of innovation that society accords any income to people who do not work for wages or receive rents for the land resources they own. A bourgeois class that receives permanent net income from its ownership of machines, factories and inventories continues to exist only to the extent that innovations do not flag.

Many of my comments will have to be critical. All of them might have been written in, say, 1934 when Schumpeter was 51 and his theory was at least a quarter of a century old. Since Schumpeter rarely discussed his own theories, and nowhere repudiated them, one's pen tends to write almost angrily: 'Do you mean to say in 1934 that . . .?' Yet the argument is really with a 1912 text. I find no useful way to evade this problem. So I must ask the reader to realize that what seems like strong criticism is not really that of a student directed against his beloved friend and benefactor, but rather is a pungent verdict by a later generation on the preliminary scientific findings of an earlier generation.

T. S. Eliot was told, 'We know more than the classics.' Much as this message pained him, if it is scientists we are talking about, Eliot must accept this fact. But even scientists must recognize the epsilon of truth in Eliot's rejoinder: 'Yes, and it is the classics that we know.' The greatest of scientists was honest in saying that he took off from the shoulders of giants. I can be as objective in weighing the merits and demerits of Schumpeter's 1912 paradigm because it was Joseph Schumpeter who taught me how to administer justice.

EVALUATING SCHUMPETER'S ZERO-INTEREST-RATE DOCTRINE

The Ramsey (1928) and Solow (1956) one-sector paradigm can illustrate Schumpeter's contentions. It was this I had in mind in earlier expositions (Samuelson, 1943, 1951). In view of Schumpeter's youthful admiration for J. B. Clark, my modelling is a fair one.

Technology

Output, $Q(t)$, is the sum of consumption, $C(t)$, and net investment: $C(t) + K'(t)$. It is produced by a first-degree-homogeneous, concave, smooth neoclassical production function whose variables are land, labour, and a homogeneous stock of capital ('leets' in Joan Robinson's sardonic lingo), $[T, L, K(t)]$:

$$\begin{aligned} Q(t) = C(t) + K'(t) &= \mathrm{F}[T, L, K(t)] \\ &= T\mathrm{f}[L/T, K(t)/T] \end{aligned} \qquad (1)$$

where $\mathrm{f}[L, K]$ is a smooth, strictly concave function.

It suffices to consider land and labour as 'primary' factors not producible within the system, instead being given in constant amounts, $[T, L]$, which by appropriate definition of units could each be taken to be unity. With the understanding that labour supply is fixed, $\mathrm{f}[L, K]$ can be written as $\mathrm{f}[K]$, with $\mathrm{f}''[K] < 0$.

Competitive Imputation

In the absence of uncertainty and technical change, [real wage rate, interest or profit rate, rent] are given respectively by the competitive marginal-productivity relations:

$$w(t) = \partial \mathrm{f}[L, K(t)]/\partial L, \qquad L \equiv 1 \equiv T \qquad (2a)$$

$$\begin{aligned} r(t) = [\partial K'/\partial K] &= \partial \mathrm{f}[L, K(t)]/\partial K, \qquad L \equiv 1 \\ &= \mathrm{f}'[K] \end{aligned} \qquad (2b)$$

$$\begin{aligned} R(t) &= Q(t) - w(t)L - r(t)K(t) \\ &= \partial \mathrm{F}[T, L, K(t)]/\partial T, \qquad [T, L] \equiv [1, 1] \end{aligned} \qquad (2c)$$

Golden-Rule State

Schumpeter's theory of a zero rate of interest in the circular-flow equilibrium posits that, for given primary factors of $[T, L]$, there is a *finite* golden-rule K^s, a Schumpeter point such that

$$0 = r^s = f'[K^s] \tag{3}$$

Before Ramsey, Meade, Allais, Phelps, von Weizsäcker, and other analysts of the 'golden-rule state of maximal per capita consumption', Schumpeter recognized that his zero-interest-rate equilibrium would maximize the aggregate steady-state real consumption of fixed-supply primary factors of production. The competitive breakdown of this aggregate between wages and rent would depend on technology and endowment of land relative to labour, w and Q/L being the greater the greater is the T/L ratio.

Falling Rate of Interest

In the absence of innovation, if $K(0)$ begins below K^s, Schumpeter may be presumed to be supposing that positive accumulation of $K'(t)$ will always be forthcoming and will soon bring the interest rate down to zero:

$$\lim_{t \to \infty} [K(t), r(t), Q(t)] = [K^s, 0, \text{maximal } Q] \tag{4}$$

And then equilibrium will persist happily ever afterwards forever.

If $K(0)$ begins above K^s, a possibility I do not remember Schumpeter having recognized, $r(0)$ begins negative and decumulation brings it up to zero.

Innovational Development

But now let us introduce the possibility of gales of creative self-destruction. A parameter of technological improvement, $\theta(t)$, is put in the production function:

$$f[L, K(t); \theta] \qquad \text{with} \qquad \partial f[L, K(t); \theta(t)]/\partial[\theta(t)] > 0 \tag{5}$$

$\theta(t)$ increases as t increases. The increases in θ may be jerky; or they may be quasi-periodic; or they could be near to random. In any case, so long as such innovations are going on, the competitive interest will be perturbed above[3] zero by development.

---

[3] Only in preparing this paper did I notice what Schumpeter did not emphasize: namely, technical change can *lower* the interest rate rather than raise it; e.g. when $\partial^2 f[L, K; \theta]/\partial\theta\,\partial K < 0$ and the prior zero interest rate turns negative as innovation makes the stock of leets become redundant.

For land and labour fixed, output will grow for two reasons: first, improved technology will raise product directly; secondly, the induced rise of the interest rate above zero will in Schumpeter's scenario cause capital to grow.

A Schumpeter Cycle

I can even construct a regular cycle of Schumpeterian developmental evolution. Thus, assume that $\theta'(t)$ is a positive periodic function of time:

$$\theta'(t) \equiv \theta'(t + \tau)$$

Or let technical advance be almost periodic. Or let it be bunchy in time like an autocorrelated error function. Or, even if technical change is purely random (as white as the driven snow of 'white noise'), the economic system will then show quasi-realistic autocorrelated fluctuations in the fashion of the Wicksell–Frisch rocking horse subject to random impulsive shocks.

The reader can verify this in the case of a quadratic production function, and where we postulate that $K'(t)$ accumulates at a rate proportional to the deviation of r from 0. This gives, after appropriate choice of units,

$$f[K; \theta] = \theta(t)K(t) - \tfrac{1}{2}K(t)^2 \qquad (6)$$

$$r = \theta - K \qquad (7)$$

$$K'(t) = \alpha r(t), \qquad \alpha > 0 \qquad (8)$$

Then, if $\theta'(t)$ is sinusoidal with period τ, it can be shown that investment becomes ultimately sinusoidal with the same period (but with a lag). Profits, growth of output, and other variables will display behaviour a bit like that observed by the National Bureau of Economic Research.

Summary

Seventy years after Schumpeter glimpsed his basic model, I have produced this instance to show that it involves no *logical* contradictions. We observe a system that evolves cyclically, displaying a rising trend of real wage and output and cyclical fluctuations in the profit rate around a flat long-run trend.

Note, however, that Schumpeter had no real need to put into his system that which economists have found to be most novel and shocking in Schumpeter. I refer to the *zero* rate of interest. How Böhm-Bawerk must have smarted at that saucy conception of Schumpeter. And we all know how vehemently Frank Knight rejected in the 1930s the very notion of a zero rate of interest.

My point is a simple one. Suppose Schumpeter had believed in a *positive* rate of subjective time preference *à la* Böhm, Irving Fisher, Pigou, Cassel, and other orthodox neoclassical writers. Call it ρ, and let it be positive (as when Pigou's representative Englishman is born with a psychological rate of subjective time preference of 4 per cent: $\rho = 0.04$).

Schumpeter's model of cyclical development would have been little different with a positive rather than a zero floor for the interest rate! Output would still grow cyclically, while real wage and interest rates would still vary in the same quasi-cycles.

To see this, replace the proportionality of accumulation to the interest rate by its proportionality to the deviation of the interest rate above the time preference rate:

$$K'(t) = \alpha[r(t) - \rho] \tag{9}$$

Then $\rho > 0$ merely gives a positive asymptote to which the interest rate may descend in the absence of innovation, rather than a zero asymptote. It is still fits and starts of innovation that create dynamic development and cycles. The scenario for the economy is still essentially a cheerful one, even if golden-rule perfection is not being attained or even aimed at.

Simplifications

Though my model is in the sense just described even more general than Schumpeter's 1912 schemata, it quite fails to catch some qualitative properties of the Schumpeterian scenarios. My transient positive profit is merely the competitive interest rate generated as innovation makes every item of capital more productive. My profit is temporary, but it is a phenomenon of perfect competition equilibrium.

Schumpeter's innovators, by contrast, are *temporary monopolists*. Their transient profiles come because rivals are not yet able to do what they can do. To understand them you need to read pages in Chamberlin on imperfect competition, or in Cournot and Marshall on monopoly.[4] As knowledge and

---

[4] Schumpeter early admired Cournot's 1838 analysis of monopoly, duopoly, and oligopoly. It was Schumpeter who edited the last symposium in which Wicksell participated, which dealt critically with A. L. Bowley's duopoly analysis. Illustrative of Schumpeter's felt need to believe in the stability of capitalism and, by extension, to rule out instability of bilateral monopoly, was the ambivalent doctrine on duopoly that Schumpeter maintained from 1925 to his death in 1950. He believed that the Cournot determinate solution is the correct one, except when it is not!—and then the collusive joint-profit-maximization solution of Wicksell is the correct and determinate solution. I am still amazed that such feckless eclecticism could satisfy him. Was it a case of the heart superseding the head?

methods are gradually imitated by rivals, oligopoly will atrophy and degenerate into competitive imputation. So to speak, I have aped with changes in *quantity* of K and its productivity what Schumpeter contrives by changes in *quality* of market structure and entrepreneurial power. Keeping this qualification in mind, we are pleased to see how much of the Schumpeterian epic this dynamic Clark–Solow model can capture.

Imperfect Competition Theory

This qualification also explains why Schumpeter should have always had so keen an interest in the analysis of imperfect competition. His laudatory views on Joan Robinson and Edward Chamberlin reflect this.

John Kenneth Galbraith's giant corporations fit well into the modified version of Schumpeter's model that he arrived at in his final years. But unlike Galbraith, Schumpeter insisted that these giants were constitutional monarchs, who reigned only so long as they desisted from trying to rule. 'What have you done for us lately?' is the question ever put to the Fortune-500 companies. Those with disappointing replies are evicted from the choice rooms of capitalism's hotel: those suites are always full, but with a changing roster of guests, each of whom must earn his place in every epoch.

The *countervailing power* that runs Schumpeter's jungle is the competition of giant seller against giant seller. And even a pygmy can challenge a giant, and hope to become a giant.

When I look at the great fortunes amassed since World War II, I understand them through Schumpeter's spectacles. David Packard or Edwin Land or Sheikh Yamani have each become as rich as Rockefeller. The Marxian paradigm of the falling rate of profit or rising organic competition of capital throws no light on the Pareto distribution of incomes and their Gini coefficient of concentration. The strictly competitive model of Hicks, Solow, and J. B. Clark, as well as the Kaldorian and Kaleckian widow's cruses, equally withhold insight on the trends and causes of income inequality.

Progression in Schumpeter's View?

I am not sure that I can document what I have described as a change in Schumpeter's view on innovators and on the welfare economics of oligopoly that took place between the autumn of 1935 when I first attended his Harvard lectures and his mature thought in his final years. In 1935 he believed Du Pont could not long hold its innovational lead. General Electric,

General Motors, IBM, and AT&T all had limited life expectancy as producers of enterpreneurial profit—which is essentially the only source of profit he then gave diplomatic recognition to.

By 1950 Schumpeter was prepared to concede that a bureaucratic corporation might be able to continue to innovate. Moreover, the *statical* deadweight loss transiently arising from the Fortune-500 innovational oligopoly power, Schumpeter came to believe, was more than compensated for by the consumers' surplus they created from their dynamic innovations. Their monopolists' Danegeld was a bargain in Schumpeter's recalculation.

Schumpeter's final logic ought to have predisposed him to accord to Hayek the final victory over Lerner and Lange in the debate over whether a socialist state could play the game of parametric pricing. To find new *cost* technologies and husband scarce knowledge as it is forever newly arriving, the letter of Walrasian equations achievable by Lerner–Lange auctioneers and bureaucrats serves as nothing compared to what Hayek's real-life speculators and profit receivers are led by the invisible hand of market competition to contribute. I do not remember Schumpeter as pronouncing on this point, but on my reading it should be congenial to his *Weltanschauung*.

How Vital is Money Creation?

The present model is unrelievedly microeconomic in its ignoring of money supply and nominal spending behaviour. It thus fails to do justice to what was considered important in Schumpeter's model, namely his insistence that innovational development be financed by money *creation*, which in turn leads to unanticipated inflation that cuts the real consumption people can purchase with their previous nominal incomes, thereby procuring the 'forced saving' that offsets the incremental innovational investment. Dennis Robertson and other writers of the 1920s on forced saving were thus anticipated by Schumpeter. Even though many orthodox economists were shocked by Schumpeter's notion that inflation could advance progress, Viner and Hayek have shown that forced-saving notions occur as early as 1803 in Henry Thornton. Keynes's *General Theory*, preoccupied with the *ex post* identity of saving with investment, needlessly denied the importance of forced saving; similarly the recent school of rational expectationists do well to insist that inflation foreseen is less effective than unexpected inflation in releasing resources from consumption for investment.

We can add money to the Solow–Ramsey model. Whether we do or do not, it confirms doubt that there *has* to be money creation for capitalism to work in its characteristic way. When the banking system keeps aggregate money inelastic in supply, innovational investment can still pull resources out of the old circular flow by competing with older kinds of investment and reinvestment for the limited quota of funds (and, in essence, resources). A disciple of Schumpeter has no need to insist upon the same degree of business-cycle overshoot relative to innovation under different policy regimes.

QUALIFICATION AND EXTENSION

Approach Towards Zero Interest Rate

My equations (1)–(4) demonstrate that Schumpeter's paradigm of an interest rate that is zero in innovationless equilibrium is not a logically impossible one. That does not mean that Schumpeter himself ever provided an adequate demonstration of this fact, and does not answer the question of whether he understood how to reply to the legitimate queries on the matter. Also, for a thing to be logically possible does not mean that it is necessarily *likely* or probably *relevant.*

There are also models, as simple as the Clark–Solow model that I have just analysed, in which the interest rate only *asymptotically* goes to zero but never quite reaches there. Frank Knight exaggerated the necessity or likelihood of such models in the 1930s, but that is no reason to refuse them careful analysis.

Thus, instead of having output attain a maximum at a *finite* stock of capital, at $K^s < \infty$, suppose $\mathrm{f}[\bar{L}, K] \equiv \mathrm{f}[K]$ only approaches its upper bound at $K = \infty$. Then

$$\begin{aligned} &\lim_{K\to\infty} \mathrm{f}[K] = B < \infty \\ &\mathrm{f}'[K] > 0, \qquad 0 < K < \infty \\ &\lim_{K\to\infty} \mathrm{f}'[K] = 0, \qquad \lim_{K\to\infty}\int_{\epsilon}^{K} \mathrm{f}'[x]\,\mathrm{d}x < \infty \end{aligned} \tag{10}$$

Any constant-elasticity-of-substitution (CES) function, with Hicksian σ less than unity, will have this property. An easy CES example is the 'harmonic mean':

$$\mathrm{F}[T, K, L] = (aT^{-1} + bK^{-1} + cL^{-1})^{-1} \tag{11}$$

This really alters Schumpeter's vision of cyclical evolution very little. True, net investment never quite ceases after innovation ceases. But it does trickle away to an ignorable infinitesimal. And quasi-periodic or even white-noise perturbations in innovation (i.e. in $\theta'(t)$ above) will still produce a quasi-regular pattern of cyclical evolution.

Therefore, even if we take the view of Schumpeter's fair-minded critic, Gottfried Haberler—namely, that it is hard to conceive of *zero* net productivity of capital being quite reached—Schumpeter's theoretical system remains intact in its important logical properties.

Unbounded Output

Knight went farther than Haberler. For him, $f'[K]$ falls very slowly indeed. That is Knight's empirical allegation, and for which he gives a bag of uneven arguments. (It is as if Knight believes σ is virtually infinite; or that $T(t)$ and $L(t)$ are not exogenously given as 'primary factors' but are, in the von Neumann fashion, themselves producible and produced at constant returns to scale *within* the economic system. Then, as Kaldor cogently noted in his critique of Knight, the innovationless system could approach positive exponential growth and an asymptote of positive interest rate would be possible.)

Whatever the slowness at which the interest rate would drop, Knight seems to assert the further view that $f'[K]$ cannot fall so fast with K as to make $f[K]$ bounded. As with the Cobb–Douglas function, where $\sigma \equiv 1$ and relative factor shares are constant,

$$\lim_{K\to\infty} f[K] = \infty, \qquad \lim_{K\to\infty} f'[K] = 0 \tag{12}$$

Again, a lawyer for Schumpeter can make good a defence for the view that this need not change his vision. Thus, if utility in a Ramsey integral attains an upper bound at finite consumption levels, investment will peter out in the absence of innovation.[5]

Now, however, there is no guarantee that pure profit falls towards zero in the absence of development. Nor is there even guarantee that the *fractional share* of profit falls towards zero. Schumpeter's startling doctrine of euthanasia of the rentier, which differs from Keynes's *General Theory* version in that Schumpeter's leads to no lasting unemployment problem and happily splashes workers and landowners with real income, now could be invalidated. My lament over this would be limited, since in any case there is

---

[5] However, now that $U(C) \leq U(f[K^s])$, with $f'[K^s] = r^* > 0$, as $t \to \infty$, we find $r(t) \to r^* > 0$. Also, as $\theta(t) \to \infty$, utility satiation will be achieved and the behaviour equations of the truly affluent society would have to be altered beyond recognition by traditional economists. If $U(\infty) = B < \infty$, and $f[K]$ is Cobb–Douglas, Ramsey's optimized integral could still be convergent, and Schumpeterian evolution would still involve an interest rate that falls towards zero except when innovation transiently elevates it.

no likelihood that innovation will cease (and perhaps no great reason to expect it to fall substantially). Why agitate oneself about a quarrel over contrafactual asymptotes?

Logical Confusions?

Even if technology could permit the interest rate to become zero, Schumpeter never spelled out correctly why and exactly how this would come about. This may have been only inadvertence. But my reading of his 1912 classic (and later discussions) raises doubt that Schumpeter perceived the problem correctly. Schumpeter seems to have had a vague notion that, in the absence of development, the interest rate *logically* could have no equilibrium other than zero.

If he held such a view, he was in error. I have used the Clark–Solow model to show that $r(t)$ going to zero is a *logically possible* case. That same model can serve to show that a zero interest rate is not *logically necessary*. It is a puzzle that Schumpeter did not perceive this and concede it.

My example of a subjective rate of time preference of $\rho > 0$ has already made the point. True, Schumpeter might have the empirical hunch that $\rho = 0$. But if that were the basis for his notion of a zero interest rate, in his polemics with Böhm-Bawerk he might have been expected to marshal the factual evidence for so unconventional a view. Instead his arguments, inconclusive as they may seem to a careful reader, appear to be theoretical in character. (Later I review some of the 1912 points.)

Suppose Böhm were to put this question to Schumpeter: 'If the physical net productivity of capital never falls below a positive constant, do you still insist that the equilibrium real rate of interest would be zero?'

It is unflattering to say so, but I fear that Schumpeter would still have answered 'yes'. Somehow, he thought, the present K input that produced the postulated future fruits would have imputed to itself so much value as to make its subsequent net yield zero. But, as I see it, no finite value for K could do that. And, unlike the case of land, which I shall deal with presently, there is no reason for an infinity to rear its head in the model's depiction of K. (I return below to Schumpeter's 1912 exposition on this issue.)

Infinite Capitalization of Land

Permanent productive land will have an infinite value when the interest rate is zero:

$$P_T T/r = \infty \qquad \text{if} \qquad r = 0 > P_T T \tag{13}$$

This would shock many critics of Schumpeter. Blunt Edwin Cannan dismissed the problem of proving that the rate of interest must be positive, taking it for granted that there has to exist a (finite) ratio between the stock value of a flow.

Suppose Schumpeter conceived of a Robinson Crusoe who lived forever. Or, better, conceived of a Swiss Family Robinson that as a clan will live forever and that empirically is free of systematic time preference. Then there is nothing absurd about land's having a value higher than any multiple of its annual net rent. Two acres of land will be worth twice one acre; but no acres will ever be permanently sold for finite annual incomes.

We think land's value must be finite because we think of each person as dying. We expect that people do not attach as much importance to their remote heirs as they do to their own old age and to their immediate children and grandchildren. Empirically, we introduce the elements of subjective time preference that seems realistic and which are inconsistent with Schumpeter's idealized scenario.

We then face a model of overlapping generations and the Modigliani life-cycle model for wealth and saving applies. As I showed in my A. P. Lerner *Festschrift* contribution, with permanent land in the picture, a Turgot–Modigliani paradigm will yield a positive interest rate that is just large enough to make the amount of wealth that people will want to hold (out of their savings and inheritances) equal to society's valuation of all earning assets. At r too low, land and leets will be worth more than people want to continue to own; as people try to sell assets and spend proceeds on increments of consumption, asset prices will drop and r will return towards equilibrium r^*. At r above r^*, people of all ages will not be able to hold on the average as much as they need to plan to hold to fulfil their expected retirement consumption needs; they will try to save more, bidding up asset values, enhancing the stock of K leets and lowering the $f'[K]$ yield back down to r^*.

So, realistically, a positive interest rate seems indicated for Schumpeter's circular-flow equilibrium. Nonetheless, since the logical issue has been debated, in the next section I shall use Ramsey's 1927 model of optimal saving to vindicate Schumpeter's *logic* of a zero interest rate.

A RAMSEY MODEL FOR SCHUMPETER

To the Clark–Solow capital technology, I add a concave utility function for Schumpeter's society. The undiscounted integral of this utility integrand, extended over the *infinite* future, is to be maximized. Thus, we have

$$\max \int_0^\infty U(c)\,dt = \max_{K(t)} \int_0^\infty U(f[K] - K')\,dt \tag{14}$$

$$K(0) = K^0 < K^s, \qquad f'[K^s] = 0 > f''[K], \qquad f[K^s] \geq f[K]$$
$$U'(C) > 0 > U''(C), \qquad U(f[K^s]) = U(B) \geq U(f[K])$$

As is well known, $K(t)$ will grow by positive accumulation from initial K^0 gradually towards the golden-rule Schumpeter turnpike K^s. This means that the interest rate falls asymptoticaly towards zero, doing so at the optimal rate given by the Ramsey–Keynes 'energy integral':

$$U(B) = U(f[K] - K') + K'U'(f[K] - K') \tag{15}$$

This first-order differential equation in K has, from each initial K^0, a solution that asymptotically approaches Schumpeter's zero-interest golden-rule state. By standard mathematical methods that I need not review here, the following asymptotic limits can be shown to hold—in close agreement with the heuristic relations (1)–(4) presented earlier:

$$\lim_{t \to \infty} \left\{ K(t), K'(t), r(t), \frac{K'(t)}{r(t)}, \frac{K'(t)}{K^s - K(t)} \right\} = \{K^s, 0, 0, \alpha, \beta\} \tag{16}$$

$$\alpha = \left\{ \frac{U'(f[K^s])}{U''(f[K^s])f''[K^s]} \right\}^{1/2}, \qquad \beta = \left\{ \frac{f''[K^s]U'(f[K^s])}{U''(f[K^s])} \right\}^{1/2} \tag{17}$$

The integral of present-discounted value of land, calculated along the system's path to equilibrium, will diverge to infinity as the interest rate decays exponentially to zero. But that is only as it should be in a system where decision-making is made on an infinite-lifetime basis.

Corrections

This concrete Schumpeter model permits us to correct any possible misapprehensions. Thus, suppose $r(t)$ or $f'[K(t)]$ can never fall below a positive number $\bar{r}$. Then with utility unsatiable, $U'[C] > 0$, Ramsey's integral will be infinite and no Schumpeter circular-flow equilibrium becomes possible. Böhm would then be right to reject any contention of a zero equilibrium rate of interest.

Also, suppose we realistically attach to Schumpeter's people finite lifetimes. And suppose that their bequeathing motivations are realistically limited: some of their Modigliani life-cycle wealth they want to leave to children and grandchildren, but they definitely fail to give like consideration to consumption by their descendants a million years from now. Then my earlier remarks about a Turgot–Modigliani model apply to negate a zero rate of interest.

Derailings

There would be some interest in dissecting Schumpeter's own 1912 expositions, to trace where his logic nods, what are his idiosyncratic definitions and views of empirical reality, and how he entraps himself in his own rhetoric. I have not the time to do this adequately. With diffidence, I mention a few of the highlights.

First, Schumpeter glimpses the golden-rule maximizing property of the zero-interest configuration. Thus Schumpeter (1912, p. 35) observes that a person who departs from the zero-interest state '. . . would discover in due course that he had obtained a smaller total satisfaction than he might have done.' This is at least a vague perception that $U(\mathrm{f}[K])$ is at its maximum when K is at the K^s where $\mathrm{f}'[K^s] = 0$. And it reflects a glimpse of the truth that $\int_0^\infty U(\mathrm{f}[K] - K')\mathrm{d}t$ is larger if $K(t) \equiv K^s$ than for any other $K(t)$ path emanating from $K(0) = K^s$.

Second, Schumpeter out-Smiths Adam Smith. He thinks that rational circular-flow competition most assuredly *achieves* the optimum glimpsed above. Only irrational 'children and primitive men', who are ignorable, will fail to be led by the invisible hand of competition to the golden-rule state. This is logically quite unwarranted, except if there is gratuitously slipped into the premises of the argument that all decision bodies live foreover and happen to perceive complete time-symmetry in their esteemings of future consumptions in 1912, 2012, and 9999...912! There is no sign that the logical issues have been thought through and sorted out from the empirical plausibilities.

Third, it can be shown that, when we specify a zero interest rate, the resulting competitive-arbitrage conditions of steady-state pricing will permit the total value of society's consumption to be decomposed into the factor-returns of labour and land (the 'primary' non-reproducible inputs). Smith asserted this (and, when the interest rate is not zero, showed how the interest return on non-primary inputs must be included as a third return). Marx, worried about the infinite regress when it takes iron to produce coal and coal to produce iron, grappled with this truth over tens of thousands of words. Schumpeter blithely asserts this truth. Since Dimitriev's 1898 Russian essay, students of Leontief and Sraffa are in a position to demonstrate that it is indeed truth.

Fourth, Schumpeter erroneously thinks that the zero-interest-rate *premise* needed for the theorem's conclusion is itself a *guaranteed* property of innovationless circular-flow competition. He errs. Competitive arbitrage has no intrinsic tendency of its own to compete interest out of existence. All it does is equalize between every effort the market-sustainable interest rate. Schumpeter (1912, p. 29ff.) gratuitously asserts that *all* final values are imputed back to land rent[6] and labour wages *alone*—a truth only true on the stipulation of zero interest rate. To deduce zero interest from a syllogism that is valid only if you have already stipulated a zero interest rate is the height of self-deception. At best Schumpeter's comments only serve to show that there is a *self-consistency* about the golden-rule state (even though, we remind him, that is only *one of an infinity* of self-consistent steady states!).

Fifth, Schumpeter falls into the attractive fallacy of automatic synchronization that entrapped J. B. Clark, Frank Knight, and Henry George. Böhm-Bawerk's turn-of-the-century polemics against Clark had to be replicated in the 1930s by Hayek's polemics against Knight to refute this fallacy. In the steady-state circular flow, the same inputs are followed by the same outputs. An observer sees simultaneously an input and an output: ergo, he is tempted to cry blunderingly that there is no time lag between inputs and outputs and no tempting temporary gain in consumption to be had by departing from the circular flow. In truth the steady state only stays steady because people choose not to fail to do that which keeps it steady.

A Lionel Robbins is wrong to assert that a zero interest rate robs people of the incentive to stay in it: our Ramsey paradigm demonstrates that Robbins is wrong.[7] But a Robbins is right to insist that staying in a steady state does require that it continues to be the more attractive of the multiplicity of choices open to you in every new period of the process.

Sixth, Schumpeter does not reconcile his doctrine that *all* value is decomposable into land rent and labour wages with a *possible* technological case: 100 rice ripen into 110 rice in one year's time without need for any labour or scarce land. (You may say, 'Surely, land is needed, eventually if not now.' Do not say it. Let Schumpeter accept the challenge and observe what he does with the rope Böhm and we give to him.)

Schumpeter's answer might start out in terms of these words (which I put

---

[6] Schumpeter on p. 166 of the 1934 English version of 1912 *The Theory of Economic Development*—my few page references will always be to this source—rejects by logic any view of Böhm that, if the interest rate is zero, the rent yield of land must evaporate: for, on an infinite base a zero yield can form a finite product: $0 \times \infty$ can equal a finite positive number. But this formality fails to meet our *empirical* rejection of infinite value for land. Our senses tell us that people do not live forever; they do buy and sell land *in the circular flow* at predictable ages and at predictable finite 'number of years' purchase'. The young Schumpeter somehow doped himself into identifying innovationless competitive equilibrium with clans that live forever!

[7] Robbins (1930) may however be considered to have more of a point in connection with the issue of *whether a decentralized pricing mechanism can sustain the golden-rule state* with each producer's integrals of present-discounted-value being *finite*. See Samuelson (1943, 1951, 1971), Whitaker (1972), and McCrae (1947).

into his mouth). 'With more rice next year, the price of each grain falls. Thus, 110 then sell for the total of marks 100 now will sell for. So 100 marks today still get you 100 marks tomorrow. The rate of interest is zero *sans* innovations. Q.E.D.' Around p. 170, Schumpeter (1912) repeatedly makes the point that (*when* the interest rate is truly zero) the greater magnitude of the forest is *already* imputed back in value to the saplings: so these foreseen changes in time only conserve the already calculated value of the process. Without labour and land, zero Kuznet product is being produced and it is correctly decomposable into zero real rent and zero real wages.

But this is pure self-deception. Real rice *is* being produced net. Kuznets can measure it. You can eat 10 rice every year and still not impair your circular-flow income. With land redundant and labour not needed, Kuznets measures national income of zero in terms of primary-factors' income. To this he adds permanent real interest income of 10 rice per year. No hocus-pocus of backward imputation—of forest to sapling, or rice grain to rice grain—evades the naive fact of productive interest.

Empirically, Schumpeter may deny to Böhm that there always exists positive technical productivity of capital at the margin. But *logically* he must throw in the towel: when 100 rice as input yields 110 rice output at the end of the year, *no* steady-state (real!, 'own'!) rate of interest can obtain other than 10% per year. A zero equilibrium rate becomes a contradiction (and settling down of the system to a steady state may no longer occur).

Seventh, and this will be my final point as patience ebbs, although Schumpeter correctly perceives the need to keep our thinking straight on the difference between (1) our being in a steady state, and (2) the process of getting into a steady state, Schumpeter himself often makes errors of logic in *denying that the differences between a magnitude in two adjacent alternative steady states may themselves be relevant for understanding what are the market pricings in each of these alternative steady states*. For a Leets model, the ratio $(f[K^2] - f[K^1])/(K^2 - K^1)$ involves only (alternative) steady-state magnitudes. But it has good relevance to the r^2 or the r^1 that you would measure in each such steady state! And, in the Leets model, it has considerable relevance to the optimal path of development that a socialist planner would aim for in maximizing the social utility over time of the ongoing society. One can hardly criticize a 1912 genius for occasional failures in understanding these subtleties. But respect for truth compels one to note in dissecting that genius's work wherein the pathologies originated.

Schumpeter à la Sraffa

My earlier 'leets' model of Solow–Ramsey type can help make clear the error in believing that competitive arbitrage makes it a requirement of steady-state circular flow that the profit rate be zero.

I replace continuous time by discrete time: $K(t)$ by K_t, $t = 0, 1, 2, \ldots$; $K'(t) = \mathrm{d}K(t)/\mathrm{d}t$ by $K_{t+1} - K_t$. For convenience I replace the net-product function $\mathrm{f}[K_t]$ by the gross-product function $g[K_t] \equiv \mathrm{f}[K_t] + K_t$. To avoid Sraffian joint products, I assume leets are used up in one use as input: we have 100 per cent depreciation and a working capital model.

Now (1) and (2b) take the form

$$C_{t+1} + K_{t+1} = g[K_t], \qquad g''[K] < 0 \tag{18}$$

$$1 + r_t = \partial K_{t+1}/\partial K_t = g'[K_t], \qquad g'[K^s] = 0 + 1 \tag{19}$$

In steady-state equilibrium, we have

$$(C_{t+1}, K_{t+1}, r_{t+1}) \equiv (C_t, K_t, r_t) \equiv (C, K, r) \tag{20}$$

Prices of consumption and leets are the same, P. The steady-state wage rate and rent rate are W and V. The interest rate per period is r.

The Leontief–Sraffa conditions of price equal to competitive unit costs—which could also be called the Ricardo–Dimitriev–Smith conditions—are as follows for the consumption-good sector and the leets sector:

$$PC = (WL_C + VT_C + PK_C)(1 + r) \tag{21a}$$

$$P(K_K + K_C) = (WL_K + VT_K + PK_K)(1 + r) \tag{21b}$$

where $L = L_C + L_K$, $\mathrm{T} = T_C + T_K$, $K = K_C + K_K$. Remember that the Ramsey–Solow 'one-sector' model involves both industries with the same technique:

$$(L_C, T_C, K_C)/C \equiv (L_K, T_K, K_K)/(K_C + K_K), \qquad L_C + L_K = L \tag{21c}$$

Schumpeter's pivotal error of imputation is to think that competitive arbitrate requires that $(1 + r)$ be $(1 + 0)$ in (21a) and (21b). We know better. We know that $1 + 0$ is only one of an infinity of arbitrage-proof equilibria. One must look to the behaviour equations of saving-investing, and not those of competition or to the definition of circular flow, to find conditions determining the relevant choice of $1 + r$ from the admissible set.

In Part I of Sraffa's (1960) classic, the six ratios in (21c) are taken as technically given. The unknowns of $(W/P, V/P, r)$ become determinate only if three further equations are specified from outside (21)–(23). However, here (21c)'s ratios are not exogenously prescribed, but instead are specified to satisfy the neoclassical production function:

$$K_{t+1} = G[T_t, L_t, K_t], \qquad K = G[T, L, K] \tag{22a}$$

$$1 = G[T_K/K, L_K/K, K_K/K] \tag{22b}$$

No competitive steady state could survive if the technique used could be replaced by a known technique that could produce a surplus profit beyond the interest rate $1 + r$. Therefore, we adjoin to (21a)–(21c) the following two marginal-productivity relations:

$$1 + r = G'[K] = \partial G[T, L, K]/\partial K \quad (21d)$$
$$W/P = (1 + r)^{-1}\,\partial G[T, L, K]/\partial L \quad (21e)$$

Along with these there is a third such marginal-productivity relation for land. But it is redundant, being implied by the formula for residual rent already implied in (21a)–(21e).

Schumpeter missed the discount factor $(1 + r)^{-1}$ in (21e)'s Wicksell–Taussig discounted-marginal-product relation. And in (21d)'s Jevons–Wicksell relation, Schumpeter failed to mention that $1 + r$ need *not* be $1 + 0$. That need obtain only in the special case where K is always guaranteed to have grown to reach K^s after innovation ceases. This is a possible case, but not an inevitable one, and certainly not so probable a case as Schumpeter's quill proclaimed it to be.

We still lack in relations (18)–(22) one final relation to make steady-state r and all our variables determinate. Schumpeter, implicitly thinking of perpetual-life actors with 'neutral' subjective time preference, supplies the missing equation by having $K(t)$ accumulate to the golden-rule level of K^s. Pigou and Fisher postulated a subjective rate of time preference, ρ, that sets the asymptote for $r(t)$. Classical economists (Smith, Ricardo) similarly closed their long-run system by having $r(t)$ fall to ρ while population grows or shrinks when $W(t)/P(t)$ differs from some postulated subsistence-wage level, $\bar{W}$. Marxians, usually ignoring land as if it were redundant, get their missing equation by similarly specifying a $\bar{W}$ level at which labour supply is reproduced from the reserve army of the unemployed.

FINALE

As I re-read my words, they strike me as overly critical and insufficiently appreciative. Joseph Schumpeter will not stay dead and exalted. His memory is so vivid, his thought so lively, that one finds oneself arguing with unseemly vigour as if he were a mere mortal.

This is not the first time I felt an urge to go back and paint in more favourable brush strokes, not for the purpose of eulogizing but simply to redress the balance properly. Thus, at Mexico City I had to say explicitly that Schumpeter was anti-Hitler and anti-Nazi, because some who read my remarks about his belief that market capitalism would not prevail unless politically imposed mistakenly equated his distrust of Stalin with sympathy for Hitler. When evaluating *Capitalism, Socialism and Democracy* (1942), and finding in the end reasons to doubt Schumpeter's belief that capitalism's *success* would be its undoing, I had to state explicitly, lest I be misunderstood, that it is a great book.

Here, in closing, I must make a similar disclaimer. My failure to agree that a zero interest rate is the inevitable equilibrium when innovation does not occur, and my discussion of some limitations in Schumpeter's mathematical expertise, in no sense lessens his claim to have been one of the few most important economic theorists of the twentieth century. His fame is secure.

ACKNOWLEDGEMENT

I owe thanks to the National Science Foundation for financial aid, and to Kate Crowley and Aase Huggins for editorial assistance.

REFERENCES

Haberler, G. (1951) Schumpeter's theory of interest. In *Schumpeter: Social Scientist* (Ed.) S. Harris, Cambridge, MA: Harvard University Press.

Heertje, A. (Ed.) (1981) *Schumpeter's Vision: Capitalism, Socialism and Democracy after 40 years.* New York: Praeger.

Kaldor, N. (1960) *Essays on Economic Stability and Growth.* London: Duckworth.

Kaldor, N. (1960) *Essays on Value and Distribution.* London: Duckworth.

Kaldor, N. (1964) *Essays on Economic Policy.* 2 volumes, London: Duckworth.

Macrae, C. D. (1974) Equilibrium, efficiency, and the golden rule. *Quarterly Journal of Economics*, **88**, 143–8.

Ramsey, F. (1928) A mathematical theory of savings. *Economic Journal*, **38**, 543–59.

Robbins, L. (1930) On a certain ambiguity in the conception of stationary equilibrium. *Economic Journal*, **40**, 194–214.

Samuelson, P. A. (1943) Dynamics, statics, and the stationary states. *Review of Economics and Statistics*, **25**, Essays in Honor of Joseph Schumpeter. Reprinted (1966) in *The Collected Scientific Papers of Paul A. Samuelson*, Vol. 2. Cambridge, MA: MIT Press.

Samuelson, P. A. (1951) Schumpeter as a teacher and economic theorist. In *Joseph Schumpeter: Social Scientist* (Ed.) Harris, S. Cambridge, MA: Harvard University Press. And (1951) *Review of Economics and Statistics*, **33**, 98–103. Reprinted (1966) in *The Collected Scientific Papers of Paul A. Samuelson*, Vol. 2, Chap. 116. Cambridge, MA: MIT Press.

Samuelson, P. A. (1971) Land and the rate of interest. In *Theory for Economic Efficiency: Essays in Honor of Abba P. Lerner* (Eds.) Greenfield, Levenson, Hamovitch and Rotwein. Cambridge, MA: MIT Press.

Schumpeter, J. A. (1908) *Das Wesen und Hauptinhalt der theoretischen Nationalökonomie (Nature and Main Content of Theoretical Economics).* Leipzig: Verlag von Duncker und Humblot.

Schumpeter, J. A. (1912) *Theorie der wirtschaftlichen Entwicklung.* Leipzig. English translation (1934) *Theory of Economic Development, An Inquiry into Profits, Capitalism, Credit, Interest and the Business Cycle* (*Harvard Economic Studies*, Vol. XLVI). Cambridge, MA: Harvard University Press.

Schumpeter, J. A. (1942) *Capitalism, Socialism and Democracy.* New York: Harper & Row.

Schumpeter, J. A. (1954) *History of Economic Doctrines.* Oxford: Oxford University Press.

Solow, R. M. (1956) A contribution to the theory of economic growth. *Quarterly Journal of Economics*, **70**, 65–94.
Sraffa, P. (1960) *Production of Commodities by Means of Commodities*. Cambridge: Cambridge University Press.
Whitaker, J. K. (1972) Private wealth as an obstacle to Pareto optimality. *Review of Economic Studies*, **39**, 325–29.

Chapter Two

Aspects of Schumpeter's Theory of Evolution

WOLFGANG F. STOLPER

INTRODUCTION: SCHUMPETER DOES NOT FIT

TO write a critical analysis of Schumpeter's theory of evolution which goes into every detail of theory and history would require a volume, and an erudition which perhaps a Gottfried Haberler or a Paul Samuelson can command. Having neither the time nor the space nor the necessary erudition, I propose to limit myself to something more manageable: to suggest that the central ideas of Schumpeter do give a broad as well as a deep understanding to the course of economic history; that they were original; and that they are neither inconsistent with ideas of other great men, nor meaningless for guessing intelligently the directions in which developments are likely to take us.

The wording of my purpose is deliberately somewhat vague. There is no question that Schumpeter saw himself as an economist and required an economist to live up to the technical standards of his occupation. But he also was a sociologist and historian of great achievement, and the requirement of being technically up-to-date did not seem to him a dispensation from having to see economic development in a broader context of social and historic change any more than having a broader outlook was an excuse for a sloppy theory. If the interaction of so disparate interests leads to a confusion of lesser lights, this may be due as much to the fact that the lesser lights lack the vision that encompass so much, as to the fact that reality is confused and confusing because no-one can understand *all* of reality.

On a political plane, the pretence to understand everything must lead to repression, since people who disagree 'obviously' simply do not 'want' to see the truth. But the theoretical consequences are also great. Since Schumpeter's 'vision'—one of his favourite words—is clearly historical (as is Karl Marx's) and as historical time is irreversible as theoretical time is (mostly) not, and as historical processes combine necessity and free-will in varying proportions while theoretical processes are essential deterministic (even when they are probabilistic), it is understandable that many economists should feel that 'The dynamic systems of the Marxists and Schumpeter leave us with a sense of frustration because they are so vague and impressionistic. We are left feeling that their tale might just as easily have been given a different ending,' and that they prefer not 'to pay [the] price . . . for this wealth of [historical] source materials' (Baumol, 1959, p. 35).

I want to suggest that perhaps the inability to formulate the Schumpeterian ideas with the precision needed for a mathematical model which is self-contained and produces all the answers in a deterministic or probabilistic manner does not involve the belief in an incompleteness of the system in some sense as, for example, Baumol suggests. It is, rather, an attempt to analyse a reality which inevitably develops in a way which in principle is not wholly foreseeable, and where the only certainty is that it will change. In this Schumpeter is perhaps unique.

Schumpeter's originality can in a way be gauged from the manner in which he is quoted in Haberler's (1946) classic *Prosperity and Depression*. There are in the 1946 edition nine references to Schumpeter, compared to 11 for Spiethoff, 12 for Hansen, 35 for D. H. Robertson, 20 for Hayek, 21 for Hawtrey, and 48 for the 'classical' Keynes. (All references refer to quotations in Parts I and II of *Prosperity and Depression*. In Part III, Schumpeter is referred to four times, Robertson seven times, Hayek and Hawtrey three times each, and Keynes, quite understandably thirteen times.) Now the point of the page count is not to adjudicate a popularity or 'importance' contest, and certainly not to criticize Professor Haberler, who in *Prosperity and Depression* straightened out so many confusions that ever since the profession has found it unnecessary to discuss the theories in the old manner. The point is that, when Schumpeter wrote after decades of development of business cycle theory, he did not seem to fit. In fact, with all the diversity of the numerous business cycle theories, they were all of a kind; Schumpeter (and perhaps Marx) were different.

Take the organization of *Prosperity and Depression* to make that point: Haberler's purpose was to review and analyse explanatory hypotheses rather than to assess the merits of various writers (pp. 1 and 13). All theories are discussed under the same headings:

1. General characteristics.
2. Explanation of the upswing (prosperity).
3. Explanation of the upper turning point (crisis).
4. Explanation of the downswing (depression).

5. Explanation of the lower turning point (revival).
6. Reasons given for recurrence, periodicity, etc.
7. International complications (op. cit. p. 13).

It is typical for all theories discussed in Parts I and II that their logic does in fact allow this kind of classification, nay, almost demands it. Certainly no one could possibly accuse Professor Haberler of having forced any of the business cycle theories discussed into an artificial mould. There are some authors who have a strong family resemblance to Schumpeter—I might mention Wicksell or Spiethoff, or even the 'classical' Keynes who accepted Schumpeter's explanation of innovation as the cause of major fluctuations of investments *expressis verbis* (Keynes, 1930, Vol. I, pp. 95–6) and with a lengthy summary quoted from Mitchell's *Business Cycles*. The point I wish to make is that, while Schumpeter has, of course, a detailed analysis of the phases of the cycle, not only are these phases defined differently than is usual, but (a) *one* explanation of the cycle refers to the cycle as a whole and is only applied to the different phases, i.e. different phases do not require different explanations, and (b) a new stimulus is required for each successive cycle which thus does not simply follow from the earlier cycle as night follows day. Nevertheless, one cycle does follow another as long as, to use a Marxist phrase, the 'capitalist mode of production' continues.

The real difference between the Schumpeterian version and that of almost all of his predecessors and contemporaries has been stated by Schumpeter himself in his posthumous *History of Economic Analysis* (1954, p. 1135):

> . . . with few exceptions, of which Marx was the most influential one, they treated cycles as a phenomenon that is superimposed upon the normal course of capitalist life and mostly as a pathological one; it never occurred to the majority to look to business cycles for material with which to build the fundamental theory of capitalist reality.

NATURE AND ROLE OF EQUILIBRIUM AS AN ESSENTIAL PART OF REALITY

This quotation and much of the writings raise questions concerning the relationships of cycles to equilibrium and of dynamics to statics. I think it fair to say that with the exception of Schumpeter, cycles and equilibrium theory were treated in watertight components, just as were equilibrium economics and the existence of the government. There is no government in the Walrasian system, and in my student days it was not uncommon to hear the opinion that the economy left to itself would work fine. Disturbances were due primarily to the bad 'interventions of the government'. And since in fact much government policy deserved and continues to deserve flunking marks, it was not impossible to prove the case.

In most business cycle theory there is also no real place for equilibrium theory, nor for the existence of equilibrium, certainly not in the Schumpeterian sense. In fact, most business cycle theorists neither believed in equilibrium theory nor made any use of it in their discussion of the cycle or, if they did, the cycle was mostly a pathological phenomenon. Once more, I can do no better than to quote Haberler's encyclopaedic *Prosperity and Depression*. Discussing 'The upturn (revival)', Haberler notes in a lengthy footnote (1946, pp. 81–2, note 1):

> It must, however, be noted that Professor Schumpeter puts forward his theory, not as an explanation of the lower turning point, but of the movement of the system away from equilibrium. . . . Serious objection can be raised against this view. But the idea that the system passes through an equilibrium, or at least approaches a normal position somewhere between the upper and the lower turning point seems to have been vaguely envisaged by many writers. . . . [I]t may be added that the fact that Professor Hayek starts his analysis from an equilibrium position seems to indicate rather a methodological principle than the proposition that the system actually passes through an equilibrium position on its way from the lower to the upper turning point.

I am quoting Haberler not only to pay tribute to a great economist, friend and teacher, but to characterize a situation. Equilibrium analysis is one of the great achievements of economic theory, and it is well known that Schumpeter considered Walras to be the greatest of all economists for his 'discovery ' of general equilibrium. At the same time he was aware that you had, as it were, a choice of either considering general equilibrium to be a figment of the imagination with no counterpart in the real world—which is what quite a few economists did and do in one form or another—or you had to explain why this wonderful construct was in fact inadequate to explain all or even the major part of reality.

To me, understanding the nature of the equilibrium is as central a part of understanding Schumpeter's approach to evolution as is the role of the entrepreneur. The equilibrium may be quite dynamic in the technical sense of the word. It is a concept which describes all the adaptive forces in an economy, forces which are very strong and which serve not only to keep an economy from going off in all directions or from exploding, but which, by the same token, require special efforts to break out of.

All the technical innovation in economic analysis is consistent with this notion: whether we have G. Cassel's progressive economy, growth paths *à la* Solow, or Harrod's dynamic economics: they all have the characteristic that nothing fundamental happens to the structure of production, there is 'balanced growth' even if it leads to growth in cycles. And in fact, Schumpeter does refer to these kinds of changes as growth. Aggregative approaches do no particular harm in such cases because what happens requires essentially only adaptation to existing and generally understood 'norms'[1] (i.e. parameters).

I think that Schumpeter would consider most policies of the Keynesian kind to be appropriate if what you want is essentially the maintenance of an equilibrium, even of a growing equilibrium. And, lest there be a misunderstanding, in this respect, monetarists are no different from Keynesians. The Schumpeterian objection to both monetarists and Keynesians is that they ignore, or rather are incapable of dealing with, the structural changes of the economy; or to put it differently, that they either assume that it makes no difference how the additional money is spent, or that somehow the economy will allocate the additional amounts in some 'sensible' way. On a somewhat charitable interpretation this may be the common sense of the more recent insistence on 'supply side economics'. It is the insistence that it matters to the development of the economy how monies are spent, but that at the same time there is no unique logical connection between new injections of money (whether through budget deficits or central bank action) and what happens in the economy (Schumpeter, 1939, Vol. I, p. 231).[2] This is a central objection by Schumpeter to both the Keynesian and monetarist approaches, as well as the reason why the disruption of the equilibrium has to be explained and becomes a central part of his business cycle theory.

Of course, money matters; in fact, it is essential. In the comment by Keynes (1930, Vol. II, pp. 95–6) on Schumpeter, in which 'Professor Schumpeter's explanation of the major movements [in the rate of investment] may be unreservedly accepted,' Keynes adds 'it is only necessary to this that the pace, at which the innovating entrepreneurs will be able to carry out their projects into execution at a cost in interest which is not deterrent to them will depend on the degree of complaisance of those responsible for the banking system' (*ibid.*). But it is a central point of the *Theory of Economic Development* (Schumpeter, 1912) that credit creation is essential to finance the innovations. And in his *Business Cycles*, Schumpeter (1939, Vol. I, p. 223) makes it even part of his definition of capitalism: 'Capitalism is that form of private property economy in which innovations are carried out by means of borrowed money, which in general, though not by logical necessity, implies

[1] 'Norms' is the Schumpeterian term used in *Business Cycles* (Schumpeter, 1939).

[2] Since Hayek was mentioned before it should perhaps be added in fairness that in this theory, too, it matters where the money is spent.

credit creation.' Yet the quotation from Keynes (1930, Vol. II, pp. 95–6) which continues

> Thus while the stimulus to a Credit Inflation comes from outside the Banking System, it remains a monetary phenomenon in the sense that it occurs only if the monetary machine is allowed to respond to the stimulus

also shows a profound difference in viewing the process of development: there is implied in the Keynes of the *Treatise*, as in Hayek and others, a demand for net investments in equilibrium with a positive rate of interest, which in Schumpeter's 'pure case' does not exist, and which, in his modified and more realistic case, does not raise any question which could not be handled by equilibrium theory. If indeed all that were happening is that you need more or less aggregative spending rather than a profound rearrangement of factor allocations the typical full employment policy would suffice. Because such a profound rearrangement of factor allocations is essential, full employment policies might be justifiable but could not be sufficient.

So the 'equilibrium' in the Schumpeterian case and its characteristics are neither just a methodological principle alluded to in Haberler's quotation concerning Hayek, nor something the economic system is passing through as the cycle is moving up and down. It is a firm and important part of reality, explaining behaviour and adjustments. And to escape from it, i.e. to destroy it, requires more than routine.

INNOVATIONS

Innovation is, of course, the 'creative' destruction of the existing equilibrium through a change in the production function, brought about by the 'entrepreneur' and financed typically by credit creation. It is central to Schumpeter's theory of the cycle and of evolution; in fact, the two are synonymous. Evolution is the continuous change in the data, and it proceeds cyclically. This is the basic difference between Schumpeter and most if not all cycle or 'trend' theorists, and it is related to the particular way in which Schumpeter looks at equilibrium.

There are several aspects to the cycle which have drawn the questioning attention of critics: the phases of the cycle; why innovations should be 'bunched'; why booms should come to an end; the multiplicity of the cycles (specifically the three-cycle scheme); who is the entrepreneur and who introduces innovations; and many more.

An economy is normally a fairly stable system. Pre-capitalist economic systems also suffer great instabilities, but these instabilities come from outside the system: crop failures, conquests, pestilences. Economic historians will point to many experiences which appear to be exceptions to this statement. To point out that he was not oblivious to these facts, it may suffice to point out that Schumpeter himself discusses early capitalism in Italy in the twelfth century or economic developments in antiquity, and would not be averse to refer to at least some of them as cycles in the modern sense. In any case, a systematic dynamics from within the system is a characteristic of what Schumpeter defines as capitalism. 'Capitalism' is a system to break through the stability from time to time to lead the economy to higher levels. It does so in a manner which differs from simple growth, the latter being an increase in the size of the economy's variables with essentially constant production functions. In the simplest case of a stationary economy, there is no net investment; gross investment is taken care of by depreciation allowances, *productive* interest is zero—as Samuelson has pointed out, this is not a logical absurdity—basically because there exists neither a demand nor a supply of 'loanable funds' in an equilibrium situation. To require a return on savings in such a situation, one would really have to assume that it takes a positive act of savings and investments just to maintain capital intact. But why should it? To be sure, there may be profligate heirs, but a normal business with proper accounting and no extraordinary problems of technical change or a radically changing value of money would be adjusted to accumulating enough funds to replace itself, and a well working money market would take care of intertemporal adjustments at an 'interest rate' representing no more than the cost of doing this kind of banking business. There would, of course, be interest on consumption loans. There is no reason to go further into these issues.

But more to the point, a system whose chief characteristic was equilibrium would not be capitalism, or an evolutionary system, though in Schumpeter's sense of the word it could be a growing equilibrium. I am not suggesting anything very original to point to the traditional hostility of the Church (or Islam for that matter) to the taking of interest, or to the fact that markets for land do not exist everywhere or at all times. For such markets to arise, there must be alternative investments producing streams of income, or else why would anyone *want* to sell the land (and its associated serfs) which does produce such an income? It is quite easily imagined (because it can be found in reality) that marginally—not in the technical economic sense but in the everyday meaning of the word as unimportant, not centrally important, existing at the edge of reality—there is always something happening that requires adjustments, just as there may always be something happening that leads to a sale of land. But this is more akin to a cyclist keeping his balance by steady adjustment from his straight path. These are the forces usually referred to in our elementary discussion which serve to re-establish equilibrium after a disturbance. It is not interesting, because not essential, to explain what happens.

The essence is precisely that something *new* happens, which requires on the one hand a special effort to carry out in the face of the stability of the environment, but which on the other will, once carried out, force adjustments to the change on a higher level of productivity and income.

The experience, for example, of the United States economy lends, I believe, considerable credence to the Schumpeterian analysis in several respects: after a considerable increase in output and productivity, productivity (i.e. output per man-hour) actually decreased. Obviously cyclical factors influence month-to-month or quarter-to-quarter changes, but it is also true that productivity increases of 3 per cent which have been taken for granted for some time (so much so that they have become almost part of folklore) have not been achieved for a long time. The explanations have in many cases the ring of rationalizations in the Freudian sense: pseudo-explanations for simple failures. I need in fact refer only to the troubles of two of the major American industries, steel and automobiles, to point out that it is more likely that wrong investment decisions rather than environmental requirements, government regulation, or 'unfair' foreign competition are at the bottom of the problems: in the case of the steel industry, the delayed adoption of the basic oxygen process (see, for example, Adams and Dirlam, 1966; Adams, 1977); and in the case of cars, the delay in building fuel-efficient and smaller cars in the face of increasing foreign sales even before the oil shocks, though surely low oil prices contributed their share.

There are reasons to mention this: the correct entrepreneurial decision (which in these two cases had obviously and flagrantly not been made) is evidently exceedingly important. And here is perhaps a case where Schumpeter has underestimated the importance of equilibrium economics in his desire to confine it to its proper bounds. Schumpeter has been quoted—correctly so—as praising big business as the source of innovation (Samuelson, 1979, p. 109). Yet there are ambiguities in this. My own interpretation of Schumpeter has been that, however important the competition of new entering firms may be in eliminating profits and assuring an optimum allocation of resources, the really important competition comes from technical change which erodes any monopoly position of any firm that does not remain in the forefront of technical change—which is another way of saying that a firm that ceases to engage in entrepreneurial activities will sooner or later run into trouble.

In my evident loyalty to the ideas of Schumpeter which we are at present discussing, I must not hide the fact that investigations about who is in fact the entrepreneur indicate that, while it may not be the smallest firm that creates the innovations, it is certainly not the biggest. The studies by Mansfield

(1977) of the chemical industry suggest that it was smaller to medium-sized firms that innovated; that Dow Chemical became big *because* of its innovative activity, and not the other way around, and that size was, if anything, a handicap to decision-making. But his studies also suggest that the *economic* decision-making on innovations was, if anything, *more* difficult than the technical one, and that everything took just about three times as long to execute as one expected. Adams and Dirlam (1966) showed similarly that Big Steel completely failed to respond to the technically and economically vastly superior basic oxygen process pioneered in Austria: it was smaller firms which 'introduced' it. Recently, new technology in the steel industry was introduced by a smaller Canadian firm into the USA with Canadian technology and Canadian management (as reported in the *New York Times*, 25 October 1980, p. 21 (Midwest Edition)). With the automobile industry it was clearly foreign competition that beat the Americans at their own game, the 'foreigners' being ironically as often American multinationals as foreigners proper. It is a not unreasonable guess that, had the Environmental Protection Agency continued to permit captive imported cars to be counted in calculating the average fuel efficiency of the cars produced by American multinationals, they would have been quite content to expand their production in Cologne or Rüsselsheim and make their profits there.

But all this is perhaps not as damaging to Schumpeter as it may appear. His explanation of reality would stand even if innovation did not come from big firms of which he thought very highly. All the better for his theory if it comes from small firms, which in the process of innovating become big. Then, if equilibrium theory turns out to be more powerful than Schumpeter expected—and personally I doubt that in view of Schumpeter's admiration for Walras, as the greatest economist—this puts all the more emphasis on the importance and achievements of entrepreneurial action to disrupt the equilibrium.

MONEY AND THE AIMS OF MONETARY POLICY

Borrowed money is an essential part of realizing the innovations, and credit creation *de facto* as essential. The reasons lie, of course, in the difficulties in breaking into the equilibrium stream. The social function of credit is to permit the entrepreneur to take resources out of the income stream before he has put resources into it. The 'complaisant' monetary authority is needed because in fact (though not by logical necessity) the equilibrium is hard to destroy.

There are important policy implications in this view which I would like to sketch. Schumpeter does not deny that lending or borrowing can take place because lenders and borrowers may have different time preferences compared to their income streams. But that would not account for development. The credit creation is needed for productive purposes, and it will normally work itself out through an inflationary process referred to as forced savings. I refrain from discussing the more realistic case in which evolution/innovation does not start from an equilibrium but already during the revival phase of a preceding cycle. In general, I shall neglect these more realistic modifications. The point of mentioning the inflationary nature of this credit creation is several-fold.

First, this kind of credit creation is self-correcting. Once the innovation yields output and sales, and hence an income stream to the innovating firm, the credit can be repaid. Whether it is offset by other loans is a separate question. Alternatively we can imagine a Keynesian multiplier process raising incomes all around (which also requires a 'complaisant' monetary system) which leads to increased savings (here there is no difference at all in the Keynesian or Schumpeterian views as far as the source of saving is concerned), which can be used to buy equity in the new firm which now is exchanged against the credit.

Secondly, this kind of credit can be justified only as a means of financing innovations. The similarity to the old banking school view of credit creation is evident. which makes neither the banking school view right nor Schumpeter wrong. The issue is not whether credit, if given for productive purposes, is inflationary or not. Schumpeter insists on the inflationary nature and the banking theory remains as wrong as ever in insisting that 'sound' credit could not be inflationary. The point is, rather, that it does make a difference what the purpose of a credit is.

Thirdly, it does make a difference what the investments are. There is a profound difference in the older view, typified by Böhm-Bawerk, and the present view concerning growth and evolution. For Böhm-Bawerk, investment has something to do with productive assets and not simply with non-consumption spending. Schumpeter differs from other Austrians, or Anglo-Saxons for that matter, in at least implying that the issue cannot fruitfully be discussed by such terms as lengthening the period of production. For the increase in productive capacity takes place not primarily through the accumulation of capital in the sense of more of the same, but through a changed structure in the sense of changed production functions.

In either case, pyramids or private housing or hospitals are not part of 'capital' in that sense. If the issue is stabilization, achieving a full-employment income through filling gaps in spending, pyramids or housing or hospitals are as good as anything else. Now no one—and Schumpeter neither—would deny the usefulness of hospitals or churches (he was an expert on Gothic cathedrals), but you do not get cycles or evolution out of them. Hicks (1974, p. 57), in another context, has pointed out that in the short run

> . . . only investment expenditure is taken into account; the productivity of the investment is neglected. (One remembers those pyramids!) Once one accepts that one form of investment is not as good as another, it follows that it is socially productive that the form of investment should be wisely chosen. It cannot be wisely chosen if it is too much hurried. The social function of liquidity is that it gives time to think.

Though the Hicksian analysis is in a slightly different context, it nevertheless is the context of 'money, interest, and liquidity', and thus germane to the Schumpeterian discussion. If the social function of liquidity is to give one time to think, one social function of credit is to help in the improvement of the productive structure.

In his chapter on the trade cycle in the *General Theory* . . ., Keynes (1964) does talk of the collapse of the marginal efficiency of capital, but the connection with Schumpeterian thought, which was so explicit in the *Treatise*, is not made. Keynes' reason for the collapse is psychological (expectation, overoptimism, etc.). The collapse precedes the increase in liquidity preference, and the reasons why it takes some time for the marginal efficiency of capital to recover are (Keynes, 1964, p. 317)

> . . . given firstly by the length of life of durable assets relation to the normal rate of growth in a given epoch, and secondly by the carrying costs of surplus stocks, why the duration of the downward movement should have an order of magnitude which is not fortuitous . . . but which shows some regularity of habit between, let us say, three and five years.

The point of quoting Keynes is not to criticize, but to point out that this kind of cycle could not account for what Schumpeter would consider development; nor could there be such a collapse of the marginal efficiency of capital for psychological reasons alone.

Yet in practical fact, Schumpeter and Keynes would be astonishingly close on what should be done in the short run, or might have been done to prevent the collapse of the economy to which Keynes was addressing himself. Schumpeter wrote about the Great Depression several times. Two articles (Schumpeter, 1931, 1946), written 15 years apart, make it clear that the Great Depression was an avoidable disaster in Schumpeter's view. The basic diagnosis is the same in both articles, but this does not concern me here. The point that Schumpeter made in 1931 (pp. 179–180) is central: even in the absence of 'unfortunate events',

> Changes in the method of production . . . necessarily create disturbances in the economic organism sufficient to produce a period of adaptation or recession. Disturbances of this kind differ . . . not only in intensity but also according to the time which must elapse before the new things created take

their full effect; i.e. in most cases before the products of the new plans reach the consumers' markets . . .

The depression which would have been due anyhow, but which might have been brought home to the nations concerned by no more serious symptoms than decreasing rates of increase has been . . . under the influence of outside factors, some of which have helped to bring it about, while others merely intensified it or made adaptation and recovery more difficult.

Of the many factors of this kind, the return to gold is especially mentioned after a warning not to exaggerate the influence for better or for worse of monetary policy. Wages are too high and sticky, yet all this means is that full employment is incompatible with the wage level, though unemployment was *not* brought about by too high wages. Short-term interest rates have not led to an appropriate reduction of long-term rates 'which must delay the emergence of those activities which usually precede general revival. The importance of this element must not, however, be exaggerated. There are wide strata of industry . . . which . . . would not borrow even if credit were offered to them for nothing . . .' (Schumpeter, 1931, p. 181). These special features of the Great Depression 'account for 90% of the values of the measurable symptoms' (*ibid.*).

Fifteen years later, some words were different, but the ideas were essentially the same: what explains a particular depression contains 90 per cent 'accidentals' in the sense of not inherently necessary to produce the capitalist process, and therefore avoidable. Since my present section deals with money and inflation, I quote that part at great length (Schumpeter, 1946, p. 5):

> . . . it is not lack of time which motivates my silence on Federal Reserve policy . . . I do not think that, broadly speaking, it made much difference one way or another. Federal Reserve policy is not entitled to praise . . .; on the other hand, it seems to me plainly absurd to blame it for not having prevented the depression. The Board was in no position to do either . . . the wider question whether more resolute inflation or else a more resolute deflation would have been indicated call for completely different answers according to the scheme of values of the man who asks them . . .

Enough on money has been said to risk a formulation of Schumpeter's view on monetary and fiscal policies in the context of evolution. Since perhaps '90 per cent of the measurable values of symptoms' are 'accidential' and not essential, yet are precisely the phenomena which hurt, policy has a major role. Since 'no decade in the history of politics, religion, technology, painting, poetry or what not ever contains its own explanation' (Schumpeter, 1946, p. 3), prevention of trouble seems as important as a cure, and both seem certainly more important than mere offsets. Money or fiscal policies can do good or harm, but are not the source of what evolution there is, and are probably perceived as much more important than they really are.

The essential role of fiscal and monetary policy is seen, I believe, not merely in ensuring that the aggregate amounts of spending are right—certainly the monetary authorities must be 'complaisant'—but in the detail in which the spending (or the restriction) occurs. Pyramids may do harm even when, at the time they are being built, the alternative is only unemployment. They may do harm if they freeze an economy in a particular direction, making future adjustments that much more difficult, setting the economy on a path in the wrong direction. After all, at the end of World War II, no one suggested to keep on producing tanks because the adjustment to a peacetime economy involved unemployment in defence industries. I well remember—and friend Samuelson will bear me out—that during the Great Depression the view could be commonly found that investments were not so important anyway, that consumption should be stimulated, and that everything would be fine if only unemployment could be eliminated.

Aggregative measures are misleading and dangerous. Of course, one wants to help unemployed workers in the steel or car industry in the USA; one even wants to help the industries. Yet import quotas or trigger prices may be as wrong as outright subsidies to the industries which are not linked to specific performance criteria. Giving unemployed workers money may be preferable to building 'pyramids', if the 'pyramid building industry' should contract.

Thus, the allocation of resources matters even when there are unemployed resources, and the overriding aim of economic policy should perhaps be the improvement in productivity, the achievement of which makes all else possible. I have felt strongly about this point for decades, ever since I was responsible for the First National Plan of Nigeria and got attacked for not making 'full employment' or 'per capita income' the major target variable.

To quote Schumpeter once more, 'analysis of the economic phenomena of any given period must proceed from the economic facts that produce them and not from the monetary aggregates that result from them' (Schumpeter, 1946, p. 3). To which I should like to add: so should the formulation of the monetary and fiscal prescriptions.

THE MULTIPLICITY OF CYCLES

The phases and multiplicity of cycles are not only a characteristic of Schumpeter's theory, but points of confusion, '*Steine des Anstosses*' for many. Not only do the phases in Schumpeter's schemes carry different meaning from other uses, the multiplicity of cycles seems unnecessary hocus-pocus even to such sympathetic friends as Samuelson. Again, the distinction between what is essential and what is accidental may help—and I believe that distinction has important policy implications.

The essential cycle has two phases. Prosperity, which starts from a break-up of the equilibrium, consists of a movement away from this equilibrium as production functions are changed by innovations and financed by credit. The downward movement, the recession, is the movement towards a new equilibrium corresponding to the parameters changed in the prosperity. It is not conceivable that this process could proceed smoothly and in a balanced fashion because adjustments take time. Balanced growth models really assume instantaneous adjustment processes, and this is really not much different from a mode of analysis usually called comparative statics. Instantaneous adjustments are not distinguishable from no adjustments: in neither case is the process of adjustment subject to inquiry. Yet it is this process which we call the cycle.

The fact that adjustments take time, i.e. that there exist lags of various lengths and for various reasons, is really sufficient to explain why evolution proceeds cyclically and why there should be cycles of varying lengths.[3] A 'crisis' is not essential in the scheme of things either in the everyday sense of a dramatic turning point or in the sense of needing an explanation why an upward movement should come to an end. Any explanation of the inter-action-of-accelerator-and-multiplier type, or Tinbergen's original economic model will do. A depression is a movement away from equilibrium, inessential though in fact quite normal, because in fact 'special' events might after all account for 90 per cent of what happens. But sooner or later this depression is bound to turn to a revival, a movement back to equilibrium, with the turning point again not requiring a separate explanation.

The essential difference to a cycle of the 'interaction-of-multiplier-and-

[3] On this point, there is no difference of opinion among economists. See, for example, p. 38 for Keynes' view in the *General Theory of Employment, Interest, and Money*. In his suggestive essay 'Business cycle and capitalism: Schumpeter versus Marx', Shigeto Tsuru quotes Schumpeter on the bunching of innovations and inserts a suggestion that matters would be different under socialism: 'But if actions to carry [major innovations] out were equally open to all as soon as they become technically and commercially possible [which will be the case under socialism] those disequilibria would not be different from . . . those which arise currently from data . . .' (Schumpeter, 1939, Vol. I, p. 97; quoted by Tsuru, 1976, p. 125, no. 16, with Tsuru's additions in brackets). Tsuru's modification of Schumpeter's argument that matters would be different under socialism would certainly be true if new processes do not become generally available for such institutional reasons as patents. But as long as actions take time, are lumpy and require scarce resources, the Schumpeterian process would also take place under socialism. That specific incarnations of the same phenomena would be different goes without saying.

acceleration' type is easily seen. In the simplest case we may get a cycle by this interaction, *provided* we get a constant stream of investments. Where that constant stream of investments comes from is not further investigated. And if it stops, the system moves back to the original equilibrium and the cycle would presumably peter out—a *perpetuum mobile* not being part of our equipment any more than it is of the phycisists!

The 'interaction' type of movements fits into Schumpeter's theoretical scheme easily enough. It gives a reason for turning points and movements away from equilibrium. In addition, however, we have a reason why there would be such a stream of investments and why it would stop. And in addition, a cessation of the stream of movements would not lead to the old but to a new equilibrium. It is easy enough to describe his process in Keynesian terms as an upward shift of the consumption function. But such an upward shift is a classical, not a Keynesian, process, even if we call it a permanent income hypothesis or use Keynesian language. It also is an essential part of the Schumpeterian scheme.

Questions have been raised why innovations should be bunched, why they should come in the 'neighbourhood of equilibrium' when things are fairly normal. I will comment on questions only very briefly.

New things are risky. We are all familiar with enormous cost overruns in military procurement, space exploration or, for that matter, investments in underdeveloped countries, all essentially for the same reason: the lack of precedence making economic calculations hazardous. We are, particularly in less developed countries (LDCs), familiar with the notion of distorted prices and their effects. Schumpeter's insistence that neighbourhoods of equilibrium are situations which minimize the risks of calculations seems plausible and consistent with observed facts.

As a planner in Nigeria, the importance of the Schumpeterian ideas was quite plain. There were, of course, the usual problems of time sequences—the brick-house problem of Hicks, or the 'Leontief Connection'—which incidentally are almost completely submerged in more aggregative types of planning. But much more to the point, there arose the problem of *when* a new investment should be introduced. This is the problem discussed, for example, by S. Chakravarty (1959) as the 'structural break'. It is precisely the Schumpeterian problem of when it is rational to break up the old equilibrium relationships. I think (though I am not sure) that the theories of the individual firm as taught and researched by business schools have something to say on this point. I am sure that Eastman–Kodak or Dupont must have some rational scheme of when to introduce innovations in production or products. Reality gives us enough examples of success and failures of such policies.

Of course, once you get away from the 'essential' two-phase to the merely more 'realistic' but inessential four-phase scheme, it is clear that far-sighted entrepreneurs will use the favourable situation of being below an equilibrium in the revival phase to introduce innovations before the economy has reached its equilibrium. There is no difficulty bringing in such reactions.

I should rather like to make some comments on the controversial three-cycle scheme, particularly as I confess to having some problems with it myself. It is usual to say that the short cycle—the Kitchin 40 months cycle—is due to inventory changes, the Juglar of 8–11 years to fluctuations in fixed investment, and the Kondratief of 45–60 years to particularly important innovations that have taken more than one cycle to execute. Schumpeter certainly could be quoted in support of such an interpretation. He does refer to the 'remarkable work' done by L. Metzler with respect to inventory cycles (Schumpeter, 1946, p. 3; which incidentally is the work admiringly quoted in the very last footnote of the *History of Economic Analysis* (Schumpeter, 1954, p. 1184, no. 29). Yet I feel slightly uncomfortable with this interpretation which I would like to supplement rather than supplant with a slightly different one.

In his *Business Cycles*, Schumpeter (1939) stresses the fact that economic life proceeds in waves and discontinuously, both because the reactions of the economic system to shocks coming from the outside are in the nature of waves—the well known rocking horse analogy—and because the shocks themselves come at discrete intervals. 'Balanced growth' as applied to the economic development of LDCs, and its equivalent in socialist theory, namely the law of proportionate development, have always struck me as very peculiar constructs. Change always starts somewhere and spreads from there. It is inconceivable to me that it should start equally everywhere. For success of everything, some other things have to have happened before others. Which is after all the basic reason why Hicks—in a somewhat different context, to be sure—insisted that the quality of investments was as important as the amount. In his picture, you must have bricks before you can build houses. Input–output analysis tells you the same story; to do something in one industry has repercussions in others, and requires that action in other industries has already been taken, all depending on the lags involved. This kind of reaction is only imperfectly dealt with by the acceleration principle.

So I have no particular difficulty in accepting that economic life proceeds in waves and that in principle there must be many kinds of waves. Whether they are observable as actual ups and downs or only as fluctuations of growth rates seems secondary now.

Schumpeter states this point *expressis verbis* in his *Business Cycles*. As his 'third approximation' Schumpeter (1939, p. 179, footnote no. 1) explicitly states:

> . . . there is nothing in our theoretical scheme . . . why the cyclical process of evolution should give rise to just one wavelike movement. On the contrary, there are many reasons to expect that it will set into motion an indefinite number of wavelike fluctuations which will roll on simultaneously and interfere with one another in the process . . . there is a theoretically indefinite number of fluctuations present in our material at any time. The word *present* meaning that there are real factors at work to produce them and *not merely that the material may be decomposed into them by formal methods*. . . . There are no particular virtues in the choice made of just three classes of cycles. Five would perhaps be better, although, after some experimenting, the writer came to the conclusion that the improvement in the picture would not warrant the increase in cumbersomeness. In particular, it cannot be emphasized too strongly that the three-cycle scheme does not follow from our scheme—although multiplicity of cycles does.[4]

I find this quotation revealing. The number three is nevertheless not quite accidental or even merely convenient. Schumpeter (1939) classifies the reasons why there should be waves of development (as contrasted with 'balanced growth') under three headings: (a) lags of gestation and absorption (pp. 166–7); (b) cycles are interdependent, not independent of each other (what I have called, using the Schumpeterian habit of giving the name of a prominent economist to an important real phenomenon, the Leontief connection) (pp. 167–8); and (c) 'processes which have also effects other than those which show in the cycles themselves' (p. 168), such as the change in other parameters. Thus Schumpeter mentions population movements as the result of railroadization (*ibid.*). For the display of these three important real phenomena, three cycles are adopted as explanatory devices 'to assure us that all of the three reasons for the multiplicity of cycles have the opportunity of coming into play, and not more' (p. 170). Shades of Tinbergen's, *Theory of Economic Policy*!

Yet Schumpeter (1939, pp. 161, 168, 169) qualified here, too, in a footnote:

> Three turned out to be the minimum number satisfying this requirement; but that does not mean that we specifically associate each of our cycles with one of those reasons. Inasmuch as the second and third reasons refer to effects which must take a comparatively long time to assert themselves, the Kondratieff will bear a particular relation to them. Otherwise it is merely a chance coincidence that, having seen three reasons for the multiplicity of cycles, we also chose to confine that multiplicity to three orders or classes.

---

[4] Italics in the original.

This seems to be a slight contradiction to the view previously expressed, though I believe it is not on some interpretation. To give my interpretation, let me, first, summarize and, secondly, make a brief and somewhat primitive methodological statement. To summarize, there are strong stabilizing forces in the economy which are described by equilibrium economics. In such an equilibrium there are also time lags involved, but the system is adapted to them. It takes a disruption of the parameters of this equilibrium to bring about evolution. The basic disruption comes from changes in production functions, typically financed by borrowed money, which move the system away from equilibrium. This movement comes to an end when the products of the changed production functions come on the market and compete with the older products and/or producers, leading to the process of 'creative destruction' upon which I have not further touched. No special explanation is needed for the turning points. A special explanation is needed to explain the next prosperity, namely a new innovation, which cannot necessarily be predicted. Recessions follow necessarily from prosperities; new prosperities do *not* necessarily follow from recessions. Two phases are the essence of the cycle, four phases are not. Waves are the essence of development, three waves are not. Four phases may be historically convenient to identify; they are inessential in the sense that two of them could be eliminated without disturbing the process of evolution.

And now my primitive methodological comment: each phenomenon we observe is unique, is an individual. To understand it, we put it into relation to others at the same time—the contents of statics—and at different times—the dynamics. The individuality is, of course, given by the specific parameters of the system. You will, of course, recognize this trinitarian scheme as Frisch–Tinbergen–Samuelson, in which a stable equilibrium is the result of a dynamic adjustment process as time approaches infinity. I am happy to pay my respects to Paul in this way as in many others.

The Schumpeterian scheme can and does accept all this, yet also goes beyond it. At any one moment in time we do deal with a single phenomenon which has been shaped by many forces. A decision to invest in period 0 must involve considerations of many kinds and many time horizons. One may make, of course, a discounted flow of income analysis to get present value, as is customary in cost–benefit analysis. But it may be worth stressing that not only would existing data be only a moderately good guide for one's action in case of innovation—the fact that others make losses would not deter me from believing that I might make profits, and such optimism would be quite rational—but short-run changes in the business cycle would not necessarily prevent me from continuing with my investment time schedule (not necessarily, i.e. the opposite could also happen). I may well feel that future energy needs require continuous increased investment in coal or nuclear energy even if energy demand falls temporarily, just as I will not stop training physicians in the face of a temporary surplus of doctors. Surely, the past decades have shown the realism of this picture. Sharp downturns and recessions have in fact been felt to be temporary and tractable in the past, as indeed they were. The present experience of stagflation is felt to be of a different kind, and optimism has turned to less than optimism once the traditional policy means did not seem to work.

Thus, in the past the recessions did not interfere with the long-term movement of investments leading to the phenomenon described as a Kondratief upswing. In 1979, on the other hand, the unexpected continuous high level of business activity did not lead firms to invest but rather to hire more labour to meet the unexpected demand. Thus, the high level of activity did not prevent a decline in long-term investment policy by individual firms which expected the downturns and future uncertainties.

Any decision made at any one moment of time is, therefore, simultaneously a decision about different time spans. Keynes quipped that in the long run we are all dead. The proper answer is, I believe, not merely the counter-quip that Keynes is dead and I am living in his long run—*Tomorrow Always Comes*, as went the title of a British novel I once read—the real answer is that the long and the short run cannot really be distinguished historically; we are always living in both.

This point, important to me, leads to a second distinction from the Samuelsonian scheme: a distinction should be made between the dynamics defined as the adjustment path of an economy to a disturbance from the outside, and a wider dynamics which insists (a) that these shocks from the outside are not really from outside the economic system but inside it, produced by a system called capitalism; and (b) that these shocks cannot be satisfactorily explained by the purely economic variables inside the system, e.g. interest rates or the need to save scarce labour, or whatever the pet theory of the moment happens to be which purports to explain the emergence of innovations.

There is a third distinction: in any existing scheme of dynamic economics, the parameters stay essentially constant. Econometricians building models make these assumptions. Investment functions are notoriously difficult to formulate, but as long as we are not trying to forecast innovations, the difficulty is not greater than with the formulation of consumer behaviour; or so I am told. It is very different with forecasting innovation, i.e. new parameters. That, as much as the fact that we are not an exact science, accounts for all models' performance having been somewhat less than perfect. But because equilibrium is real we continue to find the models useful.

Schumpeter gives not only a reason why shocks should from time to time throw the economic system out of and into a path away from equilibrium, his postulation of longer waves gives in addition very strong reasons why even the parameters of the system which are not directly affected by the innovations should themselves, irreversibly, change in time. There are more or less important feedback effects on investments which might translate into longer waves, and yet come to an end sooner or later.

Schumpeter mentions specifically the effects of railroadization on the opening of new territories. The subsequent population changes, growth of cities, of markets, etc., themselves lead to continuous investments in industries other than the railroad. Objections to Schumpeter's identification of the second Kondratief cycle with railroad building on the ground that railroad investments were not all that big and came to an end too 'early' for the proper timing of the Kondratief do not, therefore, seem to me to affect the core of his argument.

Yet, here too, there is nothing deterministic, which means that it is dangerous to project the past into the future. I have been privileged to attend at the IFO-Institut in Munich very interesting seminars about what kind of innovations on the horizon might lead us to a new Kondratief prosperity. But perhaps there will not be any such long wave, but instead a fairly smooth rise. Or possibly a collapse as the result of an inflation in the course of the strange kind of supply side economics which believes that increased funds in the hands of consumers will raise productive capacities. Perhaps time lags between new methods and their becoming universally adapted have shortened. I do not see how one can make more than informed guesses on this picture. So I cannot quite visualize how models might build changes in the parameters into their structure. Schumpeter's model promises (maybe) a better future; it does not promise a smooth path to it.

REFERENCES

Adams, W. (Ed.) (1977) 'The steel industry.' *The Structure of American Industry*. 5th Edition, Ch. 3, pp. 86–129. New York: Macmillan.

Adams, W. and Dirlam, J. B. (1966) Big Steel, invention, and innovation. *Quarterly Journal of Economics*, **LXXX** (No. 2), 167, 189.

Baumol, W. J. (1959) *Economic Dynamics*. 3rd Edition. New York: Macmillan.

Chakravarty, S, (1959) *The Logic of Investment Planning*. Amsterdam: North-Holland.

Haberler, G. (1946) *Prosperity and Depression*. 3rd Edition. Lake Success, NY: United Nations.

Hicks, J. R. (1974) *The Crisis of Keynesian Economics*. New York: Basic Books.

Keynes, J. M. (1930) *Treatise on Money*. 2 Volumes. London: Macmillan.

Keynes, J. M. (1964) *The General Theory of Employment, Interest, and Money*. New York: Harcourt Brace.

Mansfield, E. (1977) *The Production and Application of New Industrial Technology*. New York: Norton.

Samuelson, P. A. (1979) *Economics*. 11th Edition. New York: McGraw-Hill.
Schumpeter, J. A. (1912) *Theorie der wirtschaftlichen Entwicklung*. English translation (1934) *Theory of Economic Development*. Cambridge, MA: Harvard University Press.
Schumpeter, J. A. (1931) The present depression: a tentative diagnosis. *American Economic Review*, **XXL** (No. 1), 179–82.
Schumpeter, J. A. (1939) *Business Cycles: A Theoretical, Historical and Statistical Analysis of the Capitalist Process*. 2 Volumes. New York: McGraw-Hill.
Schumpeter, J. A. (1946) The decade of the twenties. *American Economic Review*, **XXXVI** (No. 2), 1–10.
Schumpeter, J. A. (1954). *History of Economic Analysis* (Ed.) Schumpeter, E. B. New York: Oxford University Press.
Tsuru, S. (1976) Business cycle and capitalism: Schumpeter versus Marx. In *Towards a New Political Economy*, Vol. 13 of *Collected Works*. Tokyo: Kodansha.

Chapter Three

Schumpeter and the Current and Future Development of the World Economy

HERBERT GIERSCH

1. IN contrast to other participants in this meeting, I never had any personal relationship to Schumpeter. Nor shall I present an exegesis of his works. But in my attempt to explain the world economy and its evolution I have nowhere found more help than in the range of ideas delivered and left to us by Schumpeter, though—as far as I know—he never dealt explicitly and in detail with the open economy and with international economic relations.

2. Schumpeter explains development and, hence, economic performance in the course of time. In order to give due weight to space, I first have to refer to another economist of the German-speaking world, Johann Heinrich von Thünen, who was born exactly 100 years before Schumpeter and also died 100 years before him.

Thünen explains the allocation of economic activity over a circularly bordered homogeneous plane with transportation costs varying in direct proportion to distance and weight. Within this system it can be proven (Giersch, 1949/50)

(a) that a city or agglomeration will emerge in the centre,
(b) that with increasing distance from the centre the density of population will decline, so that in spite of the disadvantage of transportation costs, marginal labour productivity at the periphery will attain the same level as in the centre, and
(c) that mobile capital will allocate itself, in a similar vein, so as to pass on the disadvantages of distance from the centre to immobile land, i.e. to avoid the periphery and be more concentrated in locations closer to the centre.

3. This spatial equilibrium can be depicted as an income cone with the Thünen space as its base and with value added per unit of space as its third dimension. Goods traded among locations with different distance from the centre differ in their factor proportions—as in the Heckscher–Ohlin–Samuelson model. Since Thünen was the first to recognize this phenomenon, at least with regard to the land–labour ratio, I prefer to call goods of this type 'Thünen goods', rather than 'Heckscher–Ohlin goods', as is usually done following Hirsch (1974).

4. Before bringing on Schumpeter himself, I have to turn to David Ricardo (1772–1823) as the third of the great economists who help us in explaining the world economy. His contribution lies in illustrating foreign trade by an example, in which sun-intensively produced Portuguese wine was exchanged against cloth from humid England. Neither such differences in climate nor differences in the endowment of natural resources are incorporated in Thünen's model. But as climate and the location of natural resources are so important in the world economy—especially when we ask where economic development can be generated and will take place—and what role they played in the historical process of industrialization based on coal and iron ore, we have to add a second type of goods which deserve to be called Ricardo goods (Hirsch, 1974). What is more important, however, is the fact that climate and natural resources, like the Thünen agglomeration, create economic rents—a source of income that facilitates capital accumulation and thus helps to bring about economic development.

5. By now the stage can be set for Schumpeter. The Thünen cone grows by capital accumulation but if the system produces only Thünen and Ricardo goods, capital accumulation will depress the marginal productivity of capital, in the centre as well as over the rest of the plane. The probable result will be a flattening of the income cone in the course of growth. Above all, if the real rate of interest declines and capital intensity increases, transportation costs are likely to become less important. This will intensify the tendency towards interlocational factor price equalization through trade, thus lowering the Thünen rents which are due to transportation costs.

6. 'Schumpeter goods' is the label for new goods with still secret production functions. They emerge from the production of knowledge and the application of knowledge to the production of sellable goods. In Schumpeter's words, these are 'new combinations'. Today we speak of innovations and distinguish between product and process innovations. Most of the process innovations are based on new investments goods, i.e. on product innovations at the intermediate level.

7. Where will the production of Schumpeter goods be located in the Thünen system? The answer is most probably close to the centre, where we have the highest per capita incomes due to the advantages of location, climate, and natural resources, and where the accumulation of capital which facilitates investment in basic and applied research. However, with the relative decline of transportation and communication costs, the centre loses its attractive power for these as well as for other economic activities and allows for a greater division of labour in favour of residential areas preferred by scientists. Research centres and locations of innovation may be segregated, but often the transfer of knowledge from research to industrial application will be more efficient if the advantages of agglomeration are utilized. The centre can thus be seen to include research and development activities. In this case, we capture space and time, allocation and development best, if we speak about a volcano rather than a cone.

8. In the phase of the Pax Britannica the western part of the world economy formed a single Thünen–Schumpeter system with London and England as its innovative and financial core and the Royal Navy as a means to the end of guaranteeing peace, as a necessary condition for trade. The torrent of knowledge and innovation (or lava) that emanated from the eruptions of the industrial revolution in the centre of the system (Schumpeter volcano) flew down the slope in the form of technology transfer to Continental Europe and America, where it increased factor productivities and contributed to the rise of industrial incomes.

9. The course of development during the twentieth century can best be approximated by saying that it has been governed by the Pax Americana—with the eastern seaboard of the United States of America as the top of the income cone, New York City (Wall Street) as the financial core, the New England research institutes as the innovative core, and the CIA as a replacement for the Royal Navy.

10. Since World War II two new cones have emerged: Continental Europe with the Federal Republic of Germany as its centre, and the Far East with its Japanese core region. Both have practically caught up with the USA. Whether this catching-up process can be prolonged into an overtaking is an unanswered question, at least as far as Europe is concerned. Japan seems to have accomplished the transition from imitation to innovation, and it has indeed become the centre of those storms of competition that characterize the process of creative destruction. This is genuine Schumpeterian competition. In Europe where the top of the income cone could be identified to lie in the lower Rhine area (Giersch, 1979), the centre now tends to move southwards

towards the upper Rhine valley, away from the raw material deposits so important for industrialization in the nineteenth century towards formerly poor regions where people had always been forced to base their living on human rather than natural resources. These latter regions have locational advantages for producing Schumpeter goods.

11. Let me describe the European catching-up process in Schumpeter's sense as a two-phase creative destruction with a wartime destruction at the beginning and an advanced renewal and reconstruction afterwards. With respect to the Federal Republic of Germany and her so-called 'economic miracle', the following conditions appear significant:

(a) a considerable destruction of the old capital stock, and of the jobs built into it,
(b) an influx of refugees who increased the supply of highly motivated workers, of human capital, and of Schumpeterian entrepreneurs, who caused the remaining stock of physical capital to become even scarcer,
(c) impediments to emigration, and
(d) pressure on wages generated by the scarcity of jobs in industry and the low marginal labour productivity in the overmanned agricultural sector, implying a level of wages below the marginal product of labour in industry.

12. Quasi-fixed production coefficients in manufacturing, in combination with the difficulty of fully utilizing scarce physical capital by shift-working, led to marginal labour productivity exceeding the wage rate, with a consequent 'exploitation of labour' on the one hand and a correspondingly high marginal productivity of capital on the other. An undervalued currency ensured a low wage rate and high marginal efficiency of capital in manufacturing by international standards. This served to eliminate the capital shortage by favouring those with a high propensity to save and by attracting venture capital and investors from abroad.

13. These were the conditions for rapid economic development in the form of a catching-up process. In Schumpeter's vision, old vintages of physical capital get depreciated and destroyed in the course of competition. In Germany, physical capital had been destroyed already. Schumpeter's development process is accelerated when monetary expansion lowers the market interest rate and thereby facilitates investment. In Germany the driving force of low interest rates was replaced by a high marginal efficiency of capital brought about by a wage–productivity ratio favourable to business. Schumpeter does not explicitly address the question of where new entrepreneurs may come from, but for post-war Germany the answer must be:

(a) from among the immigrating refugees, many of whom wanted to regain their economic independence;
(b) from among the millions of prisoners of war, many of whom had learned entrepreneurship, improvisation and leadership as (professional) officers, and who—confronted with barriers to entry in many professions—were able to gain their desired social status only by becoming independent entrepreneurs or by climbing up the career ladder within existing firms, not without having accumulated practical economic knowledge in the black market previously.

14. New knowledge applicable to economic decisions does not necessarily have to be produced at home in an open system. It can be imported, already in a well tested form, perhaps embodied in modern investment goods. It can also be obtained as a by-product, if trade and other commercial relations with a more developed country are intensified. This knowledge comes in automatically if the exchange rate makes domestic resources appear cheap to complementary foreign resources. You will hardly find this import of knowledge and technology registered in current account statistics, because the technological component in imported capital goods has often been paid for by early users at discriminatory prices. If foreign investors are attracted by a competitively priced currency, the imported technology will soon be transformed into export earnings, particularly if foreigners come in to establish production facilities for supplying their home markets. The country then becomes the stage for a particular sort of innovation—locational innovation. This concept immediately emerges as a combination of Schumpeter's innovation theory with Thünen's location theory and its application to open economies.

15. At this stage something fundamental has to be reiterated about relationships among the current account, the exchange rate, and economic development.

(a) A '*Sturm und Drang*' economy runs an export surplus, because its entrepreneurs unfold strong suppliers' activities on export markets, with faster domestic economic development as a by-product. A country attracting foreign resources will run a current account deficit, we suppose, but it runs into debt by strength and not by weakness. This strength is reflected in a rapid growth of domestic supply and of export supply as well. The criterion for measuring strength is international competitiveness. A country will be very competitive if its exports grow at a faster rate than world trade. In order to demonstrate, if need be, that the economy is a debtor out of strength rather than weakness, it only has to reduce domestic absorption for a time. Import demand is thereby reduced and export supply increased. This will soon convert the current account deficit into a surplus. Even for a large country, this need not be accompanied by a deterioration in the terms of trade. On the contrary, a rapidly growing country, penetrating the world market, will already have accepted less favourable terms of trade than it could have enjoyed had it not grown through penetration.[1] This may sound paradoxical or confusing within a stationary framework for a balance-of-payments and current account analysis, but is consistent with a foreign trade theory compatible with Schumpeter's theory of economic development.

(b) For less-developed countries intent to catch up, the lesson is this: You ought to have an undervalued currency in the sense that you are competitive in exporting standardized Thünen or Heckscher–Ohlin goods. Your current account might well be negative, and it must be to the extent you are absorbing complementary foreign resources in addition to domestic savings. This process of 'capital imports for export growth' amounts to an assurance of future export growth exceeding the growth of world trade, as long as the country's currency is not overvalued.

(c) It is quite possible for a rich and strong country to run a current account deficit on the strength of a boom or a structure of production dominated by highly income-elastic goods. Such countries invest beyond their domestic savings, in contrast to a widely held view which associates any current account deficit with overconsumption and weakness. This is much better for these countries—and perhaps even for world welfare—than aiming at a current account surplus at all costs. Oil-related deficits of some rich countries with highly productive investment opportunities are a case in point.

(d) If the Thünen cones of the world economy are to become flatter and the rich countries themselves are to contribute to this process, they will need current account surpluses. Measured in production costs of Thünen or Heckscher–Ohlin goods, their currencies must be overvalued. Jobs in corresponding branches are then subject to intensified destructive competition from abroad (below) and have to be transferred to less-developed countries—by locational innovations down the Thünen gradient.

(e) Within this Schumpeterian perspective, a current account surplus may well indicate weakness. This is the case if the propensity to save is not matched by a sufficiently high marginal efficiency of investment because of, say, high marginal tax rates, regulatory constraints, aggressive unions

[1] The so-called 'balance-of-payments crisis' in Germany during the Korea boom may serve as an example. The problem vanished when it became clear that the deficit was accompanied by a rapid growth of exports. If it is true that the Federal Republic had overimported then it had done so for investment rather than consumption and, in the end, for increasing exports.

and other interest groups, etc. Such countries will fall behind their catching-up colleagues.

(f) The most pathological case of a current account surplus is marked by capital flight from a country lacking profitable investment opportunities at home. Even human capital, including entrepreneurs, may leave in search of higher rewards. Their emigration is, of course, not recorded in trade statistics but it may well cause an export of complementary resources which are recorded.

16. A country exposed to destructive competition from down the Thünen gradient, notably from catching-up and newly industrialized countries, is subject to capital losses in traditional and standardized manufacturing branches which produce standardized commodities (Thünen goods). Even losses of product-specific human capital may occur. Hence, real incomes, including real wages, have to decline. If real wages are rigid, the result will be what I call Stolper–Samuelson unemployment. The political pressure to preserve threatened jobs by Stolper–Samuelson type protection is evident.

17. The positive alternative to Stolper-Samuelson protection in rich and mature economies is creative Schumpeterian innovation. It composes product innovations which open new opportunities for producers and widen the range of choice for consumers, and such process innovations which are not designed to protect the locus of Thünen goods production in high wage countries. They are all beneficial. Defensive process innovations which I have left out lead to the detrimental consequence that goods suitable for manufacturing in countries with little capital and much labour are still being produced at the original locations with more and more capital and less and less labour. The expectation of Stolper–Samuelson protection promotes such defensive investment. It may evoke precisely that reversal of factor intensities which is often used as evidence against the applicability of classical trade theorems such as the optimality of free trade and the international equalization of factor prices.

18. In order to promote creative Schumpeterian innovation and prevent Stolper–Samuelson unemployment in such countries, creative competition is necessary, in the business of scientific discovery as well as in product markets. In science as in economic life, it is supply side competition rather than defensive reactions to demand which fosters development in the long run. A parallel between scientific and economic development can be drawn by comparing the current growth of knowledge theories with the well known types of suppliers' competition (Giersch, 1980a). It is true, there is a demand-oriented growth of knowledge theory, too—put forward by Hübner

(1978)—and it is comparable with Hicks's notion of induced inventions. However, this theory fails to explain how the situation emerged (inconsistencies within the system) which is postulated to bring about scientific progress. In terms of an example familiar to economists, one would say that higher oil prices certainly induce oil-saving and oil-substituting inventions and innovations, but a comprehensive theory of development has to explain in the first place why relative prices remained as they did for quite a while and then suddenly changed.

The driving forces in supply side theories are ambitions such as curiosity, thirst for knowledge, and endeavour for reputation, social status, power, and profit. In a social setting these forces unfold in the process of competition.

19. A supplier in perfect competition has hardly any scope for innovation, since new actions promising profits would at once be imitated by his competitors so that none can expect to earn profits from innovation; on the other hand, every single mistake, in science equivalent to the falsification of a hypothesis, threatens his very existence in the market. This corresponds to the naive falsificationism in the philosophy of science sometimes read into Popper's *Logic of Scientific Discovery* (German original, Popper, 1935) where one contrary observation would suffice to refute the hypothesis.

20. Imperfect (monopolistic) competition is already more creative. In contrast to deterministic perfect competition, an entrepreneur has scope for innovative decisions which are connected with risk and chance. This setting is open to different futures; it is stochastic. In order to test innovative hypotheses, i.e. new explanations in science or new products in the market, numerous observations and tests have to take place, and each corroboration is only provisional. The supplier in monopolistic competition can take chances thanks to accumulated profits, the scientist thanks to a service contract or a scholarship.

However, in monopolistic competition which corresponds to Popper's sophisticated falsificationism there are always more hypotheses or products than seem to be necessary, and several new combinations turn out to be sham innovations. In economics this is sometimes called excessive product differentiation.

21. In a dynamic oligopoly phases of calm competition alternate with phases of stormy competition. Progress turns out to be discontinuous. This means to Schumpeter's process of creative destruction and to his thesis that economic growth occurs in waves in the wake of technological revolutions. The parallel in the theory of science is provided by Kuhn (1962 first edition and 1970 second edition) who explains scientific progress by a revolutionary

replacement of an old paradigm by a new one. A paradigm, the basic beliefs that tie together the members of a 'school' in science, looks suspiciously like a peaceful oligopoly with price-leadership, or even like a cartel. Within 'normal science', i.e. within the school or cartel, only details will be subjects of research. Colleagues write for colleagues—without regard to relevance or wider demand. Thus, normal science evolves along predetermined lines until more and more phenomena are observed which are anomalous within the old scheme. A revolutionary change of paradigm will come about only if outsiders with a new world-view tread a new path with which the former anomalies can be explained and forecast. This is the stage at which the innovators—the Schumpeterian entrepreneurs in science—coalesce. Kuhn's point in this interpretation is that progress will be discontinuous if the system allows rigidities to develop and persist. To turn to economics, Schumpeter in explaining capitalist development refers to a process of unsteady pushes interrupted by stages of relative calm: '. . . in the sense that there always is either revolution or absorption of the results of revolution . . .' (Schumpeter, 1942, p. 84, footnote 2). This parallelism between spontaneous development of science on the one hand and the capitalist production of goods on the other is remarkable indeed. Is this mere chance? Or do both forms of development have a common basis in the desire for an orderly state of affairs that can be satisfied—albeit only temporarily—by protection against irritating disturbances and adjustment pressures. The longer such an orderly situation is maintained, the more vehement will the later adjustment turn out to be. Note the abrupt nature of shifts in parities under a regime of fixed exchange rates. More generally, in science as well as in the economy, tensions are bound to arise if developments, driven from the supply side, become too independent of the demand side. Such tensions may be resolved only through a crisis if the system is too rigid.

22. Supplier's competition also seems to be the driving force in Lakatos' theory of scientific progress (Lakatos, 1970). Here, comprehensive scientific research programmes compete with each other, not merely individual hypotheses or paradigms, as with Popper or Kuhn. However, Lakatos' research programmes are comparable neither with single-product enterprises nor with cartels, but rather with multiproduct firms offering a family of products. In contrast to Kuhn, Lakatos leaves scope for continuous dynamic competition, with several research programmes (firms) existing side by side, some catching up and overtaking, others falling behind but with the chance of regeneration. This is surprisingly similar to Schumpeter's dynamic competition: '. . . competition . . . which strikes not at the margins of the profits and the outputs of the existing firms but at their foundations and their very lives . . .' (Schumpeter, 1942, p. 84).

23. These parallels suggest important consequences for economic policy.

Technical as well as economic advance requires freedom combined with suppliers' competition, albeit imperfect or monopolistic. Central direction eliminates competition in science as well as in economic life, and hence is counterproductive in both fields. In economics this is well understood. In science, policy competition is often rejected in order to avoid the apparent costs of parallel efforts. Most problematic is research planning on a national level in a protected country, where researchers are *entre nous* due to an effective language barrier. This is very similar to competition as the driving force of progress in the economy. Hence, freedom of entrepreneurship, even within firms and here at all levels, is an important public good comparable to the freedom of science and research. Hence, it deserves a similar dignity.

Centrally planned investment and even looser forms of guidance, including subsidies, require that the planners already possess the information which the competitive process has to produce. This strategy, therefore, is suitable at best for catching-up countries who can imitate the patterns of more advanced countries. It is unsuitable for countries and enterprises near the frontier of technical and economic progress. The free market for new ideas is as important as the free market for new goods. Thus, I once replied to a statement about Schumpeter made by Professor Samuelson:[2] For a Schumpeter country at the top that wants to maintain progress there exists no 'fascist solution' oppressing the freedom of thought, science, and research. Under a fascist regime an advanced country is bound to fall behind (Giersch, 1980b).

Central control of investment may be feasible if the economy is heavily protected against the storm of international competition. It is nevertheless inefficient as it requires forfeiting the enormous gains from international trade, including the cheap import of knowledge from abroad.

24. Nevertheless, government has an important role to play in Schumpeterian economic development. It can try to influence positively the attractiveness of domestic investment opportunities in worldwide intergovernmental competition

(a) by providing an infrastructure complementary to private investment,

---

[2] Samuelson (1980b) referred to the eleventh edition of his *Economics* (Samuelson, 1980a) and stated in his paper 'The world economy at century's end' presented at the Sixth World Congress of Economists in Mexico on 4–8 August 1980: '. . . Vilfredo Pareto was a clever man. And so was Georges Sorel. Reading between Schumpeter's lines, . . . we can see that the same solution as theirs was tacitly in his mind. . . . What I am alluding to is of course the fascist solution. . . . Here are the words to describe fascistic capitalism:

> Generals and admirals take power. They wipe out their leftist predecessors, exile opponents, jail dissident intellectuals, curb the trade-unions, and control the press and all political activity.'

(b) by ensuring flexibility in the labour market,
(c) by ensuring that the capital market functions in financing the formation of human a well as physical capital,
(d) by keeping open international and national product markets, and
(e) by setting tax rates and supplying public goods in such a way that the country is attractive to innovative foreign resources, including entrepreneurial and cultural talents.

If mobile resources are free to move from country to country and if currencies are fully convertible, governments in this open world economy are forced to operate in dynamic competition with one another. I am sure that Schumpeter would have fully considered this international competition of governments and of political entrepreneurs, had he not shied away from international economic relations. Whether there is an economist's Valhalla, where Schumpeter would certainly have his place, and whether he would follow my modest attempts to supplement his theory with anger or with pleasure, I cannot know, but the organizers of this conference who invited me must have presumed sympathy. For that, I have to express my gratitude.

REFERENCES

Giersch, H. (1949/50) Economic union between nations and the location of industry. *Review of Economic Studies*, **17** (No. 2), 87–97.

Giersch, H. (1979) Aspects of growth, structural change, and employment—a Schumpeterian perspective. *Weltwirtschaftliches Archiv.*, **115** (No. 4), 629–652.

Giersch, H. (1980a) Wissenschaftsfortschritt und Wettbewerb. In *Theorie und Politik der internationalen Wirtschaftsbeziehungen* (Eds) K. Borchardt and F. Holzheu, 41–45. Stuttgart, New York: Gustav Fischer. Hans Möller zum 65. Geburtstag.

Giersch, H. (1980b) Comment on P. A. Samuelson's paper: The world economy at century's end. Presented at the *Sixth World Congress of Economists*, Mexico, 4–8 August 1980. *Kiel Working Papers No. 110*. Kiel: Institute of World Economics.

Hirsch, S. (1974) Hypotheses regarding trade between developing and industrial countries. In *The International Division of Labour. Problems and Perspectives* (Ed.) H. Giersch. Symposium, July 1973, organized by the Institute of World Economics. Kiel, Tübingen: J. C. B. Mohr (Paul Siebek).

Hübner, K. (1978) *Kritik der wissenschaftlichen Vernunft*. Freiburg/Br., München: Alber.

Kuhn, T. S. (1962) *The Structure of Scientific Reductions*. 1st Edition 1962; 2nd Edition 1970. Chicago: University of Chicago Press.

Lakatos, I. (1970) Falsification and the methodology of scientific research programmes. In *Criticism and the Growth of Knowledge* (Eds) I. Lakatos and A. Musgrave, 91–196. Cambridge: Cambridge University Press.

Popper, K. (1935) *Logik der Forschung. Zur Erkenntnistheorie der modernen Naturwissenschaften*. Wien: Springer.

Samuelson, P. A. (1980a) *Economics*. 11th Edn. New York: McGraw-Hill.

Samuelson, P. A. (1980b) The world economy at century's end. Paper presented at the *Sixth World Congress of Economists*, Mexico, 4–8 August 1980.

Schumpeter, J. A. (1942) *Capitalism, Socialism, and Democracy*. New York: Harper & Row.

Chapter Four

Schumpeter's Vienna and the Role of Credit in Innovation

ERICH STREISSLER

1. WHAT was Schumpeter's Vienna like as the stage of his economic thought? What were the habits of mind he met with in his society, habits which must have coloured his work? A man's basic ideas of the world in which he lives are formed during his early manhood, particularly between his fifteenth and thirty-fifth years.[1] As he was born in 1883 we shall therefore understand by Schumpeter's Vienna his social environment exactly during the last two decades of the Habsburg monarchy. Schumpeter left Vienna for good in 1925. The first years of the inter-war period will therefore figure in our analysis only insofar as they developed trends already nascent before the breakdown of the old Empire.

2. Austria had perhaps the most rigidly aristocratic society of all the nations of Old Europe. Aristocracy should be understood as only the upper aristocracy, from Counts upwards; or what was in Schumpeter's Vienna most appropriately called the 'first society' (Brunner, 1949, p. 337). The rank of Count was, under Franz Joseph, nearly inaccessible from below. A very important cabinet minister could sometimes enter it, as did the Minister of the Exterior and the Imperial Household, Baron, later Count, Aehrenthal; now and then the same could happen to the very top generals, as for instance to the long-time Chief of the General Staff, Generaloberst Beck-Rzikowsky, who became a Count on retiring at the age of 76. Anyhow, such positions were from the start mostly open only to members of the upper aristocracy. No financier, not to mention mere manufacturers, ever became a Count in Austria after the eighteenth century, when the Fries family achieved this rank. In the narrower sense the dividing line of the upper aristocracy even went right through the ranks of the Counts: what mattered was whether one

[1] See, for this opinion, Young (1936), who constructs his 'Chronological Table' in the appendix on this supposition.

was a '*Reichsgraf*' and a '*Standesherr*' and thus had '*Ebenbürtigkeit*' with ruling Houses, a status which by its very definition could no longer be achieved by newcomers, as the old '*Reich*' had then passed away a hundred years ago. A Countess Chotek could not lawfully marry a Habsburg, though a Windigrätz could.

In the wider sense—class distinctions must not be understood to be too hard and fast—everybody who was an 'Excellency' became at least a life member of this upper upper class. All cabinet ministers were Excellencies and so were members of civil service rank III, the rank immediately below cabinet ministers, who themselves were considered members of the civil service and of rank II (they were frequently recruited out of the career civil service). Rank III included some specially promoted '*Sektionschefs*' (Permanent Secretaries, who normally would be of rank IV) and the chief provincial governors. Generals were Excellencies from *Feldmarschalleutnant* (Lieutenant General) upwards, as was Schumpeter's stepfather, Feldmarschalleutnant von Kéler. A last group of life members of the 'first society' were the members of the '*Herrenhaus*', the Life Peers; for instance in their final years all three leaders of the Austrian school of economics, Menger, Böhm-Bawerk and Freiherr von Wieser.

In spite of its social ascendancy the hereditary upper aristocracy was, however, rapidly losing both in power[2] and above all in economic strength since at least the 1870s and 1880s. What really counted was the lower upper class, or—as one then said—the 'second society'. A section of this second society was formed by the rich financiers. But most of the members of the 'second society' were rather poor; and its core was the upper civil service and the high officer class. This class was recruited above all out of the professions, whose more successful members rose into the second society. The civil service consisted of numerous employees and one 'self-employed', the Emperor, as he himself put down when filling in his file for the census of 1910. It was thus, so to speak, the Emperor's firm. One was a member of this lower upper class from rank VI in the civil service, the rank from which upwards one had to pay an inaugural visit to the Emperor upon appointment. All professional university professors were members of this class and had to stage—in uniform!—such a visit to the Emperor, who appointed them (see Lorenz, 1965, p. 129). We can well imagine Schumpeter thus visiting the Emperor. Part-time unpaid university teachers could be 'vested with the title and the character' of a university professor and thus be placed on the fringe of the upper class—a quaint idea that the Emperor could award an upper-class 'character'; as he finally did in the case of Freud, for instance, though Freud had had to pass through agonies of impatient waiting, as he repeatedly tells

[2] See, for this opinion, for instance Sieghart (1932, p. 257ff.). See also Brunner (1949, p. 338ff.).

us,[3] after he heard that in the present political constellation the minister could not think of suggesting a Jew to the Emperor.

3. Whether one held a lower aristocratic title (Edler, Ritter or Freiherr) was not really essential in order to count as part of the 'second society'. And above all, those who held these titles usually had no landed property at all. The hereditary titles had mainly been gained as honorific distinctions of upper civil servants and of quite low military ranks: from captain upwards (after 30 years' service) in the eighteenth century (see Allmayer-Beck, 1957, p. 253ff., here p. 258ff., pp. 272, 274) and from colonel upwards in Schumpeter's Vienna. The title brought no wealth with it. In certain periods, on the other hand, wealth more or less automatically brought a title, for instance in the third quarter of the last century, when hereditary rank was attached to the Order of the Iron Crown, which was later disassociated from it (see Hennings, 1963, §.30 f). Thus old established industrial and financial families held titles of the lower nobility. It is interesting that Friedrich von Hayek holds such a title from the first industrial revolution in Austria at the end of the eighteenth century though also typical that his family later followed civil service and university careers.

'*Der Mensch fängt beim Baron an*' (the human being begins with the rank of baron) was a well known saying of the upper upper class, on whose fringes some old established baronial families moved. The saying is typical, but typical also for the fluidity of the concept. A cab-driver, for instance, would call anyone who looked like a member of the lower upper class (or who tipped well) 'Herr Baron'. Distinctions were numerous but also, as in all countries of the '*ancien régime*', very vague. They were complicated by the many different nationalities which were still not fully integrated. If someone has once called France before the revolution a society of a 'cascade of contempt' (J. Droz after Hampson, 1963, p. 6), the society of Schumpeter's Vienna could appropriately be called a *maze of contempt*, a bewildering and somewhat fluid maze, but also a maze of tolerant mutual neglect.

4. It must be kept in mind that Schumpeter was the first great Austrian economist who was *not* really a member of the all important 'second society' by birth (Menger, Böhm-Bawerk, Wieser and numerous others all were); however, by education he could just 'pass'. By fortune he was much wealthier than most members of the 'second society' in their youth, which, in Austria, rather counted against him. And in character he was completely impossible; he was a brash society crasher from the start. 'Never try to

[3] Freud (1942, Vol. II/III, pp. 142, 199 and also pp. 198, 144–146, 278). Interesting in our context is the further characterization by Freud: 'the elevation to the rank of professor, which raises the physician in our society to the heights of a demi-god in the eyes of his patients'.

become famous' Count Auersperg told the civil servants below him.[4] Rudolf Sieghart (1932, p. 263), an innovative civil servant and banker, Excellency and Life Peer, though never accepted by the upper class and finally made to fail, remarks bitterly on Schumpeter's Vienna: 'People, who had a mind of their own and—*horribile dictu*—voiced it, were not suffered gladly. One had to be "popular", then one was welcome'.[5] Schumpeter tried to become famous. He tried to make a name for himself. When upbraided by a non-distinct old professor over whose head he had been promoted he terminated the conversation by asking his colleague pointedly: 'What did you say your *name* was?'

Schumpeter could just 'pass', because his stepfather, who was, as I pointed out, a lieutenant general and thus on the fringes of the upper upper class, gave him access to Austria's first school. Schumpeter entered and graduated from the '*Theresianum*', or to give it its proper name, the Maria Theresian Knight's Academy (The mass university of Vienna, on the other hand, gave Schumpeter scientific contacts but brought no social distinction). As Sieghart (1932, p. 268) summed up the point, 'The Theresianist carried the Fieldmarshal's baton in his knapsack; his origin from the famous institute in the former imperial Favorita assured him favoured treatment in the public service'.

5. And where did the entreprèneurs, the merchants and manufacturers come into the picture? In this civil service and rentier society which was Schumpeter's Vienna with a few exceptions they did not figure at all; merchants and manufacturers had hardly any social intercourse with members of the ruling classes; they were just subjects to be administered (Ehrhart, 1958, pp. 42–53).[6] Only bankers were, as I pointed out, a group on the fringes of the upper class. But they had to pride themselves on their conservatism. Freiherr von Spitzmüller, Austria's first banker when Schumpeter wrote the *Theory of Economic Development* (1912), wrote proudly: 'Profiteering and love of money were not prominent among them. The tendencies of bank policy could be called conservative' (Spitzmüller, 1955, p. 111).[7] Other entrepreneurs than bankers significantly do not figure in the high literature of the time. If in exceptional cases they do, they are usually not Austrian: Doderer's 'Wasserfälle von Slunj' describe an English manufacturing family in Austria and the sinister Kammerrat Levielle in his 'Demons' ('*Die Dämonen*') is of doubtful

[4] '*Nur nicht berühmt werden wollen*' (see Ehrhart, 1958, p. 140).

[5] In another place he calls Vienna a place '*wo man im allgemeinen für starke und eigenwillige Persönlichkeiten nichts übrig hat und glatte, bequeme Leute vorzieht*' (p. 156).

[6] Manufacturers practically do not make their appearance, for instance, in the memoirs of Ehrhart, Sieghart and Spitzmüller apart from a member of the—German—Krupp dynasty.

[7] '*Übermässige Plusmacherei und Erwerbsgier traten nicht in den Vordergrund. Die Tendenzen der Bankpolitik konnten als konservativ bezeichnet werden.*'

extraction and nationality (he stresses his title is French) as well as of doubtful occupation (von Doderer, 1956, 1963). In the 'salon' of Frau Sektionschef Tuzzi in Musil's 'Man without Qualities' ('*Mann ohne Eigenschaften*'), which is meant as a cross-section of Vienna society, only one entrepreneur figures, Arnheim, and he is German and a banker (Musil, 1931). In Herzmanovsky-Orlando's '*Maskenspiel der Genien*' (1958) the famous 'Ariadne Tapestry Works'—a pre-industrial type of manufacture and not untypically a state enterprise founded to relieve unemployment—undoes at night what has been woven in the day in order to preserve both the reputation for excellent quality and the great rarity of its tapestries.[8] In other words, Austrian manufacturers and other entrepreneurs fight shy of the judgement of the market. Bankers and civil servants stress the conservatism of the Austrian entrepreneur: What does the manufacturer really want, the President of the Vienna Chamber of Commerce asks the Prime Minister, Count Badeni, rhetorically? His answer: 'A location close to water-power, a protective tariff and the Order of the Iron Crown' (Erhart, 1958, p. 43).[9]

Such a 'need to achieve' what is called in Austria 'visible distinction', i.e. an order to be worn with dress clothes, was, however, rather presumptuous. Even during World War I, when things already went to seed and something had to be done for army suppliers and government financiers, they were awarded only rather low-brow orders of merit: they would be awarded what was popularly called the '*Comptoirkreuz des Franz-Joseph-Kai Ordens mit dem Praterstern*',[10] a term which by its local connotations suggested that it was an order fit only for Jews.

6. Technical efficiency, on the other hand, was highly honoured in Austria. The engineer Karl Ritter von Ghega, who built the railway over the Semmering Pass, came close to being an Austrian celebrity; as was also the case with Karl Freiherr Auer von Welsbach (the son of a high civil servant), who invented gas lighting and later the osmium electric bulb. He became a celebrity in spite of the fact that he even made some money out of his inventions. In general, however, Austrian inventors were not able to profit from their inventions; for instance Joseph Ressel, who invented the screw for motorships; or Joseph Madersperger, who invented a sewing machine. Like

---

[8] In addition it should be noted that the Ariadne Tapestry Works have been erected 'for reasons of economy in a nearly inaccessible location' so that 'strict commercial calculation' has shown that transport costs for removing the final product would be too high. This is a witty gloss on the crippling transport costs of many Austrian firms.

[9] '*Eine Wasserkraft, einen Schutzzoll und die Eiserne Krone*'.

[10] See Kleinwaechter (1955, p. 257); correctly, of course, the Commander's Cross of the Franz-Joseph-Order with the Star.

the Russians today, Austria claimed in Schumpeter's day, and possibly with more justification, that Austrians had invented many things first. But as Herzmanovsky-Orlando (1957) tells us in his fictitious account 'Kaiser Joseph und die Bahnwärterstochter': When the Austrians invented the steam railway, they dropped the project on British intervention in order to let the English claim priority. Or, to put it more seriously, Austrians were inventors rather than successful innovators; Schumpeter took this contrast from reality. Organizational talent seemed to be extremely scarce. The civil service prided itself on just legal solutions and on calming things down, but not so much on organization. '*Fortwursteln*',[11] to act like a puppet, was the order of the day, not only in political matters. One gains the impression that in the political difficulties of the last decade before the war, not only political but also social conservatism was in a reactionary ascendency and not on the decline.[12]

Schumpeter's eulogy of the creative entrepreneur and his significance for development, his stress that innovation not invention was decisive, the importance he assigned to organization, thus ran completely counter to all the received Austrian preconceptions. It was an anti-theory not derived from, but opposed to, the practice of the Vienna of his day. It was one of the numerous manifestations of the 'bad manners' of an '*enfant terrible*', of Schumpeter as a totally 'impossible' man in the society of his day.

7. '*Die grossen Erfolge, die sie in ihrem Aufstieg erreicht hat, dankt die . . . Grossunternehmung nicht ihrem grossen Kapital . . . denn . . . sie hat dieses in der Hauptsache erst aus ihren Gewinnen gebildet. In den Anfängen war es vielmehr die hochgespannte Führeraufgabe, welche der . . . Unternehmung den spezifischen Charakter einer bevorzugten Marktstellung gab. Die Männer, die als Pioniere die neuen Wege eröffneten, mussten Leute von auserlesener Begabung sein, die technisches Können mit Markterfahrung und organisatorischer Kraft vereinigten und noch dazu die Kühnheit des Neuerers besitzen mussten*' (von Wieser, 1914, p. 375).

> It is not capital, which brings success, for capital itself is largely formed out of accrued profits. It is its role as market leader which has brought success to an enterprise. The men who pioneered new ways had to be supremely gifted men who combined technical abilities, a sense for the market and organizational power and in addition the audacity of the innovator.

[11] A famous term invented by Count Eduard Taaffe, Prime Minister 1868–70 and 1879–1893, permanently added by him to the Austrian vocabulary. (See for instance Sieghart, 1932, p. 18.)

[12] Ehrhart (1958, p. 138ff.) condemns Sieghart with the following words: 'He liked things new at least as much as things old, he was not conservative and could not be so for he had no family tradition'. What a time if this is the worst one can think of in order to condemn a man!

This is the essence of Schumpeter's analysis of the creative entrepreneur. Unfortunately, however, the quotation is not from Schumpeter, but from his main teacher Friedrich von Wieser, that teacher with whom Schumpeter, as he himself tells us (1908, p. IX), had the closest intellectual affinity. Though published slightly later than Schumpeter's *Theory of Economic Development* Wieser's classic textbook of economics of 1914 was certainly known to Schumpeter from Wieser's lectures out of which it emerged. The elitist theory of the dominant leader, the term 'leader' (in German '*Führer*', a term of infelicitous political connotations) furthermore the term 'pioneer' and finally the term '*Neuerer*', innovator itself, terms all used by Schumpeter, are typical terms of the later years of Friedrich von Wieser, terms which were frequently used by him. Wieser was a coiner of happy phrases and prided himself on this ability. He believed that by finding an illuminating term he had cast light on a subject.[13] It is in this search for catchy phrases, too, in which the young Schumpeter followed his teacher. When one reads Wieser one cannot help feeling one ought to speak rather of Wieser's entrepreneur than of Schumpeter's. As frequently happened in the academic life of Schumpeter's Vienna, the pupil turned a good dozen pages of the teacher (Wieser, 1914, §§46, 63, 69ff.) into a book; or rather, as we shall see, into one half of a book.

Thus though the glorification of the businessman, of the creative entrepreneur, ran counter to the social values current in Schumpeter's Vienna, it apparently did not run counter to the academic tradition in economics of the University of Vienna. It was endorsed by Wieser, the acting head of the school, the successor of Menger and a highly honoured figure in his own right. But it was not even a revolutionary idea with Wieser. He himself only followed a long-established route of peculiar interest to the Menger school. Gross (1884) and Mataja (1884) had published books on 'entrepreneurial profit'. And in the first decades of our century, it was not even an unusual idea in economics outside Vienna. Willett (1901) and Hawley (1907) had written books on creative risk-taking and profits,[14] books which, as I know by oral tradition—for I was told to read them in the 1950s—were noted in Vienna. And in Germany the influential Werner Sombart had just published an article on 'The capitalist entrepreneur' in 1909 and was then writing his book on the 'Bourgeois', published in 1913 a year after Schumpeter: Schumpeter was thus apparently safely wedged in a herd of academic lemmings.

---

[13] See the article on Wieser by Weinberger (1965, p. 71ff.).

[14] There was thus immediate interest in Schumpeter's work in the United States. He received an honorary doctorate from Columbia already in 1914.

8. In fact, though, Schumpeter's idea was much more shocking than that of his fellow lemmings. It is not so much the creative role of the entrepreneur which it was shocking to urge, but the fact that the innovator wreaks *creative destruction*. '*Durchsetzung neuer Kombination*',[15] forcing through new factor combinations in—be it noted—a full-employment situation of factors is the peculiarly Schumpeterian expression and the key-note of his particular brand of analysis. Here the society crasher can be heard! Overacquainted with business cycle theories as we are, we must not forget that Schumpeter above all proposed a more or less self-contained business cycle theory centring around the creation *and destruction* caused by the innovator; and that it was one of the first cyclical theories to be proposed. This then is the more original second half of his book. 'Why does development not follow a steady path but moves in jerks?' is Schumpeter's (1912, p. 426) question. With Wieser, development pioneered by the leaders implicitly had been an orderly procession. Wieser always tended to postulate foreseen consequences.[16]

Schumpeter harked back to Menger (1871), who had stressed the impenetrability of the future and the likelihood of planning errors.[17] Schumpeter's (1912) innovators, or at least his other businessmen, do make errors of calculation.[18] And they most explicitly 'disturb static equilibrium' (Schumpeter, 1912, p. 439). If it was already bad taste in Schumpeter's Vienna to speak highly of mere entrepreneurs, it was absolutely shocking in a conservative civil service state to praise anyone for creating disorder and worst of all to suggest that the creation of unrest could have a useful social function, could further material development! And even today it is good to remember that if we invoke the Schumpeterian entrepreneur as the cure-all for declining growth, we are, if we really mean what we say, clamouring at the same time for higher instability, for greater 'jerkiness' of development. Once this is fully realized I suspect many professed adherents of the Schumpeterian entrepreneur would still be happier with his more orderly Wieserian ancestor.

9. The original brand of Schumpeter's *Theory of Economic Development* linked and intertwined three ideas, which—as such—can all be found separately in the literature before him. The uneven, the cyclical nature of development; the role of the innovating entrepreneur not only in generating development, but

[15] Schumpeter (1912, p. 158 and then repeatedly p. 184) speaks of 'force' used against the majority.

[16] Typical of Wieser is his statement: 'Value is not predetermined by the producers but only correctly foreseen' (see Wieser, 1884, p. 169).

[17] Particularly Chapter 1, §4 entitled 'Time-Error'.

[18] Chapter VI, p. 414ff., particularly p. 444ff.

in generating uneven development; and finally not only the importance of credit for development in general, not even only its influence in generating cyclical development but above all its importance in furthering innovation and through it 'jerky' or cyclical development. Exactly these ideas, by the way, are in rudimentary fashion also all present in Karl Marx's *Das Kapital*, but not so prominently displayed or coherently presented.[19] But Schumpeter in 1912 apparently did not progress so far in the ways of an '*enfant terrible*' as to take much heed of Marx then already.[20] As the other strains of Schumpeter's thought are so well known I shall, in the remainder of my paper, turn to an analysis of the role of credit in his framework.[21]

To stress the importance of credit as such was no novelty in Schumpeter's Vienna; it merely pointed out a fact of general belief.[22] Industrial nations in their early stages of development always seem to veer towards mercantilist concepts and mercantilist policies and this was decidedly the case with Austria. The importance of credit was not only noted in the popular press, it was noted in the international as well as the Austrian professional economic literature. An article by Conant in the *Journal of Political Economy* of 1898 (p. 163) said: 'The development of credit has been an almost necessary incident of the growth of capital. The great modern accumulation of capital could not be moved without credit.' And (p. 172) 'For those who conduct an enterprise it affords the supplementary capital which they need for carrying on their business.' In Austria Schumpeter's teacher Wieser (1914, p. 296) wrote, 'The economic importance of credit has always been great; it has become enormous with the modern accumulation of financial capital.' This remark, by the way, is not only more balanced but also more perspicacious than the analysis by Schumpeter. For Schumpeter somehow persuaded himself that the *sole* essential necessity of credit arises out of development[23] instead of

[19] The parallels to Schumpeter's thought in the works of Marx have been noted by Eduard März (1965, p. 363ff., here p. 382). See particularly for a detailed diffusion process of innovation Karl Marx (1867, Edition MEG XXIII, Berlin 1969, Chapter 10, pp. 335–338). The parallels with the Marxist literature of Schumpeter's own day are even closer, particularly with his fellow student in the Vienna seminars, Hilferding. See Hilferding (1910).

[20] In 1912 Schumpeter explicitly rejects the notion of a 'reserve army of labour' (*Entwicklung*, p. 159), states that crises would also characterize a communist society (p. 458 and others) and contradicts Marx explicitly in stating that the workers are among the main winners from development (p. 504).

[21] März (1965), an article from which I have particularly profited, summarizes the different ideas of Schumpeter on the role of credit (p. 374ff.).

[22] See for instance Ausch (1968, p. 27ff.). Ausch quotes from the reasons given for a parliamentary motion in 1921 which says: 'The banks hold a singular position in the economy. All economic power is concentrated in them. By awarding or denying credit they decide the fate of enterprises and even of whole branches of industry'.

[23] Schumpeter (1912, p. 212): 'The (dynamic) entrepreneur *alone* necessarily needs credit, *only* for industrial *development* is it essential'.

merely saying that development increases the relative demand for credit. Schumpeter here fell into the trap of believing that an economy which is stationary in the aggregate must then also be stationary and fully foreseeable from the point of view of all individuals in it, so that in a stationary economy individuals have no essential need for credit.

The importance of credit for causing cyclical fluctuations also lay in the air. Unaccustomed as I am to praise the work of Ludwig von Mises, I have to point out nevertheless that in the very year of the publication of the *Theory of Economic Development* (1912), Mises (1912, part 3, chapter 5, §§4, 5) in his well known monetary treatise published a substantial passage on the cyclical process engendered by credit creation, the germ of the monetary side of the business cycle analysis later developed by Hayek (1929, 1931, 1939). But with Mises credit starts an *investment* process in general, not only an innovative process, as with Schumpeter. Again, I think, the less pointed analyses of Mises and Hayek come closer to the facts.

Even the importance of credit for the creative entrepreneur finds its place in Wieser's work. Once again it is, however, less pointed, less an all-or-nothing analysis. Wieser (1914, p. 296) says: 'The rise of effective entrepreneurs, the selection of the leading persons in the realm of property, is advanced by credit in the highest degree'. Credit helps very much, but is not absolutely essential, as with Schumpeter. And therefore with Wieser (1914, p. 375) creditworthiness is a characteristic of the business leader.

The only idea of Schumpeter on the impact of credit on development for which I know absolutely no antecedents is his point that the inflationary consequences of credit do not inhibit, but rather stimulate development; in fact that development has a necessary first phase that is inflationary (Schumpeter, 1912).[24]

10. We have thus seen that of the numerous ideas propounded by Schumpeter on the role of credit in economic development only two were his own and new: the idea that the inflationary effect of a credit expansion stimulates economic growth; and the idea that credit is a necessary prerequisite for innovation, which in turn is the fundamental source of economic expansion; more particularly that credit is the medium by which new enterprises are

[24] Schumpeter (1912) does *not* use the term 'inflation' *explicitly* in the first edition of 1912. The term 'inflation' was not common usage till after the war. The analysis itself, however, is most explicit: 'Credit is essentially the creation of purchasing power for the entrepreneur, and not simply placing existing purchasing power . . . at his disposal. The creation of purchasing power essentially characterizes the method by which development is forced upon an open economy' (p. 214). 'The entrepreneur receives purchasing power from the banker to which no products circulating in the economy correspond' (p. 222). Page 437 finally speaks of a reduction in the purchasing power of money.

created which are the vehicle of innovation. Were these ideas good descriptions of Austrian reality during the last quarter century before the war, or in other words, were they derived from an observation of Schumpeter's Vienna? And are they of more than a local or specific significance, are they explanations, if not of a truly universal mechanism behind all industrial development in a free market environment, at least explanations of a more general nature, effects that are frequently important?

11. The idea that inflation even if temporary and only cyclical, had salutary real long-run effects was certainly a very brave one (Schumpeter, 1912, p. 447ff.).[25] Up to then it had been propounded by economic cranks only. Educated economists would associate such an idea with 'quacks' like John Law (whom we would judge much more leniently today than he was judged around 1900). It ran completely counter to received orthodox theory; and more particularly to orthodox economic theory in Austria. During the last century Austria had passed through a prolonged period of monetary instability and of budget deficits, which were correctly seen as the cause of monetary instability. It had become received wisdom that such monetary instability (i.e. inflation and the concomitant variations in exchange rates) caused insecurity of business, made correct economic calculation and forward looking individual planning precarious and thus vitally impeded development. Great liberal ministers, for instance Ignaz von Plener (see März, 1968, pp. 20ff., 95ff., 257ff.), had therefore made a fight against inflation an integral part of their policy. Böhm-Bawerk as Minister of Finance was a strict apostle of fiscal orthodoxy[26] and consequently considered a budget deficit as the root of all evil.[27] A comparison of Schumpeter's positive attitude towards inflation with his contemporary von Mises or Mises' pupil von Hayek and finally the immediate critique by Böhm-Bawerk[28] easily proves the point that Schumpeter here took a completely deviant attitude from the then predominant one in Austria.

The dominant attitude towards inflation recognized, of course, that inflation was in the short-run interest of government finance. But it was

---

[25] How brave it was can be seen by the fact that he was immediately taken to task by Böhm-Bawerk on this point. In defence Schumpeter developed the theory of *forced saving*. (See Schumpeter, 1913a, p. 38ff.; 1913b, p. 599ff., particularly p. 604ff.)

[26] This is deplored by Alexander Gerschenkorn (1977), who thinks that Böhm-Bawerk's fiscal rigidity stinted his Prime Minister's, Ernest von Koerber's, development programme.

[27] As he did in his path-breaking analysis of the reasons for the balance of payments deficit shortly before World War One. (See Böhm-Bawerk, 1924, Vol. I, p. 499ff.)

[28] Mises (1912, ch. 6, §1 and ch. 6, §3 ('Inflationism')). For Böhm-Bawerk's critique see note 25.

asserted that government, while hurting every other group by inflation both in the short and in the long run, also damaged itself if one took a somewhat longer view. Government credit was seriously hurt by monetary instability so that the rate of interest which government had to pay was heavily increased. Proof of this proposition could be found in the development of the 1880s and 1890s when monetary stability and 'responsible' government budgeting were finally achieved with the consequence that government interest fell drastically (März, 1968, p. 213ff., and especially p. 220ff.). Through monetary and fiscal orthodoxy Austria had at last been able to join the financial system of the industrial nations: by the currency reform of 1892 it had been able to join what one might term the 'gold standard league'.

Now inflation, which, it was asserted, hurt every reputable member of society, certainly hurt in particular the recipients of fixed incomes and members of the rentier class (officers and civil servants had to have supplementary rentier income if they married). It thus hurt in particular the interests of the lower upper class, the 'second society', to which all the Austrian economists previous to Schumpeter belonged. Schumpeter, the son of an entrepreneur, on the other hand, asserted that an inflation caused by a commercial credit expansion was to the advantage of entrepreneurs; and that their advantage became the advantage of all groups of society through their investments which brought about economic growth. Thus a variant of a process which had been thought to be not even to the real advantage of the social group causing it and certainly disadvantageous to everybody else was seen by Schumpeter as in the interest of the group which at least solicited it and through this group as advantageous also to everybody else. The shift in viewpoint thus might partly be due to the particular social origin of the economist propounding the new view.

12. The first one-and-a-half decades of the twentieth century in Austria were certainly a period of quite unusually strong inflation, as compared with the previous quarter century. It was a period of creeping, one might say of briskly creeping, inflation.

From 1904 to 1911 the price index of consumables increased by 22.5 per cent or by 2.9 per cent per annum (see Mühlpeck *et al.*, 1979, p. 676ff.).[29] Credit expansion certainly was a contributing cause in this inflation: the credit multiplier seems to have increased drastically during this period (monetarists should take note of this fact). Bank credit outstanding of the nine leading banks increased on average by 9.2 per cent per annum from 1900 to 1913,

[29] The years of the sharpest price rise were selected. From the trough of 1896 to the peak of 1913 the total price rise was 31.2 per cent or 1.6 per cent per annum.

which was more than twice as much as the increase of cash of 4.4 per cent per annum. (For the whole period 1880 to 1913 the corresponding increases are 7.0 per cent and 4.0 per cent.)[30] Finally, business profits as measured by the rate of return of Austrian corporations stood at a much higher level than in the previous decades. They averaged around 9.4 per cent with peaks as high as 10.6 per cent and 11.4 per cent in 1907 and 1912;[31] though possibly these profits are inflated by wrong accounting methods not yet adjusted to inflation. Whether the rate of growth also increased is a somewhat debated point among economic historians.[32] Nevertheless, on the whole Schumpeter seems to have had a valid point.

Whether inflation was really the *cause* of higher profits, of business prosperity and thus of economic expansion, it is now difficult to say. Real wages were certainly rising; would they have risen more relative to productivity if there had been no inflation? Higher profits, quicker economic growth and inflation were probably all due to *buoyant demand conditions*; inflation and growth were thus more properly speaking coincident rather than that one was the cause of the other.

In another sense, however, prosperity was certainly due to inflation: for had determined efforts been undertaken to keep the price level constant, this prosperity would have been seriously damaged. Much of it was due to a budget deficit caused by attempts to step up armament. This deficit, as Böhm-Bawerk (1924) showed, caused a balance of trade deficit. Had there been no budget deficit, total demand would certainly have been lower, for the armaments industry was expanding very rapidly and had strong linkage effects (März, 1968, p. 341ff.). Had the deficit been financed wholly locally in Austria there would have been crowding out of business investment. In fact it was financed to quite a large extent by borrowing abroad. Borrowing

[30] The calculations were made by Professor E. März in his 1981 monograph, using statistics of the Österreichisch-Ungarische Bank.

[31] See Materialien zur Österreichischen Produktions- und Betriebsstatistik. Zusammengestellt im Auftrag des k.k. Handelsministeriums vom k.k. Österreichischen Handelsmuseum, Vienna 1916; quoted after a forthcoming monograph of Prof. E. März. März (1965, p. 375) therefore thinks that Schumpeter's analysis of inflation was 'the observation of a genius . . . which had its roots in the Austrian reality of the first decade of this century'.

[32] Doubts have been cast on the standard view that there was an upsurge in economic growth in Austria from 1896 up to the war (a view championed above all most decidedly by Professor Eduard März and by Richard L. Rudolph 1976, p. 32ff.) and by David F. Good (1974, p. 72ff.). Good, however, draws conclusions about the real magnitudes from financial statistics only. He has, however, been partly followed by Anton Kausel (1979, p. 689ff., here particularly p. 707, p. 710ff.). According to Kausel growth rates increased from 1880 onwards and peaked in the 1890s.

abroad created a cash inflow into Austria which was the base of further credit expansion by the banks, mainly going to Austrian business enterprises.

13. Is Schumpeter's idea that inflation caused by an expansion of business credit is conducive to growth an idea of general applicability? It certainly became a very widely used idea in diverse types of economic reasoning. Hamilton (1952) applied it to the inflation of the sixteenth century. Sir Arthur Lewis (1955, p. 217ff.) distinguishes and discusses at length 'inflations whose purpose is the creation of useful capital goods'. And many have interpreted Keynesian remedies as inflationary prescriptions for economic ills.

Yet counterexamples also abound. Hamilton's essay has launched a copious and inconclusive discussion in the historical literature. Sir Arthur Lewis' idea seems, if anything, confined to certain developing nations. Recent British, Swedish and possibly also American experience arguably shows that inflation has a depressing effect on business profits and economic growth. Recent Austrian experience with much milder inflation seems to argue oppositely, and seems to show that here for the income position of any larger group, for profits and for economic growth the effect of inflation is exactly neutral. Quite considerable inflation, on the other hand, does not seem to be hurtful in Japan. In the industrial nations everything thus apparently depends most delicately on the exact reactions of the trade unions and of government and the effect of their measures on the distribution of income. General forecasts about the real effects of inflation seem to be impossible without further knowledge of the institutional matrix.

We can thus conclude: with the idea that inflationary effects of a business credit expansion had salutary effects on profits and stimulated economic growth Schumpeter put forward a more or less valid analysis of his historical environment. As a general economic explanation this idea cannot be maintained: it has been invalidated by another three quarter centuries of inflationary experience. However, *Schumpeter effectually cast doubts on the general validity of the contrary view* that inflation always harms growth. As in some other respects (for instance as regards the possible economic advantages of monopolies) Schumpeter (1947, ch. 8) can here be seen as an early precursor of the revival of *mercantilist argument* in mainstream economic theory during this century; of mercantilist ideas which are not necessarily correct under any circumstances, but neither can they be completely ignored as evidently always so absurd as the classical economists in general and Adam Smith in particular had tried to make out. The revival of mercantilist ideas is generally associated with the name of Keynes (1936, ch. 23). It is a curious fact that though among all the pre-Keynesian economic traditions it was the Austrian school which fought Keynesian ideas most violently, many of its central figures—first Menger,[33] then later even Hayek,[34] and, as we see here, Schumpeter—put forward ideas very similar to those of Keynes, ideas that were just as much at variance with what Keynes called classical economics as his own.

14. Let us now turn to the second and even better known idea of Schumpeter that credit is the vehicle of innovation and particularly that new entrepreneurs and their new enterprises, which are the main source of innovation, are financed by bank credit.

Here, I think, Schumpeter misread the Austrian experience of the last two decades before World War One. He may even have been led astray by a novice's misunderstanding of a term in the language of practical business. It is a well known fact that the industrially somewhat backward countries of continental Europe hit upon the idea of stimulating economic growth by the type of banks pioneered by the French *Crédit Mobilier*, banks which would engage in *long-term* business investment. Their type of business was called in German '*Gründungsgeschäft*', or founding business enterprises. Now it has been observed, particularly by Professor März (1968, *passim*, e.g. p. 43), that originally the Crédit Mobilier type banks in Austria, and above all the largest of them, the Creditanstalt, at their date of origin in the third quarter of the last century did not succeed in establishing themselves in the '*Gründungsgeschäft*' to a marked degree apart from the financing of railway companies; and of course those railway companies, which just employ a known technique on a new route, are the very reverse of Schumpeterian innovative entrepreneurs. Apart from railway finance the newly founded Crédit Mobilier banks originally drifted off more and more into the traditional role of financing the budget deficits of government (März, 1968, pp. 68, 79ff.). Then from 1875 to 1890 they engaged more and more in traditional short-term business finance (März, 1968, p. 240ff.). Only in the last two decades before World War One did the Crédit Mobilier banks, which were by far the most important ones in Austria, finally succeed in doing what they were originally meant for: they turned to the '*Gründungsgeschäft*' of industrial enterprises with a vengeance (März, 1968, pp. 289ff., 340ff.).[35] There was a large wave of 'foundations of new enterprises', which evidently had much to

[33] Menger's monetary theory placed precautionary balances at the fore and denied any stability to the velocity of circulation. His theory is very close to Keynes' monetary theory in this respect (see Streissler, 1973, p. 164ff.).

[34] The role Hayek assigns to the banks and the instability of the credit multiplier implied by him runs counter to classical analysis (see Hayek 1929, 1935, 1939).

[35] März summarizes p. 370: 'The years 1895 to 1914 can be called a second phase of industrial foundations in the history of Austria'.

do with the reputed upsurge of economic growth and in which the banks played the decisive role. So apparently it was just what Schumpeter had described that happened in Austria.

In fact, what happened had, with a few exceptions in the chemical, oil and electro industries, little to do with the ideas set forth in his analysis, but rather came close to being its exact opposite. The so-called '*Gründungsgeschäft*' of the two decades before the war was above all the *incorporation of existing enterprises* and the *introduction* of the common stock thus created *on the stock exchange* (this introduction frequently took some time so that initially a large amount of the newly created stock remained in the portfolio of the banks). What was commonly called the 'foundation of enterprises' thus basically was their drastic *reorganization*, not the starting of new enterprises but the act of giving old enterprises *a new start*. New ideas in organization do figure among Schumpeter's (1912, p. 159) four original kinds of innovations; but in that case it was the *banks* that were the innovators not the reorganized industrial firms. For it was the banks that took the leading role; and they were by then old established firms, not newly created enterprises. The reorganization of already more or less successful firms into corporations was certainly a very important cause of the spurt in economic growth in Austria in the first years of this century. But this expansion came about through the *economies of scale* of incorporation and the easier access to credit which it made possible. As Richard L. Rudolph (1968, p. 236) says: 'Though the banks engaged in more investment banking than appeared to the public, the keynote of the banks' policy remained that of caution. The Vienna Great Banks were not the venturesome substitutes for entrepreneurs the brothers Pereiere would have had in mind. Rather, the Great Banks appear to have selected plump, juicy firms with favourable profits, firms with the difficulties and risks of their early years already completed'. It was not so much the success of untried new ideas which brought growth but their *enlarged application* in an economically more viable way of production, capital intensive production in larger enterprises.[36] Now economics of scale of business firms were first stressed by John Stuart Mill (1848, book I, ch. 9) and are considered a central force behind economic development by Karl Marx (1867).[37] But they do not figure in Schumpeter's work. He tried to stress an idealistic causation of growth, the

[36] Again Wieser saw more clearly than Schumpeter when he said of the growth of originally innovative large-scale enterprises: 'The technical and organisational progress assured them during long periods declining costs' and adds (in 1914!) that 'older enterprises with large capital gain a superiority against which it is difficult for the talented beginner to prevail' (Wieser, 1914, pp. 375, 376).

[37] Particularly pp. 654–656; p. 655 notices the importance of credit in the creation of large-scale enterprises. See also Schumpeter's near contemporary Hilferding (1910).

heroic figure of the innovative entrepreneur exactly in contrast to a materialistic theory of development. But incorporation rather meant that the sole creative man as the focus of a whole enterprise in many cases did not gain but rather *lost* in influence. The single individual was replaced by the advice of and the teamwork in boards of directors and supervisory boards. The spurt of growth in Austria during the last two decades before World War One—if it, in fact, occurred[38]—was quite in contrast to what Schumpeter implied, a spurt due to better organization (in the sense of more systematic, more bureaucratic business organization) and a spurt due to capital investment bringing economies of scale. It was not primarily a spurt of a period of innovation by the inspired individual, the dynamic entrepreneur.

To clinch our case against the appropriateness of Schumpeter's vision of his own time we have finally to consider the attitude of the banks towards competition. According to Schumpeter the competitiveness of the new idea of the innovator in production increases competition and raises productivity all round as other enterprises find themselves obliged to follow the leader. In the last two decades of 'Old Austria' the banks on the other hand were apostles of 'orderly competition'. A major part of their organizational effort went into the formation of *cartels* (März, 1968, p. 371 and copious remarks in his recent (1981) monograph) and their enforcement and administration. Quite in contrast to Schumpeter the banks thus *impeded* competition and in consequence *decreased* the spread and adoption of new ideas in production. As it was investment in large-scale production rather than process or product innovation which was at the root of expansion in these decades, such a 'regulation' of competition did, on the other hand, not inhibit economic growth.

15. There may be some more tenuous links, however, between an increase in *credit facilities* and the foundation of new and at first of course small but highly innovative, usually unincorporated enterprises, links which do work in the true Schumpeterian pattern. As we said, the Austrian banks turned to normal short-run business finance, particularly the discounting of bills, but also to mortgage credit in the *latter 1870s and in the 1880s*. For the first time in Austrian economic history normal business credit became plentiful. Partly this was due to the rapid expansion of financial intermediaries other than the large, mainly Viennese, joint stock banks (Good, 1974, p. 85ff.). This increase of normal short-term business credit could easily have meant that newly founded, innovative enterprises found it easier to get started not because the banks financed the necessary investment in plant and equipment but because they supplied working capital. Via mortgages the banks and

[38] See the doubts of Good (1974) and Kausel (1979) in note 32.

especially the other financial intermediaries may also have financed part of the necessary building (März, 1968, p. 274).[39] Thus increased finance of a completely traditional type, finance of the non-innovative side of an enterprise, may have set free capital for the innovative investment proper. Now the 1880s were a decade of the creation of many new firms, exactly those firms which, if they proved successful, were then incorporated by the banks around the turn of the century. The need of the banks to find increased outlets for traditional finance, a need created by the dwindling opportunities of government finance (März, 1968, p. 301) may have quite unwittingly brought about a new innovative spurt. And it would be a spurt on the true Schumpeterian pattern: it started during the depressive 1880s and was due to the urgent need of the banks to find new investment outlets in a glutted credit market characterized by declining rates of interest. But it was no *conscious* effort on behalf of the banks to further innovation.[40]

Many new enterprises were certainly founded at this time in Austria, as in other countries and times, by an innovative young man teaming up with a capitalist. The banker Richard Kola, for instance, who later played a part in the sale of the common stock of the Alpine Montangesellschaft to Italian interest groups when Schumpeter was Minister of Finance, describes how he made his first 50 000 gulden. He suggested a scheme for a successful stock-exchange speculation to an elderly broker who offered him his credit on the condition that they should halve the profit (Kola, 1922, p. 111). The English cases of the firm of Bolton and Watt and of the early associates of Richard Arkwright are, of course, nearly legendary. Frequently the capitalist partner also provided much-needed managerial expertise. In the comparatively rare cases when the Austrian banks financed venture projects they usually also became partners (or rather normally, shareholders) in the newly formed business.[41] And again they provided organizational expertise of which the innovative entrepreneur was frequently sorely in need.[42] This organizational help by the banks, however, frequently ended by introducing the new firm into a cartel and thus clipping the wings of its competitive drive.

---

[39] März notes, however, particularly the mortgage credit given to 'leading industrial firms'. Even mortgage credit was more difficult to come by for the smaller fry.

[40] März (1965, p. 377) notes: 'It would be a mistake, however, to assign a very high effect to the commercial and banking houses in the industrialization of Austria. In general these forces rather exerted a conservative influence'. Spitzmüller (1955) speaks repeatedly with pride of the 'in general thoroughly conservative leadership' of the banks (p. 104; see also note 7).

[41] Professor März gives several examples for the Creditanstalt in his 1981 monograph.

[42] Kola (1922), for some time a banker, stresses in his memoirs the need for better organization of enterprises he reorganized (for instance p. 193).

And, in any case, innovation in these firms was furthered by *plentiful opportunities of finance but not by credit*: it came about through an offer of risk capital and the consequent participation of the financier in the full amount of the risks involved.

16. Why did Schumpeter assign such an important role in the process of innovation to the banks—or rather to the bankers—a role which in fact, as we saw, they did not fulfil in Austria or, if they partly fulfilled it, did so only in an indirect way? The explanation, I think, must run in terms of the perceived social roles of different groups in the social hierarchy of Schumpeter's Vienna.

As I suggested at the beginning of this paper, in Schumpeter's Vienna the banker—not dissimilar to eighteenth century England—was seen as the only really respectable businessman. The banker, and among entrepreneurs virtually only he, was a member of a certain section of the 'second society'. Furthermore, in Schumpeter's time Vienna for the first time witnessed the rise of an important *managerial elite* in business. Interestingly enough the top managers of the large incorporated banks belonged to the 'second society' just as much as the partners in important banks; or possibly even more so than the partners of somewhat dubious smaller banks. The 'second society' was dominated by the class of the top civil servants. Very significantly the first decades of this century in Austria saw the transfer of some very important civil servants into the highest managerial positions of the joint stock banks. The man who might even be termed the head of the civil service (and furthermore a member of the Vienna school of economics and thus relatively close to Schumpeter), his Excellency Privatdozent Geheimrat Sektionschef Dr Rudolf Sieghart went from the post of head of the Prime Minister's office to become governor and managing director of the noblest of the banks, the *Bodencreditanstalt* in 1910 and pursued a very aggressive bank policy there. Hofrat Dr Alexander Freiherr von Spitzmüller, later several times a Cabinet Minister, became head of the *Creditanstalt* slightly earlier. Both appointments occurred two years before the publication of Schumpeter's *Theory of Economic Development*. Earlier Hofrat Ritter von Hahn had become head of the *Länderbank*. There had been other examples, even before that date; for instance Merey Alexander von Kaposmere. As we know, Schumpeter himself during his last years in Austria followed their lead as head of the *Biedermannbank*. The links between the highest ranks of the civil service and the top bankers thus became very close.

Furthermore the banks had always been considered as organs of a semi-governmental kind of economic policy. Supervision of the banks by the Ministry of Finance meant that this Cabinet Minister could, if he wished, more or less direct the general direction of the business policies of the banks. Banking was seen as above all a *public utility* and not as mere business.

Gemeinnützigkeit, the even stronger German term for a public utility, was and still is the legal duty of the Savings Banks, which were then rapidly forging ahead; but it was seen as the moral duty of all other financial institutions as well. Spitzmüller explicitly stated that he tried 'to create a type of a so to speak social bank director who works in the public interest' (Spitzmüller, 1955, p. 112). The semi-official status of banks still continues in the Austria of today, where banks are assigned the administration of numerous investment subsidies and where a special bank gives special export credits and guarantees export risks.

Thus bankers in Austria, as in most countries, were the social elite of businessmen. It was an Austrian peculiarity that they were also part of the administrative elite. The upper-class view of 'Old Austria'—particularly in its capital, in Schumpeter's Vienna—was that Austria was superbly administered by its civil servants (in this, as in many other social and economic matters, 'Old Austria' was particularly close to French institutional arrangements and to French patterns of development (cf. Good, 1974, p. 84)). The upper Civil Service prided itself on the indirect ways of achieving its policy aims. Such an indirect policy is the stimulation of innovative activity via bank credit. Banks were public utilities. According to Schumpeter, innovation was of eminent public utility; and in this attitude he only echoed the cant of Austria's top administrators though in fact they did precious little to turn their professed convictions into practice. Can one wonder then that Schumpeter assigned to the business elite, with which the class he aspired to was closely linked, that he assigned to the banks in other words, above all to the bank managers, a leading role in germinating and fostering the efforts of the heroic entrepreneur, the dynamic innovator? Can one wonder that he asssumed that banks played their role as public utilities in the direction he thought of highest utility? He was thus misled by preconceived social clichés into seeing what, economically speaking, was hardly there or, when it occurred, occurred in different ways from those suggested by him. But he thus also obscured the real economic role the banks played in the Austria of his time, namely in achieving more efficient organization of businesses in their routine activities and in financing an expansion which brought in the harvest of economies of scale.

17. There is also another possible social interpretation of Schumpeter's theory of the role of bank credit in stimulating innovation. Schumpeter was an Anglophile, as, in fact, were most members of the Austrian school of economics. The whole analysis may just have been an idealization from afar of what he thought had happened in England. It was a well-worn cliché in Austria that the English banking community was much more developed and offered much better financial support for business enterprise. We know that

Schumpeter in a lecture in England contrasted the venturesome British entrepreneur most favourably with his sluggish and conservative counterpart in Austria and stressed the deadening influence of the bureaucracy in Austria (see Johnson, 1972, p. 83). What he described might thus be an analysis of what he thought was happening in England and what he thought did *not* happen in Austria.

Though apparently contradictory, these two explanations are in fact possibly complementary. Schumpeter was describing what *should* happen in Austria on a larger scale and for which possibly he thought he could hail the very first tentative signs. He was presenting a model of development, not its description. And he was presenting a model formed in the mould of English experience as seen with Austrian eyes, as seen by someone imbued with Austrian social conceptions.

18. In the case of the role of credit in innovation Schumpeter was thus describing something which did not happen in Austria in the way he described it and possibly never happened anywhere in this way. In his later years he himself recognized—and possibly overemphasized[43]—the important innovative role of the large corporation (Schumpeter, 1947, ch. 12). Was Schumpeter's partly counterfactual analysis of no general validity because it was counterfactual?

Curiously enough, ideas of great economists, which were counterfactual in their day, later could turn into analytical ideas of the utmost real significance. Adam Smith for instance put forward such a prescient idea which was completely counterfactual in his day: that industrial development was only possible with a higher rate of capital accumulation (when in fact in his day all that was needed was a *reallocation* of a given high capital formation).[44] Schumpeter too has created such a prescient idea. Efficient business organization becomes a matter of course once industrialization has fully developed. Economies of scale become largely exhausted: from a certain point onwards increasing costs of control compensate decreasing costs of material production; and above all the purely material side of the production of economic values dwindles in importance with rising living standards. On the other hand, a high speed of innovation is of ever-mounting importance in fully developed industrial societies with their increasing rapidity of change and the unrestrainable competiton between them. Innovation has not only become the principal engine of present growth; it has become the clue to survival.

[43] For the contrary view, that it is rather small enterprises that prove innovative, see especially Jewkes, Sawers and Stillerman (1958).

[44] See Crouzet (1972, Editor's Introduction, p. 42). See also Wilson (1965, p. 313ff.).

If we understand the role in the stimulation of innovation which Schumpeter assigned to bank credit correctly in the context of his time, he put forward an economic idea of lasting significance, which before him had not made the pages of mainstream theorizing. Banks in his context were public utilities, means of indirect government policy. What he said in fact was that innovation was much increased if there existed institutions of risk-sharing between the innovator and society. Such risk-sharing institutions need not take the form of debt instruments. They can be generous tax write-offs of all investments as in present-day Austria[45] and thus governmental forms of credit. They can be aids of and business associations with semi-public special credit institutions. They can take still other forms. What is important is the accessibility of risk-sharing arrangements for the average innovator. Also important is the unbureaucratic nature of the administration of these risk-sharing arrangements by institutions close to business problems and close to business ways of thought. Put in this way, Schumpeter first broached a question of vital significance to the present industrial world and one towards the best solution of which groping attempts are made at present in most of its nations.[46]

[45] For an English analysis of this policy see Streissler (1978, p. 255).
[46] See for instance the analysis of Herbert Giersch (1979, p. 629ff.).

ACKNOWLEDGEMENTS

I am indebted to Dr F. Baltzarek, Dr W. Neudeck and Dr P. Rosner for many most helpful suggestions. I have profited enormously from the work of Professor Dr E. März, who also lent me the manuscript of his then forthcoming publication (März, 1981).

REFERENCES

Allmayer-Beck, J. C. (1957) Die Träger der staatlichen Macht—Adel, Armee und Bürokratie. In *Spectrum Austriae* (Ed.) Schulmeister, O. pp. 253–74. Vienna: Herder.
Ausch, K. (1968) *Als die Banken fielen*. Vienna: Europa Verlag.
von Böhm-Bawerk, E. (1924) Unsere passive Handelsbilanz. In *Gesammelte Werke* (Ed.) Weiss, F. X. 2 Volumes. Vienna: Holder, Pichler, Tempsky.
Brunner, O. (1949) *Adeliges Landleben und europäischer Geist*. Salzburg: Otto Müller.
Conant, C. A. (1898) The development of credit. *Journal of Political Economy*, **VI**, 161–3, 172.
Crouzet, F. (Ed.) (1972) *Capital Formation in the Industrial Revolution*. London: Methuen.

Doderer, H. von (1956) *Die Dämonen—Nach der Chronik des Sektionsrates Geyrenhoff*. Munich: Biederstein.
Doderer, H. von (1963) *Die Wasserfälle von Slunj*. Munich: Biederstein.
Ehrhart, R. (1958) Nur nicht berühmt werden wollen. *Im Dienste des alten Österreich*. Vienna: Bergland.
Freud, S. (1942) Die Traumdeutung. In *Gesammelte Werke*. London: Imago.
Gerschenkorn, A. (1977) *An Economic Spurt that Failed*. Princeton: Princeton University Press.
Giersch, H. (1979) Aspects of growth, structural change, and employment—a Schumpeterian perspective. *Weltwirtschaftliches Archiv*, **115**, 629ff.
Good, D. F. (1974) Stagnation and 'take-off' in Austria, 1873–1913. *The Economic History Review*, **XXVII**, 72.
Gross, G. (1884) Die Lehre vom Unternehmergewinn. Leipzig: Duncker und Humblot.
Hamilton, E. J. (1952) Prices as a factor in business growth: prices and progress. *JEH*, **XII**, 325.
Hampson, N. (1963) *A Social History of the French Revolution*. p. 6. London: Routledge & Kegan Paul.
Hawley, F. B. (1907) *Enterprise and the Productive Process*. New York, London: Knickerbocker.
Hayek, F. A. (1929) *Geldtheorie und Konjunkturtheorie*. Vienna, Leipzig: Hölder.
Hayek, F. A. (1935) *Prices and Production*. London: Routledge & Kegan Paul.
Hayek, F. A. (1939) *Profits, Interest and Investment*. London: Routledge & Kegan Paul.
Hennings, F. (1963) *Ringstrassen Symphonie, 1. Satz 1857–1870, Es ist mein Wille*. Vienna, Munich: Herold.
Herzmanovsky-Orlando, F. von (1957) *Der Gaulschreck im Rosennetz—Lustspiele und Ballette*. Munich, Vienna: Langen-Mueller. 1971 edition, *Kaiser Joseph und die Bahnwärterstochter*. p. 133ff.
Herzmanovsky-Orlando, F. von (1958) *Maskenspiel der Genien*. Munich, Vienna: Langen-Mueller.
Hilferding, R. (1910) *Das Finanzkapital. Eine Studie über die jüngste Entwicklung des Kapitalismus*. Vienna: Wiener Volksbuchhandlung.
Jewkes, J., Sawers, D. and Stillerman, R. (1969) *The Sources of Invention*. London: Macmillan.
Johnson, W. M. (1972) *The Austrian Mind. An Intellectual and Social History 1848–1938*. Berkeley, California: University of California Press.
Kausel, A. (1979) Österreichs Volkseinkommen 1830 bis 1913. In *Geschichte und Ergebnisse der zentralen amtlichen Statistik in Österreich 1829–1979*. pp. 689–710. Vienna: Kommissionsverlag der Österreichischen staatsdruckerei.
Keynes, J. M. (1936) *The General Theory of Employment, Interest and Money*. London: Macmillan.
Kleinwaechter, F. F. G. (1955) *Der fröhliche Präsidialist*. Zurich, Leipzig, Vienna: Amalthea.
Kola, R. (1922) *Rückblich ins Gestrige*. Vienna, Leipzig, Munich: Rikola.
Lewis, W. A. (1955) *The Theory of Economic Growth*. London: Allen & Unwin.
Lorenz, A. (1965) *Wenn der Vater mit dem Sohne. . . .* Vienna: Franz Deuticke.
März, E. (1965) Zur Genesis der Schumpeterschen Theorie der wirtschaftlichen Entwicklung. In *On Political Economy and Econometrics, Essays in honour of Oskar Lange*. pp. 363–82. Oxford: Oxford University Press.
März, E. (1968) *Österreichische Industrie- und Bankpolitik in der Zeit Franz Josephs I*. Vienna, Frankfurt, Zurich: Europa Verlag.
März, E. (1981) *Österreichichische Bankpolitik in der Zeit der grossen Wende 1913–1923*. Vienna: Verlag für Geschicte und Politik.
März, E. and Rudolph, R. L. (1976) *Banking and Industrialization in Austria–Hungary*. Cambridge: Cambridge University Press.
Marx, K. (1867) *Das Kapital*. 1st edition, Volume 1. Hamburg: O. Meissner.
Mataja, V. (1884) *Der Unternehmergewinn*. Vienna: Hölder.
Menger, C. (1871) *Grundsätze der Volkswirtschaftslehre*. Vienna: Braumüller.

Mill, J. S. (1848) *Principles of Political Economy*. 2 Volumes. London: Longmans, Green.
Mises, L. von (1912) *Theorie des Geldes und der Umlaufsmittel*. Munich, Leipzig: Duncker und Humblot.
Mühlpeck, V., Sandgruber, R. and Woitek, H. (1979) Index der Verbraucherpreise 1800–1914. In *Geschichte und Ergebnisse der zentralen amtlichen Statistik in Österreich 1829–1979, Festschrift*. pp. 649–676. Vienna: Kommissionsverlag der Österreichischen Staatsdruckerei.
Musil, R. (1931) *Der Mann ohne Eigenschaften*. Hamburg: Rowohlt.
Rudolph, R. L. (1968) *The Role of Financial Institutions in the Industrialization of the Czech Crownlands, 1880–1914*. Ph.D. Thesis, University of Wisconsin. p. 236. University Microfilms, Ann Arbor, MI.
Schumpeter, J. A. (1908) *Das Wesen und der Hauptinhalt der theoretischen Nationalökonomie*. Leipzig: Duncker und Humblot.
Schumpeter, J. A. (1912) *Theorie der wirtschaftlichen Entwicklung*. Leipzig: Duncker und Humblot. English translation (1934) *Theory of Economic Development*. Cambridge, MA: Harvard University Press.
Schumpeter, J. A. (1913a) Zinsfuss und Geldverfassung. *Jahrbuch der Gesellschaft Österreichischer Volkswirte*, p. 38ff.
Schumpeter, J. A. (1913b) Eine 'dynamische' Theorie des Kapitalzinses. Eine Entgegnung. *Zeitschrift für Volkswirtschaft, Sozialpolitik und Verwaltung*, **XXII**, 599ff.
Schumpeter, J. A. (1947) *Capitalism, Socialism and Democracy*. London: Allen & Unwin.
Sieghart, R. (1932) *Die letzten Jahrzehnte einer Grossmacht*. Berlin: Ullstein.
Sombart, W. (1909) Der kapitalistische Unternehmer. *Archiv fuer Sozialwissenschaften und Sozialpolitik*, **XXIX**, 689.
Sombart, W. (1913) *Der Bourgeois—Zur Geistesgeschichte des modernen Wirtschaftsmenschen*. Munich, Leipzig: Duncker und Humblot.
Spitzmüller, A. (1955) . . . *Und hat auch Ursach', es zu lieben*. Vienna: Frick.
Streissler, E. (1973) Menger's theories of money and uncertainty—a modern interpretation. In *Carl Menger and the Austrian School of Economics* (Eds) Hicks, J. R. and Weber, W. p. 164. Oxford: Oxford University Press.
Streissler, E. (1978) Measures to promote capital formation. In *Capital Shortage and Unemployment in the World Economy* (Ed.) Giersch, H. p. 255. Tübingen: J. C. B. Mohr (Paul Siebeck).
Weinberger, O. (1965) *Handwörterbuch der Sozialwissenschaften*. Volume XII. Stuttgart, Tübingen: J. C. B. Mohr (Paul Siebeck).
Wieser, F. von (1914) Theorie der gesellschaftlichen Wirtschaft. In *Grundriss der Sozialökonomik I/1, Grundlagen der Wirtschaft*. Tübingen: J. C. B. Mohr (Paul Siebeck).
Wieser, F. von (1884) *Über den Ursprung und die Hauptgesetze des wirtschaftlichen Werthes*. Vienna.
Willett, A. H. (1951) *The Economic Theory of Risk and Insurance*. Oxford: Oxford University Press.
Wilson, C. (1965) *England's Apprenticeship 1603–1763*. London: Longman.
Young, G. M. (1936) *Victorian England, Portrait of an Age*. Oxford: Oxford University Press.

Chapter Five

Schumpeter's Model of the Decay of Capitalism

ARNOLD HEERTJE

Zionism is above all, an enterprise of creative construction
(Ezer Weizman, *The Battle for Peace*, London: Bantam, 1981)

SCHUMPETER'S VISION

IN his book *Capitalism, Socialism and Democracy* of 1942, Schumpeter tries 'to show that a socialist form of society will inevitably emerge from an equally inevitable decomposition of capitalist society' (*CSD*, p. 409).[1] Both, according to Schumpeter, are equally inevitable. To use his own words, '. . . value judgements about capitalistic performance are of little interest. For mankind is not free to choose' (*CSD*, p. 129).

In his book Schumpeter develops a set of economic, social and historical observations and refined arguments to illustrate his vision. Some observations are essential for the whole reasoning. Others are only dealt with because they are essential in the eyes of the general public or because they belong to the mainstream of economic theory, but are in fact, according to Schumpeter, misleading.

Since the publication of Schumpeter's prediction so many years have elapsed already that a provisional verification of the theory is possible through a confrontation of his conclusions and arguments with the actual developments, although Schumpeter may have taken an even longer view (*CSD*, p. 163) We might arrive at the conclusion that Schumpeter has already been proved right, either because of the reasons he himself gave, or as a consequence of other causes. The other possibility is that, up to now, his vision of the decay of capitalism has not come true. Again, it is conceivable that his arguments are correct in the qualitative sense, but that their empirical

[1] All references are to the fifth edition by Professor T. Bottomore, and will be referred to as *CSD*.

relevance up to now did not carry enough weight to produce the effects that Schumpeter predicted. In other words, a falsification of his theory after 40 years does not exclude the possibility that in the long run Schumpeter will prove to be right. It is also possible that the empirical evidence, gathered so far, differs in many or all respects from the picture sketched by Schumpeter. For these reasons, it is therefore not sufficient to compare his prediction about capitalism with the present state of affairs, but it is necessary to discuss in full the essence of the reasons on which his conclusions are based. Such a discussion may help us to gain insights as to what we can expect in the future.

THE MARXIAN DOCTRINE, CAPITALISM AND SOCIALISM

Schumpeter's prediction about the decay of capitalism is prefaced by a discussion of Marx's analysis of the inevitable breakdown of capitalism and is followed by the description of the socialist alternative to capitalism. This may have inspired many commentators of Schumpeter to deal also with Marxism and socialism, even if the problem they have set themselves is restricted to the analysis of Schumpeter's model of the decay of capitalism in the strict sense (see, for example, Heertje, 1981). To bring in Marx is a natural consequence of the fact that both Marx and Schumpeter argued that permanent changes in methods of production and the constant appearance of new products are basic features of capitalism and that the breakdown of capitalism is inevitable. In this contribution I shall restrict myself to an analysis of Schumpeter's view on the decay of capitalism. I also avoid the temptation to deal with socialism in this connection. If socialism is considered to be an attractive alternative to capitalism, it may aid Schumpeter to make his point. The attraction of an external alternative to capitalism may contribute to its undermining but, in order to be convincing, the explanation for the decay should—in my view—be based mainly on internal causes. My procedure boils down to an attempt to grasp the essence of Schumpeter's vision and to develop a critical analysis of the gist of his theory, on the basis of which a possible scenario of future developments may be derived.

MAIN ARGUMENTS

A few quotations from *Capitalism, Socialism and Democracy* are needed in order to get a clear picture of Schumpeter's ideas.

> Capitalism, then, is by nature a form or method of economic change and not only never is but never can be stationary. . . The fundamental

impulse that sets and keeps the capitalist engine in motion comes from the new consumers' goods, the new methods of production or transportation, the new markets, the new forms of industrial organisation that capitalist enterprise creates. . . . The opening up of new markets, foreign or domestic, and the organizational development from the craft shop and factory to such concerns as U.S. Steel illustrate the same process of industrial mutation—if I may use that biological term—that incessantly revolutionizes the economic structure *from within*, incessantly destroying the old one, incessantly creating a new one. This process of Creative Destruction is the essential fact about capitalism. It is what capitalism consists in and what every capitalist concern has got to live in. . . . [T]he function of entrepreneurs is to reform or revolutionize the pattern of production by exploiting an invention or, more generally, an untried technological possibility for producing a new commodity or producing an old one in a new way, by opening up a new source of supply of materials or a new outlet for products, by reorganizing an industry and so on. . . . To act with confidence beyond the range of familiar beacons and to overcome that resistance requires aptitudes that are present in only a small fraction of the population and that defines the entrepreneurial type as well as the entrepreneurial function. This function does not essentially consist in either inventing or otherwise creating the conditions which the enterprise exploits. It consists in getting things done (*CSD*, pp. 82, 83 and 132).

The main characterizing feature of capitalism is the behaviour of economic actors, who introduce new combinations financed by banks that provide money, and who, therefore, are called entrepreneurs. Schumpeter's entrepreneur operates in an uncertain world, has the courage to start ventures, and must be strong enough to swim against the tide of the society in which he is living. Almost by definition the decay of capitalism is the decay of the entrepreneur. Or, the other way round, the decay of the entrepreneur is the decay of capitalism. So, the basic question in Schumpeter's book is: Why has the entrepreneur to disappear? To understand Schumpeter's answer, one has to realize that the entrepreneurial function is connected with a permanent increase of total output. Economic performance is measured by total output during a year. If people do not want more or technology cannot advance further, a stationary state will emerge.

There would be nothing left for the entrepreneurs to do. . . . Profits and along with profits the rate of interest would converge toward zero. The bourgeois strata that live on profits and interest would tend to disappear. The management of industry and trade would become a matter of current administration, and the personnel would unavoidably acquire the characteristics of a bureaucracy. Socialism of a very sober type would almost automatically come into being. Human energy would turn away from business (*CSD*, p. 131).

The assumption of absolute saturation is not realistic for the foreseeable future, according to Schumpeter. But similar effects on the structure of society may also come about through another channel. 'Progress itself may be mechanized as well as the management of a stationary economy, and this mechanization of progress may effect entrepreneurship and capitalist society as much as the cessation of economic progress would' (*CSD*, p. 131).

The increase and qualitative change of production is brought about by entrepreneurs, who revolutionize the pattern of production by exploiting new technical possibilities. The entrepreneurial function consists, in Schumpeter's view, of getting things done. Now, Schumpeter argues in 1942 that this social function is losing importance and that it will lose even more importance in the future. Innovation itself will be reduced more and more to routine; and personality and will-power will be less relevant as people become accustomed to change. 'Thus, economic progress tends to become depersonalized and automatized. Bureau and committee work tends to replace individual action' (*CSD*, p. 133). And just to present another quotation: 'Since capitalist enterprise, by its very achievements, tends to automatize progress, we conclude that it tends to make itself superfluous—to break to pieces under the pressure of its own success' (*CSD*, p. 134).

The hollowing out of the entrepreneurial function, especially in the big monopolistic firms, during the development of capitalism is the main and, in my view, the only factor which in Schumpeter's theory counts for the decay of capitalism. At this stage in his book Schumpeter has already excluded other possible causes for the decay of capitalism from the scene on various grounds: monopolistic practices and the vanishing of investment opportunities. On the other hand, the disappearance of small and medium-sized firms and traders weakens the political structure of capitalism and makes the prospect of capitalism even more dependent on the vanishing role of the Schumpeterian entrepreneur in big business. This process pushes the institutions of property and free contracting into the background and develops into an atmosphere of universal hostility to the capitalist order, fed by the feeling of the have-nots that they can get something from the haves. A special role is played in this respect by the intellectuals, of which the educational process produces so large a number that huge unemployment is unavoidable. The already deteriorating position of the entrepreneur is surrounded by growing hostility. 'Thus the same economic process that undermines the position of the bourgeoisie by decreasing the importance of the functions of entrepreneurs and capitalists, by breaking up protective strata and institutions by creating an atmosphere of hostility, also decomposes the motor forces of capitalism from within' (*CSD*, pp. 161–162).

So, the decay of capitalism is not only due to the bureaucratization of the entrepreneurial function, it is identical with it. Given Schumpeter's interpretation of capitalism, of its goals and achievements and of the entrepreneurial function, the relationship between the decay of capitalism and the vanishing role of the entrepreneur may also be reduced to a tautology. Given the narrow scope of Schumpeter's measure for economic performance within a capitalistic setting, namely the rate of increase of total output, the relationship is a matter of definition. Entrepreneurs look for new, profitable combinations, which lead to higher production, through individualistic activities. They cease to be entrepreneurs as soon as their work has been routinized, which puts an end to capitalism and rings the bell for the march into socialism.

EVALUATION

Has Schumpeter proved to be right, already? I do not think so. Even those who like to point to the increasing role of the state in modern economics and to the bureaucratization of big, monopolistic firms would not pretend that Schumpeter's vision has been confirmed by actual developments in modern societies. Even if one has a country like France in mind, where socialist tendencies are very strong nowadays, one would be inclined to argue that the bulk of the entrepreneurial activity is not a matter of routine and, therefore, that capitalism has not yet died. That conclusion leaves us with the question whether the tendencies foreseen by Schumpeter have not carried enough weight so far or whether the empirical evidence differs in a more fundamental sense from the Schumpeterian theoretical picture.

In order to deal with the first question, it seems fair to remain within Schumpeter's framework by accepting for the time being the rate of total production as the only yardstick for the outcome of entrepreneurial activity. The essence of this activity then is the exploitation of new technical possibilities with a view to making profits. These restrictions enhance the probability that Schumpeter's predictions become true, as may be gathered from the behaviour of a large company just arriving at higher output through the application of new technical methods and the introduction of new products. This description suggests that collective routine has taken over from individual creativity and will-power.

It can be admitted that in particular in large firms the emergence of new technical knowledge is mechanized to a certain extent and that the decision-making process about its application, both in the sphere of production and marketing, is often hampered by bureaucratic features, threatening the static and dynamic efficiency of the firm and therefore the level of output. But these decisions still take place in a world of uncertainty and financial risk. These latter aspects of the decision-making process come more to the fore as the size of the firm becomes smaller. Within these firms, individuals who take final and major decisions and bear the responsibility for profits and losses do still exist. If in certain cases Schumpeterian developments occur due to a lack of these individuals, one often experiences after some time a reaction in the form of new dynamic leadership. Many small firms still exist or come into being in order to gain a place in the market. Their managers take initiatives and often have to overcome resistance of consumers to achieve their market goals. It may be true that nowadays nearly everybody is confronted with change and new developments at a very high rate, but this does not imply that everybody accepts this state of affairs. So, on the whole, there are traces of a Schumpeterian development in our Western economies, but mechanization and routinization of the entrepreneurial function is by no means the general picture. Our economic life is still a melting-pot of conflicting tendencies, ups and downs, major risks and minor certainties. In short, it is the dynamic, ever-changing scene for entrepreneurs who have to be inventive and sensitive to new opportunities. Those entrepreneurs who follow the Schumpeterian line will be punished by the market, that is by competitors who are prepared to take risks and to bear losses.

On balance I am inclined to argue that innovation as a process of development, application and diffusion of new technical possibilities has not been reduced to routine. Nor have people become so reconciled with change that personal characteristics such as will-power and perseverence are no longer needed to break through traditional patterns. However, as has been pointed out above, a falsification after 40 years does not imply a falsification for ever. It therefore seems appropriate to look more carefully at the empirical evidence about the entrepreneurial function and about the acceptability of the level of output as the sole yardstick for economic performance. This may enable us to look into the future of capitalism, as well.

THE FUTURE OF CAPITALISM

Is the essence of the entrepreneurial function really the exploitation of new technical possibilities or of new opportunities in general? On the basis of Schumpeter's distinction between inventions and innovations, it is natural to identify entrepreneurial activity with innovative activity. But in the no-man's land between invention and innovation there is a missing link, found by Kirzner (1977, pp. 72–74, 80–82 and 129; 1979). Kirzner points out that the alertness to information, the awareness for new opportunities that exist already and are waiting to be noticed, and the response to possibilities offered by the market system are the essential entrepreneurial components in human action. Although in many cases those who are on the look-out for new opportunities are the same men and women who exploit them, I think that Kirzner's refinement of Schumpeter's characterization of entrepreneurship is of the utmost importance. It may be argued that certain stages of the application and execution of new ideas can be routinized, but the property of being alert to marketable applications of what is already there, but generally overlooked by others, is still an individualistic characteristic, not one for being automatized. Even if we comprehend in the definition of the entrepreneurial function the application and implementation of new combinations, it is still true that one first has to be alert to what may be applied. In this sense entrepreneurship never was and never will be a matter of routine.

Turning now to the level of output as a measure for welfare, it is clear from Schumpeter's writing that he is fully aware of the limited significance of output. He acknowledges that the satisfaction of wants not only depends on the quantity but also on the quality of production (see, e.g., *CSD*, pp. 66 and 190). In fact, he is an adherent to the broad concept of economic welfare, which refers to the satisfaction of wants insofar as this satisfaction is dependent on dealing with scarce resources. The broad concept of economic welfare is formal and subjective. Schumpeter nevertheless has restricted the analysis laid down in his book to a material interpretation of welfare.

A common feature of modern Western economies is people's attempt to make the broad concept of welfare operational. People want technology with a human touch, a better environment, a higher quality of life and better working conditions. Here lies a new challenge for entrepreneurs who are alert to new possibilities, the application of which may improve the level of satisfaction of the people. There is then a profitable market for new products. It needs no emphasis that the subjective yardstick of economic performance makes it even less probable that entrepreneurial activity will become mechanized, as the social outcome of activity is no longer measured only in objective terms of output but also on a subjective basis.

The subjective basis may be the theme of widespread discussion, since it is determined by individual preferences. In our pluriform society these preferences are heterogeneous and constantly changing. The optimal allocation of resources is more complicated if individual preferences are no longer only concerned with more goods, but also by a large number of welfare considerations. In recent years several major social problems have cropped up in our capitalistic world, specifically problems of energy, environment, employment and technical change. Many have thought that the solution of these problems is provided by the government. This expectation has not come true and in my view will not come true. Although the state may play a role, the concrete solution of these problems has to come from new technology, new resources of energy and new types of investment. In this connection entrepreneurial behaviour still has to play a crucial role. This insight is generally accepted now and is taken as a fact of life. It is, so to speak, condensed experience. The reason is that decentralized decision-making in an environment of competition and uncertainty appears to be the best stimulus for creativity and an efficient allocation of resources. And creativity is needed to solve social problems, such as the environmental problem. One cannot expect from governments that they develop new technical methods with more positive external effects than the old. The entrepreneur has the technical and managerial power to allocate resources so that solutions are presented which are socially acceptable and which are brought about by the incentive of making profits. The fact that it is not only the market that determines what is socially acceptable, but also public authorities, does not harm entrepreneurial activities as long as entrepreneurs respond to the new challenges and know how to make profits, even if immaterial welfare effects have to be taken into account.

In order to solve the many problems of today both in the private and the public sectors, entrepreneurial activity on a large scale, based on a sensitive and innovative attitude, guided by a broad concept of welfare, is needed even more than before. There is no attractive alternative, and therefore an upswing instead of a decay of capitalism is a better bet for the future. Changes are to be expected in the field of decision-making and in the distribution of the profits gained. Our real challenge is how to attain the integration of capitalism in the sphere of production with a socially acceptable distribution of profits and other incomes.

Let me add a few words about decision-making. In a simpler world, economic decisions were easy. It was a private matter for private firms. Decisions about innovations were based only on financial considerations and the managers alone were qualified and responsible for making such decisions. In our more complex modern world this is no longer the case. Managerial decisions now also take into account the welfare of the general public, the consequences for the labour market, the availability of raw materials and energy and the effect on the environment. If a firm is faced with a number of alternative techniques, it may be clear which alternative is best from a financial point of view. But technique A may be more labour-saving than technique B; and technique C may promote job satisfaction while D is the choice of the environmentalists.

Techniques may be ranked on a financial basis, but they differ also in other respects, which are important for the welfare of individuals. It is obvious that there are public welfare effects as well. Pollution is also a public welfare effect of the choice of technique. As for the effect on employment, private and public welfare effects are interconnected. From the different aspects of the choice of techniques, it follows that from a social point of view the choice is not optimal if based only on private welfare effects of a financial character. A tension may develop between this social optimum and the optimal choice for the firm. Traditionally, firms only react to preferences of individuals, which are expressed in the market. The question arises whether it is in the long-run interest of the firm to move in the direction of the social optimum, by taking into account preferences of individuals which are expressed outside the market. Without suggesting that the tension between the social and individual optima will be completely removed, we are inclined to argue that a firm can strengthen its long-run market position by widening the structure of the decision-making process through the introduction of 'non-marketable' or immaterial welfare effects. On the one hand a certain level and persistence of profits is a condition for taking into account welfare effects which operate outside the market; on the other hand the perspective with regard to profits depends to a certain extent on the firm's social behaviour.

The traditional task of the entrepreneur has been to take decisions on the basis of cost–benefit calculations mainly of a financial character. Insofar as individual preferences which cannot be translated into financial terms have to be taken into account, the cost–benefit calculation is more complicated. The information about the costs and benefits can no longer only be derived from the market, but has to be extracted directly from the individuals. Here a new task for the entrepreneur of the future comes to the fore. In order to prepare a final decision, he has to organize the decision-making process so that a weighing-up of the different competing material and immaterial welfare effects becomes possible. To achieve this, more direct consultations with personnel than he is used to are needed. Here starts a tendency towards decentralization in decision-making.

Being alert to new methods of production and to new products, combined with alertness to the challenges that arise from the empirical significance of the broad concept of economic welfare, seems to me the driving force without which most present-day problems cannot be solved. Alertness to new possibilities that may yield positive results in market or social terms being an even more essential characteristic of the entrepreneur than getting things done, the fear of a possible automatization of the entrepreneurial function loses its appeal.

Capitalism survives because it is the only system in which the essential entrepreneurial activity of being alert to new developments is brought into practice, leading to positive material and immaterial results. It may contribute to the revival and rehabilitation of the entrepreneur and therefore to the reorientation of capitalism that the public is becoming more and more aware of the fact that social behaviour of public figures can be explained—at least partly—by individual motives and aims. In other more technical words, the public awareness of the empirical significance of methodological individualism contributes to the revival of capitalism because a less negative attitude towards private enterprise may be expected. It is of some interest to note that Schumpeter not only introduced the term 'methodological individualism', but also defended the approach as a proper method to understand social phenomena (see Schumpeter, 1908, 1961). If it is true that politicians try to maximize votes and that bureaucrats try to maximize their budgets, it implies that their first concern is not the general interest and that therefore they do not differ in principle from entrepreneurs in the market who look for profits. The fundamental correspondence between the behaviour of individuals in the public and private sectors is clearly expressed by Schumpeter's definition of democracy as 'that institutional arrangement for arriving at political decisions in which individuals acquire the power to decide by means of a competitive struggle for the people's vote' (*CSD*, p. 269).

CONCLUSION

An identification of capitalism with entrepreneurial activity can only lead to the conclusion that capitalism is still alive. The future of capitalism is very promising insofar as the entrepreneurs remain in a position to respond to new challenges. The alertness to a profitable allocation of resources in a changing world of technical development and social attitudes is still the essential entrepreneurial feature. Alertness in this sense is not programmable, but it is still the pioneering property and creative act of a few who are in this respect gifted by Nature or God. The exploitation of new combinations with a view to making profits does not exclude the possibility that society suffers, especially if competition does not work properly. For this reason, restraints are put on individual behaviour in the market, so that one does not lose sight of the social optimum. It is, however, not only the private sector for which such restraints are considered appropriate and effective. Individual aims and motives are, in fact, also the driving force in the public sector. And this may just as easily lead to socially unacceptable developments, in particular if monopolistic situations arise in the public sector.

In predicting the decay of capitalism, Schumpeter was wrong and will remain wrong, although the social developments on which his prediction was based had and still maintain a certain appeal. The forces that counteract the tendencies that point in the direction of routine, risk-avoidance and rest seem to be the stronger.

ACKNOWLEDGEMENT

The author wishes to express his sincere thanks to Professor Dr P. Hennipman for critically reading the manuscript and for his stimulating comments.

REFERENCES

Heertje, A. (Ed.) (1981) *Schumpeter's Vision: Capitalism, Socialism and Democracy after 40 Years*. London: Praeger.
Kirzner, I. M. (1977) *Competition and Entrepreneurship*. Chicago: University of Chicago Press.
Kirzner, I. M. (1979) *Perception, Opportunity and Profit*. Chicago: University of Chicago Press.
Schumpeter, J. A. (1908) *Das Wesen und der Hauptinhalt der theoretischen Nationalökonomie*. Part 1, Ch. 6, p. 88ff. Leipzig: Verlag von Duncker und Humblot.
Schumpeter, J. A. (1942) *Capitalism, Socialism and Democracy*. New York: Harper & Row. 5th Edition (1976) (Ed.) Bottomore, T. London: Allen & Unwin.
Schumpeter, J. A. (1961) *History of Economic Analysis*. 4th Edition, p. 889. London: Allen & Unwin.

Chapter Six

Schumpeter's Contributions to the Study of Comparative Economic Systems

MARTIN BRONFENBRENNER

A man so various that he seemed to be
Not one's, but all mankind's, epitome
(Dryden, *Absalom and Achitophel*)

INTRODUCTION

A GENERATION has elapsed since the death of Joseph Alois Schumpeter (1883–1950). His name and reputation survive, and show every indication of continuing survival, in each of the three branches of economics to which he contributed at least one major work. These three fields are, of course: economic dynamics, including both growth and fluctuations—the 'Schumpeterian system' of Clemence and Doody's (1950) appreciative essay following his death;[1] the history of economic thought, particularly in its analytical aspects; and my present subject, comparative economic systems.

Comparative economics is the subject matter of *Capitalism, Socialism and Democracy* (Schumpeter, 1942).[2] This book retains wider readership among the general public than any of Schumpeter's other major works (whatever

[1] 'The manuscript of this book was virtually completed at the time of Professor Schumpeter's death . . . He was, moreover, aware of the fact that we were writing it.' However, 'we worked quite independently of his counsel, and he never saw any of our results' (Clemence and Doody, 1950, Preface).

[2] The English text of the third edition is the original; the first (1942) edition is reproduced without change, but with addenda covering developments of 1942–49. (We shall refer to this volume as *CSD*.)

may be the case among professional economists). Despite the time lapses since its publication and Schumpeter's death, it is more widely read than when it was new. Many teachers continue to use it as a textbook, in commemoration of its having revolutionized its subject as a teaching field. I am among these teachers, although I never shared in the benefits of personal contact with Schumpeter himself.[3]

THE SCHOLAR OF SOCIALISM

Schumpeter was educated at the University of Vienna during the glory days of both the Austrian School in standard economics and the movement now called 'Austro-Marxism' in socialist thinking.[4] His teachers included major contributors to the first of these; his friends and classmates included major contributors to the second. His interest in the problems of socialism Schumpeter himself dates from this period. He gave a series of public lectures on 'Social classes' and 'Economic democracy' as early as 1910 in Czernowitz (now Chernovtsy, USSR) and a course on 'Social classes' during his first American academic appointment (as Visiting Professor at Columbia) three

---

[3] This regretful admission does not propose to disparage several major scholars whose lectures on comparative economic systems I *did* attend. These were Paul Douglas, whose course I took as a Chicago graduate student, and Selig Perlman, whose lectures I visited as his junior colleague at Wisconsin. (I was also an unofficial student of Oscar Lange and A. P. Lerner at Chicago in the late 1930s.)

[4] If Leninism be mainstream Marxism, the Austro-Marxists were Right-wing Deviants. Many of them believed tendencies to overproduction (rather than to a falling rate of profit) would be the major cause of capitalist decay; as for imperialism, they saw its primary economic motive in marketing 'surplus' consumer goods (rather than investment opportunities for 'surplus' capital); some of them even thought capitalism would soon collapse without the messinesses of war, revolution, and proletarian dictatorship (cf. Sweezy, 1942, Ch. 11ff.). Schumpeter's own account of the Austrian Social Democratic Party and its principal leader is acidic (*CSD*, p. 348ff.):

> Rising slowly from small beginnings, it established itself under Victor Adler, who had succeeded in welding together the socialists of all the nations who inhabited that country, and who was to lead them for another 30 years. This party was officially Marxist. The little circle even contributed substantially to the development of Marxian doctrine. At the same time, everyone knew that Adler would stand no nonsense. [H]e was able to allow them all the Marxism they wanted in their cafés without letting them interfere with what really mattered to him, the organization and the party press, universal suffrage, progressive legislation, and, yes, the proper working of the [Habsburg] state. This combination of Marxist doctrine and reformist practice answered admirably. Austrian governments discovered a factor that from its own interest was bound to support the central authority in its perennial struggle with filibustering national oppositions. These governments thereupon proceeded to extend favors to the party, which reciprocated in full.

years later. His best-known essays on 'socialist' topics (prior to *CSD*) date from 1919 and 1926.[5] But he seems never to have taught comparative economic systems formally in Austria or Germany as part of an academic curriculum. In this limited sense at least, Schumpeter's famous 'Socialism' course at Harvard was a product of his 'American' period (1932–50), and *CSD* itself represents the expansion and development of his lectures in that course.

I summarize the fragmentary evidence by concluding that Schumpeter was a lifelong student and scholar of socialism. The pressure of academic-propriety and the gestation of the Schumpeterian system reduced comparative economics, outside relatively brief intervals, to the status of second or third strings to his academic bow until approximately 1939, when his two-volume *Business Cycles* appeared. (His second and third strings could however fire more and better arrows than most people's first strings!) In the last decade of Schumpeter's life, comparative systems shared the first place with doctrinal history. It was altogether fitting and proper for his final (unfinished) essay to bear the tital 'March into socialism',[6] although his principal research activity of the later 1940s had been the attempt to complete the *History of Economic Analysis*.

THE 'RICH MAN'S KARL MARX'

Schumpeter is neither the first[7] nor the last, but for my purposes decidedly the greatest, of a group of scholars whom I think of as 'rich man's Karl Marxes',

[5] These are 'The sociology of imperialisms' and 'Social classes in an ethnically homogeneous environment', translated by Heinz Norden as *Imperialism and Social Classes* (Schumpeter, 1951).

[6] Delivered from notes to the American Economic Association, New York, December 1949, and included in *CSD* (pp. 415–425).

[7] The first may have been the unfortunate Eugen Dühring (1833–1921), best known from Friedrich Engels' denunciation of 1877–78 in *Anti-Dühring* (full title, *Herrn Eugen Dührings Umwälzung der Wissenschaft*). Engels' denunciation included a definitive statement of various Marxian positions as approved by Marx himself, who was still alive. (This excerpt is widely known as *Socialism Utopian and Scientific*.)

Dühring was basically a philosopher of science in the (non-dialectical) materialist strain of Ernst Mach and Richard Avenarius, but also a Utopian idealist in social philosophy. After attacking (unread!) Dühring's *New Foundations for Rational Physics and Chemistry* because 'the laws of physics and chemistry there set forth are worthy of being placed alongside Herr Dühring's discoveries [in] economics as a measure of the ignorance and arrogance of Herr Dühring', Engels impartially attacks the University of Berlin for the 'despicable wrong' of withdrawing Dühring's licence to teach, following a dispute between Dühring and his senior colleagues (Engels, 1907, pp. 26 and 29). Such devotion to academic freedom is rare on either side of every curtain!

however vehemently most of them would resent the appellation. Their number includes (in addition to Schumpeter) Böhm-Bawerk, Pareto, Spencer, Max Weber, Veblen, Tawney, Myrdal, Parsons, possibly also Bulding and Galbraith. What do these disparates have in common?

A 'rich man's Marx' must possess, to some slight approximation of Marx himself, an encylopaedic mind at home in the higher reaches though not necessarily the latest fads and fashions of more than one or two humanistic or social disciplines (history, literature, philosophy; anthropology, economics, politics, sociology). Not only must he transcend the 'narrowness' limitations of single-field technical virtuosity—'knowing more and more about less and less, and finally everything about nothing'—he need never attain or retain such virtuosity. (Marx and Engels appear to have disdained as 'vulgar economics' the marginalist revolution of the 1870s and many economists—not all of them Marxists—approve their disdain.)

But more than this: the 'rich man's Marx' must devote considerable attention to the corpus of Marxian doctrine both before and since Marx's own death in 1883. He need not devote much of his effort to direct wrangling with Marx's ghost or Marx's disciples. He must, however, be basically unconverted, even if he admires Marx (as I also do) as the greatest secular social scientist who has yet lived. And he must, I think, be capable of occasional side-glances at Marx and Marxism when his conclusions are at variance with theirs.[8] He need not be pro-capitalist, or conservative, or reactionary, or liberal in the nineteenth-century sense, or fascist in any sense.[9] He may indeed be a socialist albeit not a Marxian one, or an anarchist of an individualist or libertarian sort. He should not, however, be a clear and present danger to the Powers That Be. And his activism, if any, should likewise be subdued, academic and preferably footnoted.

THE STRUCTURE OF *CSD*

CSD is divided into five parts, entitled respectively 'The Marxian doctrine', 'Can capitalism survive?', 'Can socialism work?', 'Socialism and democracy', and 'A historical sketch of socialist parties'. The second and fourth parts embody the book's major contributions to comparative economics, but we consider the other three initially and in passing.

---

[8] An example from the economic-development literature is Walt W. Rostow's *Stages of Economic Growth*, bearing the subtitle, *A Non-Communist Manifesto*.

[9] Other than 'objective fascist', of course. Any non-'movement' type whose net effect is seen as weakening the 'movement's' particular variant of Marxism may be called an 'objective fascist'. Example: The Marxist Trotsky at the hands of the Marxist Stalin.

Part 1, on Marxism, is reprinted in *Ten Great Economists from Marx to Keynes*;[10] it constitutes Schumpeter's most nearly definitive treatment of Marx. (The numerous references in his *History of Economic Analysis* (Schumpeter, 1954)[11] are briefer, scattered, and diffuse, the major one being at pp. 383–392. Even here, for the analysis proper Schumpeter refers the reader (p. 392, note 15) to Paul Sweezy's *Theory of Capitalist Development* (1942, parts 1–3)[12] in preference to attempting his own substantive presentation.)

Schumpeter's Marx is a human being, neither God nor Devil. Such presentation is not easy, short of full-length biography—and not all full-length biographies succeed—in view of Marx's genius, universality, pedantry, intolerance, rule-or-ruin personality, and of course the idolatry of the faithful. On the other hand, Schumpeter's key 'sociology' and 'economics' chapters in this section leave much to be desired, particularly in view of the new 'young Marx' materials which have become available since they were written.

Never having studied sociology in formal fashion, I would do well to evade or avoid discussion of Schumpeter on 'Marx the sociologist'. A further and impersonal argument against rushing in 'where angels fear to tread' follows from Stalin's outliving Schumpeter by three years and *CSD* by a decade. Schumpeter lacked what his readers, Marxist and non-Marxist alike, now possess—experience of the post-Stalin flowering of Marxian thought, including substantial accretion of Marx's own *Nachlass*. If Schumpeter on Marx now seems dated, as I fear is the case, the fault is not primarily Schumpeter's.

What, more precisely, seems dated in Schumpeter on 'Marx the sociologist'? For one thing, adequate discussion of the evolution of Marx's thought: whether a 'young Marx' was or was not outgrown by a 'mature Marx', how seriously the early manuscripts should be taken in view of *Das Kapital*'s neglect of their contents, the role of the *Grundrisse* as bridge between 'two Marxes', and so on. We note merely that the controversy flourished after Schumpeter's death, and pass on to more substantive matters . . .

More important in calling Schumpeter's criticism 'dated' is its functionalist

[10] Schumpeter, J. A. in Schumpeter, E. B. (1951) This posthumous work was edited by Schumpeter's widow, Elizabeth Boody Schumpeter.

[11] Mrs Schumpeter also edited this incomplete and posthumous work from her husband's manuscripts.

[12] Sweezy, a confirmed Marxist and currently (1980) senior editor of *Monthly Review*, was for many years the anti-Marxist Schumpeter's graduate assistant at Harvard. (It speaks to the quality of Schumpeter's mind that he tried and failed to secure for Sweezy a permanent post at Harvard despite the wide divergence of the two men's viewpoints.)

theory of classes, of social mobility, and of the circulation of elites. While exposited most fully in 'Social classes',[13] this functional theory also underlies *CSD*'s second chapter. To Schumpeter, classes rise and fall within society as families rise and fall within a class. As a class's function rose or fell in importance, and as the class's performance of its function rose or fell in efficiency, so that class would rise or fall in social position. Marx is accordingly faulted for overstating the importance of cataclysmic revolution in this process, and (more importantly) for underestimating the importance of social mobility both within and between such broad classes as the bourgeoisie and proletariat. What I see as occurring in Marxian thought since Schumpeter's heyday has been unconcern with numerical evidence on social mobility as summarized by such sociologists as Seymour Martin Lipset and Reinhard Bendix (Lipset and Bendix, 1966) as compared with stress on the *mechanism* of mobility (following hints in Marx himself). Rising by co-optation, as via the Harvard Law or Business Schools, is a quite different and on balance less significant phenomenon than rising by radical politics, the trade union movement, or developing a bicycle repair shop into the Ford Motor Company.

Nor is the precise position of the economic and business element in a generalized materialist interpretation of history quite so important a matter as Schumpeter, and as anti-Marxists generally, consider it. Whether the economic elite is the 'dog' of the ruling class with the political, military, and other elites as 'tails' or 'fleas on the tail', or whether some other elite is 'dog', or whether several of the elites are more or less on a par with each other, seems largely irrelevant in contemporary Marxism as compared with another consideration, namely, the extent to which the individuals comprising the several elites, which between them comprise the ruling class, have come to know each other, to associate with each other socially, to intermarry with each other, and to compromise their differences much of the time in varieties of imperfect and incomplete alliance. We may call such an alliance a 'power elite' following Wright Mills (1956), or simply a ruling class as more conventional Marxists do; this is a secondary or even tertiary consideration. (By the by, Schumpeter's own 'atavism' theory of imperialism, as expounded in 'Sociology of imperialism', loses much of its anti-Marxist bite and force when one considers more fully than Schumpeter did the intermingling and intermarriage between the 'atavistic feudal remnants' of the military elite

[13] Schumpeter's judicious limitatioin of his analysis to the 'ethnically homogeneous environment' is more confining than he may have realized, in view of the association between particular ethnic (religious, sexual) groups and particular class statuses—not only within societies like his own Austria–Hungary and contemporary America, but on a world scale with less-developed countries in proletarian roles.

with the upper circles of the bourgeoisie. This feature, however, may have been less prevalent in Habsburg Austria and Hohenzollern Germany than it has since become.)

A similar 'dated' quality extends, more surprisingly, to Schumpeter on 'Marx the economist'. Here *CSD*'s (unrevised) first edition of 1942 was fortuitously ill-timed. In that same year, 1942, were also published the two seminal works[14] which between them have almost double-handedly lifted English-language criticism of Marxian economics out of a half-century-old rut of dismissal in the manner of Böhm-Bawerk (1941) as simply flawed price theory. Schumpeter refrains from any $(n + 1)$st repetition of that old story, but (if we accept his widow's testimony)[15] had already become involved too deeply in the manuscript of his posthumous *History of Economic Analysis* to do anything more with the newer work. As a result, no foreshadowing can be seen in *CSD* of the post-war flowering of modern economic restatements and extensions (and criticisms) of Marx's economics.[16] (It is however reasonable to doubt that Schumpeter would ever have written him off as an economist by calling him 'a minor post-Ricardian' as Samuelson did.)

SOCIALISM AND SOCIALIST PARTIES

'Can Socialism work? Of course it can. No doubt is possible about that once we assume, first, that the requisite stage of industrial development has been reached and, second, that transitional problems can be successfully resolved.' Thus Schumpeter in 1942 (*CSD*, p. 167).

And so what else is new? 'The requisite stage of industrial development' may be considerably less than Schumpeter believed; he may have been too cautious in ignoring possibilities of 'fraternal' aid from established socialist regimes. My pencilled headnote on *CSD*'s part 3 (on socialism) reads in part: 'The least satisfactory part of the book. Atmosphere of "Utopia-Man meets Lenin and Stalin".' Schumpeter's ghost could do better now, with Chinese,

[14] In addition to Sweezy's (1942) *Theory of Capitalist Development* (already mentioned in footnotes 4 and 12) I refer to Joan Robinson's *An Essay on Marxian Economics* (1942). Maurice Dobb's 'A lecture on Marx', forming Ch. 9 of his *Economic Theory and Socialism* (1954) also dates from 1942 despite its 1954 publication date. Oscar Lange's briefer and less influential 'Marxian economics and modern economic theory' (1935) was a precursor of all this literature, but was not referred to in *CSD*. (A later Schumpeterian reference, at p. 884 of the *History of Economic Analysis*, cites it only as evidence that Lange remained a Marxist only in economic sociology.)

[15] *History of Economic Analysis*, 'Editor's Introduction' (by Elizabeth Boody Schumpeter), p. v.

[16] A few selected references, in roughly chronological order: Horowitz (1968), Samuelson (1957, 1971), Baran and Sweezy (1966), Hunt and Schwarz (1972), Morishima and Seton (1961), Morishima (1973), and Bose (1975).

Cuban, and Yugoslav experience to draw upon, let alone post-Stalin USSR.

While not basically wrong, this judgement is too harsh, I now believe in 'the cold pale light of dawn'. The Schumpeter of 1939–41 was spitting in the face of two intellectual trends, the first of which part 3 of *CSD* did its bit to demolish. (The second was demolished more effectively by history.)

(1) The first trend, represented by the work of Oscar Lange (1938)[17] and Abba Lerner (1944),[17] embodied the belief that the theorems of the purely competitive costless-information model of the market economy could be largely translated into precepts for action by socialist managers under the supervision of socialist governesses (called Planning Boards) to yield results much closer to both hearts' desire and Pareto optimality than can be expected from monopoly-ridden and imperfectly informed capitalism. Lange, later to rise to the Vice Presidency of a socialist Poland, was the more emphatic in his socialism. Lerner's primary allegiance was to the rules themselves; whether their enforcer was to be nominally capitalist or socialist was to him both a secondary and a distracting side issue.

(2) The other fashion combatted in *CSD*'s part 3 was the position that the ridiculed '57 varieties' of socialism differed only on tactics for getting 'from here to there', but that socialism-in-practice, or at least scientific-socialism-in-practice, was planned from the outset to be, or at least to culminate in, a monolith represented for all essential purposes and in all countries by the USSR as it had evolved from Lenin to Stalin. The prevalent attitude remained that proclaimed by Lincoln Steffens after the October Revolution, that he had already seen the future and that it was already working. Also, the Webb's (1937) two-volume affirmative answer to their question: *Soviet Communism: A New Civilisation?*[18] was still accepted widely (both for better and for worse) following the Stalin Constitution of 1936 and despite the next five years of the Moscow show trials and Hitler–Stalin Pacts.

When Schumpeter tells us that socialism works, he includes in 'working' anything from Utopia to the mere avoidance of breakdown. Thus a Post Office 'works' in his sense so long as (eventual) mail delivery continues between postal strikes, and so long as the taxpayers continue to fund the postal deficits. An army 'works', too, so long as it fills its ranks by conscription or otherwise, maintains for at least its higher officers the social status and glamour anticipated 'when they first put this uniform on', and avoids annihilation by some enemy force foreign or domestic. In both these senses, socialism 'works' for Schumpeter; only this, but little more. (Also

---

17 Lange's most influential essay and the definitive Lerner work, with preliminary papers covering the preceding decade.

18 But see also, for a completely contrary view, Trotsky (1972) who accuses the Webbs of 'conservatively pedantic socialism' at p. 2.

little less. As we shall see, Schumpeter's socialism need not degenerate into Hayek's serfdom.)

CSD's part 5 is on the post-Marxian history of socialist parties. We pass over it quickly, not because of any outright deficiencies but because its task is done better elsewhere. For the period prior to 1917, Edmund Wilson's (1940) *To the Finland Station* was an approximate contemporary of *CSD*. Beautifully written by a literary critic and intellectual historian, it also includes substantial material at 'the other end' of the story, i.e. on the intellectual backgrounds of Marx and Marxism. For the period since 1917, Wright Mills' (1962) *The Marxists*, less detached than Schumpeter, carries the story forward an important 20 years into the period after World War Two.

CAN CAPITALISM SURVIVE?

'No, I do not think it can', answers Schumpeter, to open part 2 of *CSD*. Neither the question nor the answer is new with Schumpeter, but repetitions with explicit reference to Schumpeter's work have been rumbling through the comparative-economics literature ever since. As I prepared to write these lines in the spring of 1980, an essay crossed my desk by a former chairman of the US Council of Economic Advisers (McCracken, 1979),[19] bearing Schumpeter's title and starting from Schumpeter's treatment in *CSD*.

We should note at the outset something which Schumpeter's critics occasionally forget, that Schumpeter is merely assessing 'the weight of the evidence' as he saw it in the last decade of his life under the influence of the 'disappointing Juglar' of the 1930s.[20] It is not, in other words, an exercise in fatalistic prophecy of the crystal-ball or tea-leaf variety.

The crude outlines of Schumpeter's position are common knowledge. Capitalism digs its own grave with three shovels. These shovels, however, do *not* include either its lapses from pure and perfect competition in the static microeconomy or any inherent Keynesian[21] or Marxian type stagnationist

---

[19] Professor McCracken acknowledges his debt to Schumpeter, who was one of his teachers at Harvard in the 1940s.

[20] This is the title of Section G of the 15th and final chapter of Schumpeter's *Business Cycles* entitled 'The world crisis and after'. Subsection G(5), pp. 1032–1050 of vol. 2, should be read as a preliminary sketch for this basic argument of *CSD*. Erich Schneider (1975) traces the argument back yet further, to a 1918 essay on 'The crisis of the tax state'.

[21] Schumpeter's opposition to the Keynesianism of the *General Theory* is well known, although the standard treatment by Arthur Smithies (1951) seeks to paper over the hostility between the two. McCracken (1979, p. 144) is more forthright in recalling Schumpeter's contempt for the 'Keynesian nursery' conducted by his Keynesian colleagues at Harvard. (He claimed that the economic content of a year's course could be learned in two weeks.)

tendencies in the macroeconomy. They arise from capitalism's successes rather than its failures. They are part technological, part sociological: (1) capitalism reduces the vital element of innovation (not invention!) largely to a routine capable of carrying on by hired managers or technicians (again, just like the Post Office or the Army);[22] (2) it does not prevent—indeed, it may sometimes accelerate—the demise of what might otherwise be 'protecting strata' within the pre-capitalist military and landowning aristocracy;[23] and (3) most importantly it earns the active opposition of the class or stratum of the intellectuals—particularly those who, as social critics, deserve rather the title of 'emotionals'—by displacing them from positions of social status—'if you're so smart, why aren't you rich?'—who then become the active agents of its own threatened demise.[24]

Primarily from the alienation and disaffection of the intellectuals, Schumpeter believes, result the concrete legislative excesses which themselves cause capitalist decline and stagnation. These excesses include high progressive taxation, one-sided pro-union labour legislation, anti-monopoly legislation, price fixing on the public utility model, and inflationary pursuit of full employment. Both the rise of environmental legislation and the post-thalidomide burgeoning of ostensible consumer protection have come since Schumpeter's death; both would have been grist for Schumpeter's mill. Given these millstones around its neck, capitalism lives on only in the

[22] 'Since capitalist enterprise . . . tends to automatize progress, we conclude that it tends to make itself superfluous—to break to pieces under pressure of its own success' (*CSD*, p. 134).

On invention and innovation: Much scholarship has been in my view misplaced in analysis of patent and other statistics, with a view to showing that private individuals and small firms continue to be responsible for a substantial part of *inventive* activity. But Schumpeter's argument relates not to invention *in vitro* but innovation (application) *in vivo*, which is where the large oligopolistic firm's advantage lies.

[23] 'In breaking down the pre-capitalist framework of society, capitalism broke not only barriers that impeded its progress but also flying buttresses that prevented its collapse' (*CSD*, p. 139). The economic collapse of the 'buttresses' (rentiers) is accelerated by monetary inflation, which (along with his Austrian experience of hyperinflation in 1919–24) explains Schumpeter's strong antipathy to inflation. Schneider (1975, p. 47) goes so far as to list inflation among the independent forces making for the collapse of capitalism in Schumpeter's thinking.

Schumpeter's view may be compared and contrasted with that of Barrington Moore; Moore (1967) argues that capitalism coexists with democracy where its rise overthrew pre-capitalist society more violently, and with democracy where the rising capitalists form viable alliances with, e.g., the feudal aristocracy.

[24] Neither distrust of the ntellectual as an alienated element in society nor respect for his potential prowess as a corrosive element is novel in the sociology of the intellectual. Huszar (1960), for example, traces one or both of these strains back to Plato and Ibn Khaldun. Primarily economic precursors of Schumpeter include Thorstein Veblen (1921) and, with special reference to Marxism and its rivals within the labour movement, Selig Perlman (1949).

'oxygen tent' of government deficit spending and other forms of inflationary finance, and is easy prey for socialist critics.

I would not call myself a Schumpeterian, however, and raise two sorts of demurrer to his analysis as outlined above.

Rather than spelling out or otherwise elaborating my major demurrer, let me merely suggest a thought experiment. Suppose a liberal capitalist parliamentary democracy, with visibly unequal distribution of wealth, income, and consumption. In this society social mobility is limited to the co-operation cases, but 'certified' intellectuals, lay and clerical, are readily bought off or otherwise co-opted. Per capita GNP is sufficient to permit a significant portion of the working class to be supported well above the subsistence level when unemployed or on strike. If I understand Schumpeter correctly, the logic of his system would require him to consider such a society largely impervious to socialist propaganda because the potential propagandists have become tame cats of the ruling capitalists. I, on the other hand, would expect otherwise. In such a society, I should expect one or more labour, farmer, or other movements to arise almost spontaneously, and to grow or generate its own dissident intellectuals, including its own emotionals and mindless fanatics. Under this home-grown leadership both in the large—e.g. the labour press or farm organizations—and in the small—e.g. the shop steward on the factory floor—I should expect both crippling strikes and anti-capitalist legislation to approximate what we see around us. (I grant that this home-grown leadership will be more like Samuel Gompers, John L. Lewis, Huey Long, or Adolf Hitler than like Marx, Engels, Lenin, or Trotsky.)[25]

My minor demurrer relates to Schumpeter's disregard for the *tertium quid*, meaning non-socialist alternatives to capitalism. Fascism, in particular, was at its zenith while Schumpeter was writing *CSD*, but he ignores its ideology almost completely in that volume. His earlier *Business Cycles* (especially Vol. 2, pp. 695–700), however, may indicate why he did so.

However fascist parties may have been founded and financed originally, Schumpeter sees fascism as eventually equivalent to socialism in its anti-capitalist stance. It may be in part an atavistic throwback to the feudal past, but it is less an atavism than an insignificant way station on 'the road that leads from capitalism to orthodox socialism' (Schumpeter, 1939, p. 697). The reader is reminded of the comedian's summary of the Nazi 'Left' (before its annihilation in Hitler's 1934 purge): 'Rare roast beef—brown outside, red inside'. And on the other side of the globe, John Dower wonders with

[25] Concern for the 'more, more, and more' ideology of the home-grown labour leader, as distinguished from the self-consciously intellectual Socialist one, underlies Henry C. Simons', 'Reflections on syndicalism' (1944) and Charles E. Lindblom's, *Unions and Capitalism* (1949).

reference to Japan's militant young officers of the 1930s, 'How far Left is Right?'

Such a 'convergence hypothesis' between fascism and socialism may have made sense with regard to Hitler, Mussolini, and especially their Japanese allies.[26] But what of the less flamboyant and glamorous, more methodical and insidious civilian semi-fascism of technocratic planning by a government–big business alliance, possibly with the farmer as junior partner but with the worker and consumer left out in the cold except for 'trickle-down'? ('Japan, Inc.' is my model here, but it post-dates Schumpeter by many years.)

SOCIALISM AND (LIBERAL?) DEMOCRACY

Let us relocate *CSD* in time. The 1942 date of the first edition comes after Mises on the impossibility of rational (non-dictatorial) economic calculation in a socialist state, after Hayek's promulgation of the Mises doctrine among English readers ignorant of German, and after the 'market socialism' rebuttals by, *inter alios*, Lange and Lerner (Mises, 1920; Lange, 1938). But 1942 comes before Hayek's *Road to Serfdom* (1944), which would catapult the controversy into public limelight and which Schumpeter would later review in a prestigious scholarly journal. *CSD* cannot therefore be viewed in terms of a contribution to a 'Hayek' or 'serfdom' controversy already under way, to which his 'conclusion *ex ante*'[27] would satisfy partisans on neither side.

Schumpeter's treatment of democracy, in particular, is controversial from its very definition. He not only accepts what lawyers call a 'procedural'

---

[26] Schumpeter's interest in entrepreneurship and its developmental role inspired a long-term and long-distance love affair with the Japanese economy, including its big-business *zaibatsu* elements. Had Bonn not called Schumpeter to Germany in 1925, after the failure of his venture into private finance as President of the Biedermann Bank in Vienna, he might have moved to Japan. (Indeed, he had already accepted a visiting appointment there when the Bonn offer arrived.) Schumpeter actually visited Japan only once, for several months in 1931.

Schumpeter's sympathy for Japan was reciprocated by a school of Japanese Schumpeterians led by Ichiro Nakayama and Seiichi Tobata, who had studied with him at Bonn and translated his *Theory of Economic Development* into Japanese. It is interesting to speculate on the possible consequences for economics East and West of Schumpeter's transplantation from Europe to Japan rather than America, both before and after the young officers eliminated the zaibatsu focus of anti-militarism by the assassinations of 15 May 1932.

[27] 'Between socialism as we defined it and democracy as we defined it there is no necessary relation: the one one exist without the other. At the same time there is no incompatibility: in appropriate states of the social environment the socialist engine can be run on democratic principles' (*CSD*, p. 284).

definition along representative lines[28] but explicitly parts company with the 'substantive' and mystical definition in terms of the 'common good' or 'people's will', which we associate particularly with Rousseau. Thus democracy means just democracy, as distinguished from liberalism, from libertarianism, and even from liberal democracy. Schumpeter emphasizes the point with historical accounts of illiberal and extremist horrors which either had, or might easily have had, popular approval in their own days.[29] An elitist—one might almost say a congenital elitist—Schumpeter harbours no illusions about 'The People, Yes.' ('You cannot fool all of the people all of the time', as Lincoln said, but what of a majority of the people a majority of the time?)

Schumpeter goes on to elaborate four conditions under which procedural democracy can, in his view, be relied upon to yield satisfactory—not 'optimal'—results as viewed by the social critic and the man from Mars (*CSD*, pp. 290–295):

> The first condition is that the human material of politics should be of sufficiently high quality. [T]he only effective guarantee is the existence of a social stratum, itself the product of a selective process, that takes to politics as a matter of course.
>
> The second condition for the success of democracy is that the effective range of political decision should not be extended too far. [Beyond certain limits] government and parliament will have to accept the specialists' advice whatever they may think themselves.
>
> As a third condition, democratic government in modern industrial society must be able to command the services of a well-trained bureaucracy, endowed with a strong sense of duty and no less strong *esprit de corps*. Such a bureaucracy must be in a position to evolve principles of its own and sufficiently independent to assert them.
>
> The fourth set of conditions may be summed up in the phrase Democratic Self-control. [T]he democratic method cannot work smoothly unless all

---

[28] '[T]he democratic method is that institutional arrangement for arriving at political decisions by which individuals acquire the power to decide by means of a competitive struggle for the people's vote' (*CSD*, p. 269). The rival 'classical' or 'substantive' theory of democracy is, according to Schumpeter 'that there exists a Common Good, the obvious beacon light of policy, which is always simple to define and which every normal person can be made to see by means of rational argument' (*CSD*, p. 250). For a critique by a Schumpeter student with more traditional American faith in democracy, see David McCord Wright (1951).

[29] Autobiographical digression: The writer has lived through one minor example, Wisconsin under Senator Joseph McCarthy, who was 'Our Joe' to the end of his chequered career in almost every Wisconsin county except Dane (Madison) and perhaps Milwaukee.

> the groups that count are willing to accept any legislative measure so long as it is on the statute book and all executive orders issued by legally competent authorities. Above all, electorates and parliaments must be on an intellectual and moral level high enough to be proof against the offerings of the crook and the crank. The voters must respect the division of labor between themselves and the politicians they elect. They must understand that, once they have elected an individual, political action is his business and not theirs. Finally, effective competition for leadership requires a large measure of tolerance for difference of opinion. [T]olerance cannot be absolute. But it must be possible for every would-be leader who is not lawfully excluded to present his case without producing disorder.

As we saw so recently as the quotation in footnote 27, Schumpeter sees no contradiction whatever between socialism and democracy. To this extent, he differs sharply from the Hayek of *The Road to Serfdom*. Socialism and even moderately successful democracy, however, may be another matter. If, as Schumpeter believes, a developed society is required for democracy to function and flourish, a socialist Tanzania or Botswana can hardly become a successful democracy in the twentieth century despite the hopes of their British Labourite enthusiasts—but neither can a capitalist Tanzania nor Botswana! Other things equal, socialist efforts at democracy have, Schumpeter suggests, one important advantage over capitalist ones. That advantage relates to history, and primarily to intellectual history. Thanks less to capitalism's intrinsic weaknesses (in his view) than to 'treason of the intellectuals', important groups in many still-capitalist countries—'intense minorities', 'militants', 'terrorists'—will take to the streets and sabotage both 'measures still on the statute books' and 'executive orders issued by legally competent authorities' when these statutes and orders appear supportive of capitalists as a class or contrary to their notions of 'participatory' or 'industrial' democracy,[30] whereas their capitalist equivalents in socialist countries prefer to take refuge across the border or overseas. As an offset to this advantage, a socialist government (especially in an early post-revolutio-

[30] 'Participatory democracy' in the sense of direct decisions by crowds assembled voluntarily or otherwise for the purpose of making such decisions freely or otherwise, has had its current revivals only after Schumpeter's death, and he has nothing to say about it. 'Industrial democracy', however, he characterizes (*CSD*, p. 300): 'Industrial or Economic Democracy is a phrase that figures in so many quasi-utopias that it has retained very little precise meaning. Mainly, I think, it means two things: first, the trade-union rule over industrial relations; second democratization of the monarchic factory by workmen's representation on boards or other devices calculated to secure them influence on the introduction of technological improvements, business policy in general and, of course, discipline in the plant in particular, including methods of "hiring and firing". . . . It is safe to say that much of this economic democracy will vanish into thin air in a socialist regime.' (Compare Poland 1980–1982.)

nary atmosphere) is apt to lack both high-quality politicians and bureaucrats in sufficient numbers for successful democracy—and also the patience to await their development. The urge to substitute for democracy one or another cult of one or another personality, or alternatively to congeal the heroes of the revolution into a *New Class* (Djilas, 1957), may easily but not necessarily be too strong to resist in post-revolutionary and incompletely pacified milieus. Better, perhaps, a dictator to bang heads together, check inflation, and make trains run on time than a democracy, however socialistic, bent on tearing itself to pieces. Was it not Voltaire who would rather be ruled by one lion than by a hundred rats?

While democracy, and particularly unsuccessful democracy, was entirely compatible with socialism in Schumpeter's analysis, liberal democracy was not. State monopoly of the media and state control of 'factory discipline' would see to that,[31] and Schumpeter's system did not comprise persistent rivalries between and within the civilian bureaucracy, the Army, and the Party as reliable offsets. Socialist democracy, still in Schumpeter's vision, would be a pallid and narcotized imitation of what his critics, such as McCord Wright (1951), consider the genuine article.

Schumpeter's socialist democracy differs only in degrees—although I think in several significant degrees—from either Hayek's *Serfdom* or Orwell's *Nineteen Eighty-Four*. It is less inevitable; the overtones of concentration camp and *Gulag Archipelago* are missing; nothing is hinted about perpetual war or continuous decline in civilian living standards. Nevertheless basic sympathy with the Hayek position is there. It is no surprise to find Schumpeter's review of *The Road to Serfdom* to be favourable, even laudatory.[32] And as for a rival scenario, the possible 'convergence' of American-style capitalism and Soviet-style communism to an apparently social-democratic *via media*, we may make bold to read Schumpeter's posthumous mind. Convergence rose to (temporary) prominence only after both Schumpeter's and Stalin's deaths, but Schumpeter—unlike, for example, the great Dutch economist and planner

[31] 'After all, effective management of the socialist economy means dictatorship not *of* but *over* the proletariat in the factory. The men who are there so strictly disciplined would, it is true, be sovereign at the elections. But just as they may use this sovereignty to relax the discipline of the factory, so governments may avail themselves of this discipline to restrict this sovereignty. As a matter of practical necessity, socialist democracy may eventually turn out to be more of a sham than capitalist democracy ever was. In any case, that democracy will not mean increased personal freedom' (*CSD*, p. 302, from the final paragraphs of part 4).

[32] Schumpeter faults Hayek only for not having asked *why* those particular socialistic ideas had come to flourish, which he (Hayek) felt would end in dictatorship. 'If [Hayek] had gone into the historical conditions from which those ideas arose which he dislikes so much, he could not have helped discovering that they are the product of the social system which he does like' (Schumpeter's review of Hayek (1944) in *Journal of Political Economy* (1946), p. 270.)

Jan Tinbergen[33]—would actively have opposed the ordinary convergence hypothesis of the 1950s and 1960s in favour of the one-way convergence implied in Hayek's work.

INSTEAD OF A CONCLUSION

I have brashly stated both hypothesis and conclusions on the run, section by section and sometimes even paragraph by paragraph. Instead of any overall conclusion, therefore, let me merely acknowledge the factual and historical assistance of two biographical studies. Neither appreciation stressed Schumpeter's contributions to the study of comparative systems quite so much as I might have hoped, but both made Schumpeter (whom, as I said, I never knew personally) come alive as no conventional academic obituary could have done. The older of these two studies is Gottfried Haberler's 'Joseph Alois Schumpeter, 1883–1950' (Haberler, 1950; Spiegel, 1964); the more recent is the late Erich Schneider's memorial (1975), translated under the title *Schumpeter, Life and Work* by W. E. Kuhn.[34] Whichever is more accurate in their unavoidable points of minor disagreement,[35] I am grateful for the assistance of both.

[33] On convergence, see the three selections comprising Part Vd of Morris Bornstein (1974). These selections are numbered 28 (Millar), 29 (Linnemann, Pronk, and Tinbergen), and 30 (Mesa-Lago).

[34] Haberler's account is fuller in matters of extra-curricular detail.

[35] One focus of possible disagreement relates to the extent and nature of Schumpeter's formal classroom teaching of comparative economic systems in Germany and Austria. Compare Haberler (pp. 339, 341, note 2) with Schneider (p. 29). The Haberler version suggests more such teaching than the Schneider one.

REFERENCES

Baran, P. A. & Sweezy, P. M. (1966) *Monopoly Capital*. Ch. 3–7. New York: Monthly Review Press.

Böhm-Bawerk, E. von (1941) *Karl Marx and the Close of His System*. Sweezy edition. New York: Kelley, Original German edition 1896.

Bornstein, M. (1974) *Comparative Economic Systems: Models and Cases*. 3rd Edition. Homewood: Irwin.

Bose, A. (1975) *Marxian and Post-Marxian Political Economy*. Parts 1, 3. Harmondsworth: Penguin.

Clemence, R. V. & Doody, F. S. (1950) *The Schumpeterian System*. Cambridge, MA: Addison Wesley.
Djilas, M. (1957) *The New Class*. New York: Praeger.
Dobb, M. (1954) A lecture on Marx. *Economic Theory and Socialism*. Ch. 9. New York: International Publishers.
Engels, F. (1907) *Landmarks of Scientific Socialism*. (Tr. and Ed.) Lewis, A. Chicago: Kerr.
Haberler, G. (1950) Joseph Alois Schumpeter, 1883–1950. *Quarterly Journal of Economics*, August. Abridged version in Spiegel, H. W. (1964).
Hayek, F. (1944) *The Road to Serfdom*. London: Routledge. Reviewed by Schumpeter (1946) *Journal of Political Economy* (June), p. 269ff.
Horowitz, D. (Ed.) (1968) *Marx and Modern Economics*. New York: Monthly Review Press.
Hunt, E. K. & Schwarz, J. G. (Eds) (1972) *A Critique of Economic Theory*. Parts 4–5. Harmondsworth: Penguin.
Huszar, G. B. de (Ed.) (1960) *The Intellectuals, a Controversial Portrait*. p. 5. Glencoe: Free Press.
Lange, O. (1935) Marxian economics and modern economic theory. *R. E. Stud*. June.
Lange, O. (1938) On the economic theory of socialism. In *On the Economic Theory of Socialism*. (Ed.) Lippincott, B. E. Minneapolis: University of Minnesota Press.
Lerner, A. (1944) *Economics of Control*. New York: Macmillan.
Lindblom, C. E. (1949). *Unions and Capitalism*. New Haven: Yale University Press.
Lipset, S. M. & Bendix, R. (1966) *Social Mobility in Industrial Society*. Berkeley and Los Angeles: University of California Press.
McCracken, P. W. (1979) Can capitalism survive? In *Dilemmas Facing the Nation* (Ed.) Prochnow, H. V. New York: Harper & Row.
Mills, C. W. (1956) *The Power Elite*. New York: Oxford University Press.
Mills, C. W. (1962) *The Marxists*. Ch. 8–14. New York: Dell.
Mises, L. von (1920) Die Wirtschaftsrechnung im socialistischen Gemeinwesen. *Archiv für Socialwissenschaften*. Translated by Adler, S. as Economic calculation in the socialist commonwealth for Hayek, F. A., (Ed.) (1935) *Collectivist Economic Planning*. London: Routledge & Kegan Paul.
Moore, B. (1967) *Social Origins of Dictatorship and Democracy*. London: Allen Lane.
Morishima, M. (1973) *Marx's Economics*. Cambridge: Cambridge University Press.
Morishima, M. & Seton, F. (1961) Aggregation of Leontief matrices and the labor theory of value. *Econometrica*, April.
Perlman, S. (1949) *A Theory of the Labor Movement*. Ch. 1 and 8. New York: Kelley. Originally published 1928.
Robinson, J. (1942) *An Essay on Marxian Economics*. London: Macmillan.
Samuelson, P. A. (1957) Wages and interest: a modern dissection of Marxian economic models. *American Economic Review*. December.
Samuelson, P. A. (1971) Understanding the Marxian notion of exploitation. *Journal of Economic Literature*. June.
Schneider, E. (1975). *Schumpeter, Life and Work* (Tr. W. E. Kuhn). pp. 25 and 48. Lincoln: Bureau of Business Research, University of Nebraska.
Schumpeter, E. B. (Ed.) (1951) *Ten Great Economists from Marx to Keynes*. pp. 3–74. New York: Oxford University Press.
Schumpeter, J. A. (1939) *Business Cycles*. 2 Volumes. New York and London: McGraw-Hill.
Schumpeter, J. A. (1942) *Capitalism, Socialism and Democracy*. New York: Harper & Row. 3rd Edition, 1950. New York: Harper.
Schumpeter, J. A. (1951) *Imperialism and Social Classes*. Sweezy edition. New York: Kelley.
Schumpeter, J. A. (1954) *History of Economic Analysis*. New York: Oxford University Press.
Simons, H. C. (1944) Reflections on syndicalism. *Journal of Political Economy*, February.

Smithies, A. (1951) Schumpeter and Keynes. *Review of Economics and Statistics*, May.
Spiegel, H. W. (1964) *The Development of Economic Thought. Great Economists in Perspective*. Abridged Edition. pp. 432–460. New York: Wiley.
Sweezy, P. M. (1942) *The Theory of Capitalist Development*. New York: Oxford University Press.
Trotsky, L. D. (1972) *The Revolution Betrayed*. New York: Pathfinder Press. Originally published 1936.
Veblen, T. (1921) *The Engineers and the Price System*. Condensed in Lerner, M. (Ed.) *The Portable Veblen*. New York: Huebsch.
Webb, S. & Webb, B. (1937) *Soviet Communism: A New Civilisation?* New York: Scribners.
Wilson, E. (1940) *To the Finland Station*. Part 2, Ch. 1–4, Part 3. Garden City, NY: Doubleday.
Wright, D. McC. (1951) Schumpeter's political philosophy. *Review of Economics and Statistics*, May.

Chapter Seven

Schumpeter and Socialism

KURT W. ROTHSCHILD

INTRODUCTION

TO deal with the relationship Schumpeter–Socialism is no easy matter. Not only has socialism acquired so many different shades and meanings—witness the miraculous capacity of the Left to split and resplit on 'fundamental' issues—that the question 'What sort of socialism?' arises. There is also the difficulty that Schumpeter's capitalism is not of the usual sort. And there is finally the baffling question as to the exact message of Schumpeterianism. Like all great social scientists, Schumpeter was fully aware of the complexity of the real world and made—quite deliberately—ample use of qualifications, of 'buts' and 'ifs', so that it is not always easy to state uniquely 'what Schumpeter *really* meant'.

Even the answer to the rather simple question whether Schumpeter was a socialist seems not to be so obvious as one would think. Edgar Salin, in his introduction to the German translation of *Capitalism, Socialism and Democracy* states firmly 'Schumpeter is a socialist' though he hastens to add that 'no socialist, be he a Marxist or a Fabian, will detect his socialism in Schumpeter's writing' (Schumpeter, 1950a, p. 8). At the other end of the scale Joan Robinson (1943), after having read the very same book, finds that 'Professor Schumpeter, as many tart phrases reveal, has little love for socialism, and none at all for socialists' (p. 381).

While I believe that there can be no doubt that on this point Joan Robinson was much nearer to the truth than Salin,[1] there remains the fact that

[1] 'I do not advocate socialism.' Thus wrote Schumpeter in a manuscript on whose final edition he worked on the day before he died (see Schumpeter, 1950b, p. 447). Although Schumpeter often hesitated to advocate (rather than explain), it is certain that all through his life he adhered to the above attitude on the basis of his convictions.

Schumpeter could evoke such different impressions among his expert readers. And even more important is the fact that—whatever Schumpeter's attitude may have been—his writings had an important and stimulating influence on the deliberations of socialist economists; much more so than the works of other 'bourgeois' economists. Thus we find in Paul Baran's important neo-Marxist analysis of *The Political Economy of Growth* (1957) that Schumpeter is quoted quite as often as Engels, viz. 14 times, as compared with 36 quotations from Marx, 18 from Lenin and seven from Keynes.

The reasons for this ambivalent status of Schumpeter are not difficult to find. All through his life Schumpeter was attracted to the same kind of questions and problems which had been foremost in the minds of Marx and some of the classical economists: to the 'magnificent dynamics'[2] of economic development. This and the openness of a tolerant mind brought him into close contact with Marxian thinking and the capitalism–socialism problem.

If we want to oversimplify we could say that while there exists any number of people who are non-Marxist socialists, there are very few specimens who can be regarded as non-socialist Marxists. Schumpeter is one of them. Or at least nearly so, because Sweezy is probably right when he defines more carefully that the 'Schumpeterian system (is) comparable in its scope to Marxian social science, though not to Marxism as a whole' (Sweezy, 1951, p. 120). At any rate it will be advisable to deal separately with Schumpeter and Marx (in the third section) and with Schumpeter and socialism (in the fourth section). The two aspects are, of course, in many ways interwoven. But the differentiation is useful. In the first case we meet warmth and sympathy (intermingled with Schumpeterian irony), in the second aloofness and cool analysis. But before going into these matters I want to say a few words on Schumpeter himself.

SCHUMPETER HIMSELF

To understand fully Schumpeter's special position *vis-à-vis* both Marx and the capitalism–socialism problem, one has to be aware of his background and of the values that underlie his 'grand designs'. Such a biographical and psychological detour not only helps us to get a clearer insight into Schumpeter's ideas but it is also in the best Schumpeterian tradition. In his brilliant biographical essays (Schumpeter, 1951) as well as in his monumental posthumous *History of Economic Analysis* (Schumpeter, 1954) he usually introduces biographical and historical material to make the evolution and contents of specific theories more intelligible.

[2] The term is used in Baumol (1961).

From what one knows about Schumpeter[3] there seem to me to be two outstanding characteristics which leave their mark in all his work and in his likes and dislikes: a certain old-world 'romanticism' and a stupendous intellect. While the intellect was a gift of Nature, the romanticism grew out of the circumstances of his upbringing. In his formative years he was exposed to the full blast of the feudal remnants and the glamour of the Habsburg empire which must have seemed outdated to many Western observers even in those days. The ten-year-old boy, coming already from a well-to-do background, is presented with a titled stepfather high up in the military hierarchy. The values he derives from (and probably admires in) him are fortified by the aristocratic–conservative influence of the *Theresianum*, the exclusive school to which he is promptly sent and which greatly impresses him. After taking his doctorate at Vienna University he spends several months in England where—at least on his visits to Oxford and Cambridge—he is again in touch with an aristocratic–individualistic atmosphere. Finally, his first academic appointment which came after a prolonged stay in the monarchic circles of pre-capitalist Egypt, takes him to a chair in the University of Czernowitz, a town in the less-developed, semi-feudal east of the Habsburg empire.

Thus, up to the age of 28—and by that time the young genius had already worked out the main lines for his future research—Schumpeter, the great theoretician of capitalism and its development, was steeped in an atmosphere of aristocratic and pre-capitalistic sentiments which he liked and which shaped him. This led to a persevering nostalgia for his young days, for Czernowitz, and later—when he had moved to the United States of America—for Europe. It must also have contributed to some of his lovable habits of chivalry, good conversation, exquisite dress, etc., which had an air of bygone days.

But, above all, this basic make-up coloured his theoretical interests and his work. His elitist and romantic views lie behind his very idiosyncratic picture of the heroic entrepreneur–pioneer who is the prime mover of development and around whom capitalism is more or less defined. This point will come up when we deal with the capitalism–socialism problem. His aristocratic aloofness,[4] together with his intellectual honesty, also eased his openness towards Marx. Just as some aristocratic circles in old Austria found it easier than the immediately threatened petty bourgeoisie (for which the aristocracy

---

[3] See in this context various contributions in Harris (1951), particularly Haberler, and further Schneider (1970), Kirsch (1979) and März (1964). The last-mentioned work also contains an interesting section on Schumpeter and Marx.

[4] 'In his personal life he refused to compromise with bourgeois or proletarian standards of respectability' (Smithies, 1951, p. 13).

had little esteem) to understand the social question and the socialist aspirations of the working class, so Schumpeter felt less tied than many of his colleagues to the possessing bourgeoisie (*Besitzbürger*) as such and felt no obligation to 'refute' or ignore Marx and socialism.[5]

SCHUMPETER AND MARX

The two economists who were held in particularly high esteem by Schumpeter were Walras and Marx.[6] In them he found the two qualities which he valued most, developed to highest perfection: analysis and vision. Walras had come nearer to a natural-science-like system-analytic[7] structure of economic transactions than anyone before. But it remained a static picture. Marx, on the other hand, had—again more than anyone before—provided a grand vision of the movement of the economic and social system as a whole and had done it—in contrast to the Utopians—as a scientist, because he provides the underlying analysis.

That Walras usually got the highest marks in Schumpeter's evaluation of economic doctrine, higher not only than Marx but also higher than Smith, Ricardo and Mill (although Schumpeter's work was more akin to Marx) is again, I believe, to be explained from the personal background. The quality admired in Marx—vision (paired with analysis)—was not in short supply among Schumpeter's talents. In this respect he surpassed his contemporaries by head and shoulders all through his life. When it came to 'exact' formal-mathematical analysis, his other beloved child, he did—in spite of all his achievements—come up against difficulties and could not quite reach the exacting standards he had set himself (see on this Samuelson, 1951). So Walras' achievement impressed him most, because it seemed so difficult to obtain. There is thus no contradiction between this extreme admiration for Walras and Schumpeter's famous dictum that if he had to choose only one of the three qualifications essential for a good economist—viz. theoretical analysis, statistics, and history—it would be history (see his remarks in Schumpeter, 1949a), which moves him, of course, nearer to Marx than to Walras.

---

[5] 'Schumpeter had been the enfant terrible of the Austrian school of economists. Steward to an Egyptian princess, owner of a stable of race horses, onetime Finance Minister of Austria, Schumpeter could look at the prospects for bourgeois society with the objectivity of one whose feudal world had come to an end in 1914' (P. A. Samuelson in his *Newsweek* column in 1969, quoted in Samuelson (1980)).

[6] See the Foreword of Elisabeth Boody Schumpeter to Schumpeter (1951, p. ix).

[7] Already in his early work on the essence and contents of theoretical economics Schumpeter had a clear idea of the need for system analysis (see Schumpeter, 1908, pp. 28–9).

The vicinity to Marx in the grand design of Schumpeter's life work is quite obvious. Like Marx and in sharp contrast to the spreading neoclassical allocation theory he always kept the vision of an endogenous dynamic movement of the entire economic system foremost in his mind. Static analysis may open up useful insights into particular problems and it may be a necessary stepping-stone in building a dynamic theory, but it can never be a substitute for it. Marx and Schumpeter were also more or less of one opinion with regard to the underlying force which leads to constant economic change. It is technical progress and innovation in the widest sense, the development of the productive forces.

From this common basis of a dynamic, long-term approach follows a whole series of further similarities. The long-term dynamics free the onlooker from a narrow preoccupation with a given historic system and from the tendency to regard given conditions as the absolute standard. Every system is in a state of flux and liable to change. This is no less true for capitalism than it was for feudalism. Thus to regard socialism as a *possible* follower to capitalism was to Schumpeter—again in stark contrast to many of his neoclassical, static, and partly apologetic colleagues—quite an obvious viewpoint. That he also regarded socialism as the *likely* or *necessary* sequel to capitalism was by no means obvious and here the vicinity to Marx is—as we shall see later—spurious, because the expected mechanism is quite different.

The stress on long-term endogenous change is also responsible for similarities in methodology. If economic systems change in the course of history, historical and sociological problems cannot be relegated to a 'given' framework. They have to be included into the analysis. This explains why Schumpeter did not join in the *Methodenstreit* in which his colleagues from the Austrian school were so heavily engaged, and why he always had a high regard for Gustav Schmoller (see Schumpeter, 1926). But what he missed in Schmoller and what he found (and admired) in Marx was the combination of historical vision and economic analysis. And though Schumpeter did not aim at the extreme synthesis of history, sociology and economics,[8] which we find in Marx, he nevertheless was always aware of their interrelationship and gave them due consideration.

His two classical sociological essays on imperialism (Schumpeter, 1919) and social classes (Schumpeter, 1927) carry particular weight in this respect. Not only do they show his capacities in this field, they also carry programmatic character in showing that an understanding of change in economic systems requires an active knowledge of sociological and historic forces. In their *content* these essays are not in line with Marxist literature but they certainly are written in a Marxian *context*. In the essay on imperialism, Schumpeter

[8] See his remarks on the relationship, but separateness of economics and sociology in Schumpeter (1908, pp. 539–41).

examines critically the neo-Marxist views of Otto Bauer, Emil Lederer, and Rudolf Hilferding, who had been his debating partners in his student days in Böhm-Bawerk's seminars; and in the essay on social classes, the perennial Marxist question regarding the transition from one epoch to another is treated with special reference to the transition from feudalism to capitalism.

In the more restricted field of the dynamics of the capitalist process itself we again find some decisive similarities between the viewpoints of Schumpeter and Marx. The weight given to technical progress and growing capital intensity helped them to recognize the in-built tendency towards large-scale organization and monopoly. Although they differed in their *evaluation* of this tendency, they were at least free of prevalent illusions about a possible return to a competitive and romantic world of small-scale free enterprise.

Again, their dynamic outlook helped them to recognize the unavoidable shifts and shocks in economic and social structures, and prevented them from viewing the economic process merely in terms of equilibrium. Disturbances and adjustments are essential elements in this picture; and so they could accommodate business cycles in the core of the economic process at a time when other economists relegated this theme to specialists, outsiders, or historians. It is not by chance that Schumpeter made *Business Cycles* (1939) his magnum opus and gave it the significant subtitle *A Theoretical, Historical, and Statistical Analysis of the Capitalist Process*.

But here again, though making the cycle a *normal* element of the capitalist economy is a common characteristic of Schumpeterian and Marxian thinking, they are far apart with regard to the explanation of the cyclical mechanism. Schumpeter finds it in more or less exogenous waves of technical inventions which then go through the fluctuating endogenous process of innovation (by the 'true' capitalist leaders) and imitation (by the rest). As far as Marx has a business cycle *theory*, it is an endogenous theory with underconsumption and wage-cost elements.

Finally, on a more philosophical plane, the holistic and interdisciplinary approach which Schumpeter shared with Marx made both of them sensitive to the role of ideology in social theorizing. Schumpeter never doubted that 'vision' without 'ideology' is impossible, and he had full understanding for Marx's stress on ideological elements. He only scolded him for not being sufficiently aware of and critical *vis-à-vis* his own ideological bias. The same can, by the way, also be said of Schumpeter, at least with regard to some elements in his thinking. He may also have missed the Marxian argument that the ideological commitment of a *disprivileged* class eases the way towards a 'realistic' vision, while entrenched interests tend towards mystification.

So far we have stressed—in 'desperate brevity' (to use a favourite Schumpeterian expression)—the 'Marxist' streak in Schumpeter. Before I go on to point out a few of the major differences, I want to venture a hint about the way in which Schumpeter himself may have seen his relation to Marx. When one reads the chapter on the Marxian system in the *History of Economic Analysis* (1954, Part III, Ch. 1) one cannot help noticing the warmth with which Schumpeter tries to explain the personal achievement of Marx to an audience whom he probably assumed to be hostile, indifferent, or dogmatic when it comes to Marxian economics.

Particularly in section II of this chapter he stresses Marx's incessant zest for work and study—not always under favourable conditions—leading from philosophy and sociology to economics, and the enormous amount of knowledge acquired and utilized. All this knowledge—so said Schumpeter—was subordinated to the lifelong task of throwing more light on the fundamental problems of capitalist and general economic evolution, the main vision and ideas of which had already been acquired at the early age of 29 when Marx wrote the *Communist Manifesto*. Though always drawn by his alert mind ('in which scholarly coal did not put out the fire') to many other problems, the analytic urge drove Marx always back to his basic theme. His main writings are to be seen as a constant attempt to revise, improve, and extend the 'great vision', and it was natural that with such an enormous task at hand, which could not be fulfilled in a lifetime (if ever), there should remain behind contradictions, lacunae, and 'heaps of disorderly manuscripts' (Schumpeter, 1954, p. 387). To understand what Marx wanted to say and did say, it is not sufficient—so Schumpeter insists—to read excerpts from his writings. One should go carefully through all the volumes of *Das Kapital* and of the *Theorien über den Mehrwert* (*Theories of Surplus Value*).

Does this account not fit to an an amazing extent the life, work, and aspirations of Schumpeter himself? The incessant devotion to work, the early semi-intuitive vision and insight into a comprehensive scheme of things, and the steady return to its central problems, the undying enthusiasm for new knowledge and further analysis, a life which is too short to give the finishing touches to a theoretical work, and a structure which has to be seen as a whole to be fully appreciated. The parallels are obvious. And although Schumpeter leaves no doubt that he does not agree with most of the details of Marx's analysis, and although he certainly did not approve of Marx's aggressive polemics, one cannot help feeling that Schumpeter was not only impressed by Marx's stature but to some extent tried to shape himself in a similar manner.[9]

But let us return to the theories themselves and point out some of the major

[9] In contrast to Marx, Schumpeter wanted to remain purely analytic in his scientific writings and leave the formulation of aims and policy recommendations to the reader. (See for instance his programmatic remarks in this respect in the Introduction to *Business Cycles* (1939).) But, of course, being a human being—and one with strong personal values at that—he did not always manage to stick to these standards.

differences between Marx's and Schumpeter's approach to economic development. On the methodological plane the main difference is that Schumpeter's approach—and here he betrays quite distinctly his affinity to the Austrian school—is individualistic, while Marx starts from a collectivist or group basis. For Schumpeter macroeconomics should be based on microeconomics. For Marx the sociological groups are the central objective of research.

This difference is clearly revealed in the diverging views of the capitalist entrepreneur and the process of technical change. Schumpeter's picture is—as mentioned before—a heroic–romantic painting of a small band of gifted, innovating entrepreneurs who are the driving force behind economic growth. They are not necessarily capital owners. But in a free-market capitalist society with credit creation they can get hold of resources and through their innovative advance they can create firms, temporary monopolies, high profits, and so *become* capitalists or *remain* capitalists in the usual sense. The block of 'imitator-capitalists' try to follow up and *may* thus be able to survive. The individual entrepreneur (in the narow Schumpeterian sense) is thus the motor of technological progress and of the steady (though cyclical) rejuvenation of capitalism. His initiative comes from such aristocratic motives as love for a dynastic future, will to victory, but—of course—also from interest in material gain.

In the Marxian view it is technical progress that is the driving force. It is the 'natural' product of a thinking and working mankind, though it may be helped or hindered by more or less appropriate institutions. In competitive capitalism a capitalist class which is characterized by ownership of the means of production has the ability to introduce innovations and is—by threat of economic ruin—driven to do it. Profit and accumulation are the aims of a capitalist class that wants to survive in such an environment, though the social and power status flowing from ownership is also recognized as a motive for innovative expansion.

Technical progress and the innovating capitalist play, therefore, a decisive part both in Marx's and Schumpeter's dynamics (see on this in particular März, 1964, pp. 384–5), but their roles tend to be reversed; and Schumpeter's innovating capitalist is a rather special phenomenon.[10] To some extent

[10] It may be worth while to indicate the other dominant prototypes of the capitalist in economic theory. In static neoclassical theory the capitalist is owner and manager combined, acting in a transparent world. His desire for profit makes him a perfect accountant. He sees to it that resources are efficiently allocated according to the best technical knowledge currently available. The Keynesian entrepreneur is seen as acting in the dynamic environment of the short and medium period with uncertainty as the dominating feature. His wish for survival and profits is hemmed in by existential fears caused by an uncertain future which he overcomes when his animal spirits are strong enough or when institutional and policy action reduce uncertainty. A special distinction between pioneering and imitative behaviour *à la* Schumpeter is not decisive.

perhaps Marx *and* Schumpeter have underrated the force and the *problematique* of technical progress. Marx did not see—as Schumpeter 80 years later easily could—that the terrific growth in productivity would permit exploitative capitalist relations to be accompanied by sharply rising living standards among the working class. Schumpeter underrated the economic impetus issuing from the *diffusion* of technical progress, and the autonomous force of technical expansion in old as well as new, in 'entrepreneurial' as well as in bureaucratic–managerial enterprises. Both were, therefore, rather blind (in their 'prophecies') with regard to the *general* problems of high industrialization and rapid technological change beyond the capitalism–socialism question, to the problems of the speed and direction of technical change which seem to gain in importance in our days.

SCHUMPETER AND SOCIALISM

We now turn to Schumpeter's socialism. Again we shall have to be very brief. Once we leave Marx aside the idea that Schumpeter *personally* had any likings for socialism can be quickly dropped. He made no secret of it that he had an 'ingrained dislike of socialism' (Harris, 1951, p. 45). But—unlike many of his colleagues—he never turned into primitive anti-socialism and he tried to keep an open mind with regard to both the theoretical and the practical aspects of socialist economics. His non-dogmatic thinking permitted him to be both against nationalization and in favour of a capital levy and a mixed economy in post World War I Austria. He thus managed to be *persona non grata* to socialists and to conservatives alike (Kirsch, 1979, pp. 147–8). His *Capitalism, Socialism and Democracy* (1942) 'is full of ironic twists that provide cold comfort for anyone who agrees with him. Capitalists, socialists, and intellectuals are all provided with strong emotional grounds for rejecting the argument' (Smithies, 1951, p. 16).

His dislike of socialism did not prevent him from arriving at his famous conclusion that capitalism will give way to socialism. In this point where he seems to be near to the beliefs and aspirations of Marxist and non-Marxist socialists he is in fact further away from them than anywhere else. This is so because not only is he more saddened than exhilarated by this prospect, but above all because his reasoning is socialist thinking turned upside down: capitalism—according to Schumpeter—peters out not because of its inadequacy or because of its inherent faults but because of its success.

When it comes to this question of the long-term 'March into Socialism' (Schumpeter's (1950b) last address to the American Economic Association) we should be aware of the very special terminology used by Schumpeter. He deals with the—to him likely—movement from *Schumpeterian* capitalism to *Schumpeterian* socialism. 'Capitalism' as he defines with admirable brevity in his *Business Cycles* 'is that form of private property economy in which innovations are carried out by means of borrowed money' (Schumpeter, 1939, p. 223). Capitalism is, therefore, endangered and on the decline when the environment becomes unfavourable to the unfettered development of the private, innovation-prone individual.

Socialism, on the other hand, is seen as a system in which the control over the means of production and over production itself is exercised by a central authority, or where—more generally—the economic affairs of society belong to the public sphere rather than to the private one (Schumpeter, 1942, p. 167).

The main thrust of Schumpeter's argument has always been that there are strong forces to move from the above-mentioned prototype of capitalism to the above-mentioned prototype of socialism. He realizes, of course, that there are other types of socialism and all sorts of mixed forms; but starting from his 'vision' of capitalism he sticks to his conclusion that 'there is a long-run tendency towards socialism in our sense'.[11] This tendency does not stem from any inherent incapacity of present-day capitalism to 'produce and distribute the goods'. It comes from the self-destroying forces created by the very success of Schumpeterian capitalism.

There are four main factors at work. They are:[12]

1. The success of private business in creating a high level of production has laid the foundation for high living standards and bureaucratization and has undermined the social and political position of an obsolescent business class.
2. The 'rationality' of capitalist activity destroys the habits of subordination which preserved the hierarchy at the firm and society level.
3. The growing administrative tasks have created a political system and an intellectual class which tend to be hostile to large-scale business.
4. '[I]n consequence of all this, the scheme of values of capitalist society, though causally related to its economic success, is losing its hold not only upon the public mind but also upon the "capitalist" stratum itself' (Schumpeter, 1950b, p. 449).

These factors spoil the environment in which the 'true', unfettered capitalist–innovator can initiate that creative destruction of old structures which is the essence of Schumpeterian capitalism. Stabilization policies, attempts towards reducing income inequality, antitrust legislation, public controls in labour

[11] This quotation comes from Schumpeter (1949b, p. 375), where he discusses labourism as a first step towards socialism.

[12] This concise enumeration follows Schumpeter's (1950b) summary of his ideas (pp. 448–9). Some of the following remarks also refer to the very typical statements contained in this article.

and money markets, security legislation, a growing sphere of public enterprise, all these are seen as a decay of (Schumpeterian) capitalism and as a steady movement towards socialism of which one may approve or not.

What seems to me to be important is not that these Schumpeterian contours of the long-run tendencies of capitalism are—terminologically, emotionally, and above all with regard to the envisaged processes—in obvious contrast to almost all 'schools' of socialism. This could only be a challenge to discuss more intensively the diverging viewpoints. The real difficulty with Schumpeter seems to me to lie in his peculiar delineation of 'true' capitalism and his views of the state.

Because of his narrow definition of dynamic capitalists and capitalism on the one hand and his concentration on the textbook example of centralized socialism on the other, Schumpeter leaves a rather wide grey zone in between on which he is rather vague. According to his view we have already left capitalism proper but have certainly not yet reached the other pole. While Schumpeter realizes that in this in-between zone different things may happen—labourist capitalism, a Catholic-inspired organization on the basis of *Quadragesimo Anno* (Schumpeter, 1949b, p. 373, 1950b, p. 447), etc.—he seems to have no doubts that all these are only stages on the way to socialism.

Had he seen the capitalists first and foremost as the property-owning class they are, rather than as two distinct groups of innovators and imitators, he might have pondered more about the primitive fact that privileged groups are not prone to give up their privileges. The consequences of this have to be seen in relation to the role of the state. On this point Schumpeter is again much nearer to Marx than to most conventional economists or to Keynes. He never falls into the error of viewing the state as the impartial arbiter administrating the common good. He sees the people and the power influences behind governments and bureaucracies. But the pioneering role he played in analysing the motives of politicians and bureaucrats and in laying the foundations for the new *Economic Theory of Democracy* (Downs, 1957), while no doubt very important and enlightening, led him too far away from the Marxist–socialist concern about the role of the state in the class struggle. The possibilities and mechanisms of using the state in the interest of privileged groups do not get sufficient weight in Schumpeter's analysis.[13]

Thus he has little to say on the questions which agitate socialist factions when they try to evaluate present-day developments, e.g. with regard to the existence or non-existence of state-plus or state-contra monopoly capitalism. In particular, once history has left the special brand of Schumpeter's competitive, heroic, conquering capitalist–innovator behind, he is so hypnotized by the avenue heading towards socialism that he pays little attention

[13] For an interesting non-Marxist view on these matters, see for instance Barlett (1973).

to possible side-ways, round-about ways, etc., which can in the meantime lead to other 'capitalisms' leaving the basic power structure intact. This, I think, explains the strange ommission of a proper economic analysis of the fascist past and of possible fascist futures in Schumpeter's writings.

It cannot be stressed sufficiently that the 'strictures' contained in the last few paragraphs apply exclusively to the main contours of Schumpeter's vision. When one goes into the details of his writings there is a wealth of ideas, hints, and information that is of immediate relevance for current debates on capitalism and socialism. Schumpeter's observations on the proper time and the personal requirements for a successful transition to socialism, on bureaucracy and democracy in socialism, on socialism and labourism, are always stimulating and well worth considering whether one agrees with them or not. And, above all, when one enjoys Schumpeter's enlightened—though by no means indifferent—analysis making full use of 'bourgeois' and Marxian contributions one begins to divine what economic science could have been and could be if people like him and a few others—like Lange, Kalecki, Joan Robinson—had dominated the scene.

REFERENCES

Baran, P. A. (1957) *The Political Economy of Growth*. New York: Monthly Review Press.

Barlett, R. (1973) *Economic Foundations of Political Power*. New York: Free Press.

Baumol, B. (1961) *Economic Theory and Operations Analysis*. Englewood Cliffs, NJ: Prentice-Hall.

Downs, A. (1957) *An Economic Theory of Democracy*. New York: Harper.

Haberler, G. (1951) Joseph Alois Schumpeter, 1883–1950. In *Schumpeter—Social Scientist* (Ed.) Harris, S. E. pp. 24–47. Cambridge, MA: Harvard University Press.

Harris, S. E. (Ed.) (1951) *Schumpeter—Social Scientist*. Cambridge, MA: Harvard University Press.

Kirsch, H. (1979). Joseph Alois Schumpeter. *Journal of Economic Issues*, **13**, 141–57.

Kowalik, T. (ed.) (1964) *On Political Economy and Econometrics. Essays in Honour of Oskar Lange.* Warsaw: Polish Scientific Publishers.

März, E. (1964) Zur Genesis der Schumpeterschen Theorie der wirtschaftlichen Entwicklung. In *On Political Economy and Econometrics. Essays in Honour of Oskar Lange* (Ed.) Kowalik, T. pp. 363–87. Warsaw: Polish Scientific Publishers.

National Bureau of Economic Research (1949) *Conf. on Business Cycles*. New York: National Bureau of Economic Research.

Robinson, J. (1943) Review of *Capitalism, Socialism and Democracy*. *Economic Journal*, **53**, 381–3.

Samuelson, P. A. (1951) Schumpeter as a teacher and economic theorist. In *Schumpeter—Social Scientist* (Ed.) Harris, S. E. pp. 48–53. Cambridge, MA: Harvard University Press.

Samuelson, P. A. (1980) The world economy at century's end. Paper given at the *Sixth World Congress of the International Economic Association*, Mexico (to be published).

Schneider, E. (1970) *Joseph A. Schumpeter. Leben und Werk eines grossen Sozialökonomen.* Tübingen: J. C. B. Mohr.

Schumpeter, J. A. (1908) *Das Wesen und der Hauptinhalt der theoretischen Nationalökonomie*. Berlin: Duncker und Humblot.

Schumpeter, J. A. (1919) Zur Soziologie der Imperialismen. *Archiv für Sozialwissenschaft und Sozialpolitik*, **46**, 1–39, 275–310.

Schumpeter, J. A. (1926) Gustav v. Schmoller und die Probleme von heute. *Schmollers Jahrbuch für Gesetzgebung, Verwaltung und Volkswirtschaft im Deutschen Reich*, **50**, 337–88.

Schumpeter, J. A. (1927) Die sozialen Klassen im ethnisch homogenen Milieu. *Archiv für Sozialwissenschaft und Sozialpolitik*, **57**, 1–67.

Schumpeter, J. A. (1939) *Business Cycles. A Theoretical, Historical, and Statistical Analysis of the Capitalist Process*. 2 Volumes. New York: McGraw-Hill.

Schumpeter, J. A. (1942) *Capitalism, Socialism and Democracy*. New York: Harper & Row. Quotations from 4th Edition, 1965. London: Unwin University Books.

Schumpeter, J. A. (1949a) Historical approach to the analysis of business cycles. In *Conf. on Business Cycles*. pp. 149–62. New York: National Bureau of Economic Research.

Schumpeter, J. A. (1949b) English economists and the state-managed economy. *Journal of Political Economy*, **57**, 371–82.

Schumpeter, J. A. (1950a) *Kapitalismus, Sozialismus und Demokratie*. Einleitung von Edgar Salin. München: Francke. 3rd Edition, 1972.

Schumpeter, J. A. (1950b) The march into socialism. *American Economic Review, Papers and Proceedings*, **40**, 446–56.

Schumpeter, J. A. (1951) *Ten Great Economists*. New York: Oxford University Press.

Schumpeter, J. A. (1954) *History of Economic Analysis* (Ed. from manuscript) Schumpeter, E. B. New York: Oxford University Press.

Smithies, A. (1951) Memorial: Joseph Alois Schumpeter, 1883–1950. In *Schumpeter—Social Scientist* (Ed.) Harris, S. E. pp. 11–23. Cambridge, MA: Harvard University Press.

Sweezy, P. M. (1951) Schumpeter on imperialism and social classes. In *Schumpeter—Social Scientist* (Ed.) Harris, S. E. pp. 119–24. Cambridge, MA: Harvard University Press.

Chapter Eight

Schumpeter, Political Economist

BRUNO S. FREY

SCHUMPETER SAID EVERYTHING ALREADY

READING Schumpeter's *Capitalism, Socialism and Democracy* (5th Edition, 1976, to be referred to as *CSD*) is a revelation. First published in 1942, it contains the essence of what has been developed in 'public choice', a well developed field with a large number of adherents and a correspondingly large literature, since the beginning of the 1960s.[1] Sometimes called the 'economic theory of democracy', public choice is based on Schumpeter's definition of democracy as

> [T]hat institutional arrangement for arriving at political decisions in which individuals acquire the power to decide by means of a competitive struggle for the people's vote (*CSD*, p. 269).

This definition masterfully captures the main features of democracy as seen from the economic point of view. Firstly, democracy is looked at as a method or mechanism for *arriving* at social outcomes, i.e. it is not defined *in terms* of outcomes. What matters is that the content is arrived at in a well defined way. Whatever the content of the decision, it has to be accepted as long as the institutional decision-making mechanisms have been observed. The democratic method is seen as one of several different ways of reaching social decisions, and as a very good method when compared to the alternatives (*CSD*, pp. 288–90). Schumpeter thus develops a *comparative theory of*

[1] Not to mention his contribution to political sociology in the field of imperialism and social classes (Schumpeter, 1918–19, 1927) and the fiscal crisis of the state (Schumpeter, 1918).

institutions—something which has been undertaken by modern economic theory only very recently.

Secondly, Schumpeter's definition of democracy makes it clear that this institutional agreement is closely related to *economic* competition. Political as well as economic competition may be more or less perfect, and the properties of the processes observed vary accordingly. If the political entrepreneurs are not free to enter the 'market' for votes, it cannot be expected that the process of translating the people's will into political decisions will work well. Institutional conditions must be established to guarantee that the barriers to entry for both political and economic competitors are minor.

Thirdly, the favourable outcome of the competitive struggle for the people's vote is a *side-product* only, exactly as is the case in the competitive struggle for money. Politicians do not strive for a 'better world'; they struggle to gain power and therewith to satisfy their own utility. This does not mean that politicians are particularly wicked or immoral people (as little as are economic entrepreneurs); they may endeavour to gain power in order to be able to put their own ideas and preferences into practice, but they will only be able to do so if they can attract sufficient votes to be elected into office. Consequently, parties are 'groups whose members act in concert to win power' (*CSD*, p. 283).

Schumpeter draws two conclusions from this definition of democracy which have been elaborated and stressed in modern public choice analysis:

1. The competitive struggle for votes forces the politicians to adopt a short-run outlook because voters judge their performance and/or promises by their immediate effect. It is thus difficult for politicians to pursue long-term interests (*CSD*, p. 287). This shortsightedness of the democratic process has been central to the politicoeconomic models developed since the mid-1970s (see, for example, Nordhaus, 1975, or Frey, 1978a).
2. The competition for votes forces the parties to advance positions which closely resemble each other. Schumpeter does not belabour this point but only mentions it as an aside (*CSD*, p. 283), while in public choice it is one of the most central and most often treated propositions (see, for example, Riker and Ordeshook, 1973).

Capitalism, Socialism and Democracy also deals thoroughly with the behaviour of *voters*, again closely anticipating what was done in public choice 20 years thereafter. Schumpeter again uses the comparative method, confronting the individual's behaviour in politics and in the market. There is little difference in behaviour in the political and economic spheres when local affairs and political issues that directly and unmistakably concern individuals and groups are involved (*CSD*, p. 260). In general, however, little effort is made by people to master political problems. In Schumpeter's words, 'the typical citizen drops to a lower level of mental performance as soon as he enters the political sphere' (*CSD*, p. 283). Public choice theory completely agrees with Schumpeter in his evaluation of the comparative performance of individuals in politics and the market, and attributes it to exactly the same reason: an individual only marginally affects the outcome of political decisions by casting her or his vote, and a reasoned act of voting costs the person much time and effort which he/she is unwilling to expend in this public good context.

Schumpeter realizes, however, that it is well worth participating actively in politics if one has the chance noticeably to influence the decision, and if the policies arrived at can be moulded to one's own advantage. This applies to professional politicians, economic interest groups and idealists as well (*CSD*, p. 263), as for instance the environmental movement today.

The third major contribution by Schumpeter, and an idea central to modern public choice, is the importance attributed to *constitutional rules and institutions*. Democracy can only function if the vast majority of the citizens observe the 'rules of the democratic game' (*CSD*, p. 301) and agree on the fundamentals of the institutional structure. Schumpeter stresses that the constitution must limit the power of the state; democracy does *not* mean every aspect of life is subject to political decisions (*CSD*, p. 292).[2] It has only been in the last few years that this important aspect has been recognized in public choice (see Buchanan, 1975a, 1977, and Frey, 1982).

Besides these three major ideas, *Capitalism, Socialism and Democracy* contains a host of other ideas also common to public choice. One is the importance of the *political entrepreneur*, which makes it possible that 'latent volitions . . . are called to life by some political leader who turns them into political factors' (*CSD*, p. 270). Non-organized wishes in the population may thus become part of political programmes and actions, such as for example the wishes of the elderly, or environmental concerns. It is noteworthy that it has taken a long time for public choice to recognize this idea (Wagner, 1966). Another idea clearly spelled out by Schumpeter is that *small political units* are important for a working democracy (*CSD*, pp. 261, 267) because the voters are by nature better informed and have more of an incentive to participate and to assimilate new information. Schumpeter is thus a founder of the economic theory of federalism, now a flourishing field within public choice (see, for example, the contributions contained in Oates, 1977).

Finally, Schumpeter foresaw the idea of *rent-seeking* which has very recently been put forward in the economic literature (Krueger, 1974;

[2] Wright's (1951) criticism of Schumpeter's political philosophy is therefore quite misplaced.

Tullock, 1967; Posner, 1975). He speaks of the 'tremendous loss of energy which the incessant battle . . . imposes on the leading men' (*CSD*, pp. 286–87). Though acknowledging their importance, Schumpeter characteristically does not look at these costs in isolation but rather compares them with the potential costs and losses inherent in *other* social decision-making mechanisms.

PUBLIC CHOICE DOES NOT NEED SCHUMPETER

In view of the fact that Schumpeter's *Capitalism, Socialism and Democracy* contains the essentials of what constitutes today's public choice, it would be natural to expect him to occupy a prominent place in the field. This, however, is not at all the case. It can, on the contrary, be argued that:

1. To a large extent public choice has been developed *independently* of Schumpeter.
2. Public choice has gone much *beyond* Schumpeter and can therefore learn nothing from him.
3. Schumpeter advances some ideas which according to public choice are *mistaken*.

These three points will be elaborated in the following.

Public Choice Has Been Developed Independently of Schumpeter

This proposition may be tested by consulting the public choice literature.

Turning first to the classic contributions in the field it turns out that Schumpeter is rarely quoted and, if he is, it is more as a standard reference than a direct use and adoption of his ideas. Kenneth Arrow in his *Social Choice and Individual Values* (1951) makes no reference to him at all; Anthony Downs in his most influential book, *An Economic Theory of Democracy* (1957), which can be considered an elaboration of Schumpeter's view of democracy as the competitive struggle for votes, mentions him but twice. Downs (p. 29, no. 11) acknowledges in general terms that he is greatly indebted to Schumpeter for his 'profound analysis of democracy' and mentions the side-product effect of democratic competition; later (p. 284) he repeats this indebtedness again. James Buchanan and Gordon Tullock in their book, *The Calculus of Consent* (1962), concern themselves with the constitutional aspects of democracy along very similar lines as Schumpeter does, but do not quote him in the main text at all. In Appendix 2 on 'Theoretical forerunners', which comprises seven pages, Schumpeter is mentioned in only one sentence, saying that he 'made contributions' (p. 335), but without imparting to the reader at all what these contributions were. Mancur Olson in his book, *The Logic of Collective Action* (1965), quotes Schumpeter twice. In one case (p. 108, no. 30) he suggests that the reader consult him for an opinion differing from Olson's (without saying what Schumpeter's opinion is); in the second instance (p. 159), he refers the reader in general terms to Schumpeter's view of rational behaviour in the market and in politics.

We may summarize by saying that the classic works in public choice (which are themselves referred to in almost all other works in the field) have obviously not relied on Schumpeter's much earlier and original contributions to the subject.

The survey books on public choice present the same picture. Dennis Mueller (1979) notes Schumpeter's 'slight *direct* influence' as a 'curiosity' (p. 1, no. 1). Mueller himself mentions Schumpeter only once and then not directly but rather quoting another author who refers to the fact that Schumpeter found tolerance and democratic self-control important. In comparison, for example, he quotes Knut Wicksell 16 times! Hans van den Doel (1979) mentions Schumpeter four times but in the usual fashion, only in reference to his definition of democracy. Norman Frohlich and Joe Oppenheimer (1978) make no reference to Schumpeter as a political economist, mentioning his theory of the entrepreneur in a purely economic context (p. 68). William Riker and Peter Ordeshook (1973) again do not mention him at all, and I myself (Frey, 1978b) only note him twice, once as an 'unorthodox political economist' (pp. 55–56) and then as a precursor of Downs' vote maximization model (p. 66).

As for survey reviews, such influential papers covering the development and state of public choice as those by Vincent and Elinor Ostrom (1971), Michael Taylor (1971), James Buchanan (1975a) and Tomás Esteve Serrano (1979) completely disregard Schumpeter. It may be concluded that public choice practitioners have developed their field quite independently of Schumpeter and that no immediate influence whatsoever can be detected. If they are aware of his contributions it seems to be *ex post*, i.e. after the theories have been worked out they realize (probably with some surprise) that Schumpeter had already developed the same ideas more than 20 years earlier.

Being myself a case in point, I hasten to add that *nobody* seems to have been aware that Schumpeter developed many of the most central ideas in modern political economy. All biographers stress at length that he was an important sociologist (and even philosopher),[3] but no one seems to note that he also made—if anything—even more important contributions to political science

[3] Thus Samuelson (1951, p. 49) mentions '*sociological* hypotheses concerning phenomena on the fringes of politics and economics' (emphasis added); similarly Haberler (1951, pp. 24, 28, 44).

(public choice can be considered to be part of both economics and political science). Thus Wolfgang Stolper in his *International Encyclopedia of the Social Sciences* biography (1968) mentions Schumpeter's definition of democracy among his 'sociological writings' (p. 71), and Reinhard Schäder in his biography for the *Handwörterbuch der Sozial- und Wirtschaftswissenschaften* (1956) also refers to his definition of democracy but adds immediately that this idea does not count among his noteworthy contributions (p. 156). Among the memorial articles, Wassily Leontief (1950) and Arthur Spiethoff (1949) for example do not refer with even one word to him as a political economist; and even more surprisingly, Erwin von Beckerath (1950) reviews *Capitalism, Socialism and Democracy* at length and most thoughtfully but still manages not to mention his contribution in the field of political economy. The conclusion thus holds that neither the public choice practitioners nor traditional economists do justice to Schumpeter in his role of political economist, and none seems to have taken up his ideas. It is as if he had never written on political economy—and yet we have shown that his work contains much of what is 40 years later an established field of its own.

Public Choice Has Gone Much Beyond Schumpeter

It can be argued that Schumpeter's contributions are irrelevant from today's point of view because public choice has developed much beyond his work and can therefore learn nothing from him.

It is indeed true that public choice has pushed its analysis of the topics treated by Schumpeter much further. With respect to the competitive struggle for votes, for example, a large literature has evolved (see, for example, Riker and Ordeshook, 1973, Chaps 11 and 12; Frey, 1978b, Chap. 7; Mueller, 1979, Chap. 6) studying in depth what happens under varying objectives (e.g. vote maximization or majority maximization), whether there is an equilibrium for party programmes and, if so, what its characteristics are. How this equilibrium depends on particular assumptions about voting behaviour has also been analysed, in particular what party programmes look like when the citizens abstain from voting. We now know precisely under what conditions the programmes of two competing parties will converge towards the median of the distribution of the voters' preferences. Equal analytical effort has also been devoted to the study of the voters' behaviour (see, for example, Riker and Ordeshook, 1973, Chap. 3; Frohlich and Oppenheimer, 1978, Chap. 5). Under the assumption of utility maximizing individuals, it is shown under what conditions people will vote for a particular party.

Public choice has developed a great deal over the last 10 years with respect to empirical research. Some of the propositions derived analytically have been subjected to extensive empirical testing, but more importantly a branch has developed—politicoeconomic modelling—which combines formal models with econometric testing. In a sense, Schumpeter's method of closely combining theoretical and empirical analysis has materialized here in political economy; but again, all this took place without him having any direct influence.

Schumpeter Advances Ideas Which Are Mistaken from the Point of View of Public Choice

In his *Capitalism, Socialism and Democracy* Schumpeter is at variance with many ideas found in today's public choice. This is not surprising because he loved to be unorthodox and to advance minority views, while public choice under the leadership of American economists has largely degenerated to the application of neoclassical orthodoxy to the realm of political questions. In this context, two of his unorthodox views will be given by way of example.

The first refers to the individual's conceptions of reality and therefore his/her expectations of future events. Schumpeter argues that people may have completely mistaken ideas about the causal relationships that exist in the real world, and that these misconceptions may be kept over a very long period of time. There is thus no mechanism that automatically tends to correct such wrong views. For this he gives an example from the field of public health (*CSD*, p. 259). Generation after generation, people have failed to associate the spread of some of the most severe infectious diseases with their habits of personal and communal hygiene. As long as no such link is established, the objective consequences (including regularly occurring epidemics) will not produce a subjective experience that will correct the mistaken conception. Schumpeter suggests that a correction of wrong perceptions is even more unlikely if people are reluctant to recognize causal relations or where there is some interest which actively agitates against recognizing them.

Schumpeter's view is incompatible with what has received so much attention today under the unfortunate name of 'rational expectations'. According to neoclassically oriented public choice (and general economic) theory, it is not possible for objectively wrong perceptions to be maintained over an extended period of time. The information available on the objective relationships will induce people to correct their wrong expectations such that on the average the errors are unrelated to available information; i.e. all that is profitable to know will be used to make forecasts.[4]

[4] McCallum (1980) and Kantor (1979) give useful surveys of the present state of the rational expectations theory.

Another example of where Schumpeter's views are completely opposite of those of public choice is his evaluation of public bureaucracy. The modern economic theory of bureaucracy—as developed for example by William Niskanen (1975) and Gordon Tullock (1965)—stress that, due to a lack of property rights, which results in limited possibilities for control and inexistent or biased incentives for the individual members, bureaucracy will tend to oversupply the public goods and produce them in an inefficient manner. It has therefore been proposed that public supply should be made by private firms as much as possible, or that the public bureaux should at least be subject to as much competition as possible (see, for example, Niskanen, 1978, 1980).

Schumpeter has a much more positive view of public bureaucracy (*CSD*, pp. 205–10 and 293–94). He actually considers bureaucracy to be the main counterforce to amateurish democratic government! He is well aware that public bureaucracy does not function in an ideal way, but 'the readers should not allow themselves to be unduly influenced by the associations the term carries in popular parlance' (*CSD*, p. 293, no. 6). Schumpeter points to the example of well functioning public bureaucracies in Europe which are based on tradition and whose members are well educated. While public choice stresses the aspect of insufficient control leading to shirking, Schumpeter draws attention to the fact that devotion to work cannot simply be 'hired' by money. Thus he and public choice have quite opposite conceptions of the value of the public bureaucracy.

Thus the conclusions to be drawn by neoclassical public choice would be harsh: that public choice has developed independently of what Schumpeter wrote, and that theoretical and empirical analyses have also gone much beyond the ideas he produced. Furthermore, as it can be easily shown that some of his ideas are at variance with the theoretical structures of today's public choice, they would have to be rejected from that point of view as well. The conclusion would seem to be that Schumpeter today is of no importance for political economy.

SCHUMPETER HAS MUCH TO OFFER US

The conclusion that Schumpeter is of no importance today has been drawn from the point of view of neoclassical public choice. The question of course arises as to whether public choice is or should be the one and only theoretical framework for political economy. We will argue in this section that once we leave the straightjacket of today's public choice theorizing, Schumpeter's ideas have indeed a great deal to contribute. Four theses will be advanced, the first two concerning his way of thinking about political economy, and the next two concerning matters of content.

Thesis 1

> *In modern political economy, it is more important to advance new and stimulating ideas than to elaborate single points in great depth.*

This thesis of course runs counter to the present understanding and practice in public choice and in general economics, which are almost exclusively concerned with formally proving or econometrically estimating some small variant of a well established theory. Thus a large part of public choice has in the last 25 years been concerned with proving the possibility or impossibility of preference aggregation when one of Arrow's conditions is slightly changed. Another favourite topic has been to show whether the median voter solution resulting from the competitive behaviour of parties still holds if the assumptions about the parties' or voters' objective functions and the distribution of the voters' preferences are slightly changed. As a result, scientific journals containing articles on political economy—in particular *Public Choice*—have become less and less interesting to read for anybody who wants to know about the real world and the interrelationship between the economy and the polity rather than one more variant of a theorem within a well known theory. The formalistic analysis of some old theory with very few exceptions does not advance our knowledge, and is of little interest for empirical research. Indeed, whenever an interesting new idea does appear—as for example the new voting mechanisms (e.g. Tidemann and Tullock, 1976; Mueller, 1978) or politicoeconomic models—it has been developed *despite* and not because of the existing theoretical structure.

Schumpeter is a political economist who can teach us a quite different way of thinking, one constantly open to new ideas and seriously concerned with the problems of reality. His style of thinking is that of a Schumpeterian entrepreneur in the realm of scientific endeavour. He develops and takes up new ideas, checks and exploits them, pursuing them further until they reach the point where rapidly diminishing returns set in. Moreover, the reader is led through an exploration with an unknown goal—quite unlike much of today's theorizing (for example, that of the Chicago school) where the result is often known before the analysis has started.

Thesis 2

> *The analysis of grand relationships in political economy is more important than the precise elaboration of some small part of a theory.*

This thesis is again in contradiction to what is current practice in political economy, which in common with general economics almost exclusively considers the rigour of an argument rather than its relevance. Schumpeter's thinking—though not loose—was certainly not rigorous according to today's standards; he was much more interested in having an approximate understanding of the large questions in political economy. He tried to study the overall relationships existing between capitalism, socialism and democracy—an attempt which would not be undertaken within today's public choice, or only by outsiders.[5]

There are two very simple reasons why the overall relationships must be tackled by political economists even if this is not possible in a rigorous way. Everyone who thinks about political economy, and especially those who undertake formalistic analyses of small theorems, has a quite different concept of these relationships in the back of their minds. But as it is not considered to be 'scientific' to deal with these background assumptions, they often remain very vague and amateurish. To change slightly Schumpeter's phrase quoted in the first section, the typical public choice analyst drops to a lower level of mental performance as soon as he enters the sphere of larger political questions. Anyone who has tried to discuss 'practical' political problems with a specialist in preference aggregation will immediately realize what is meant.

The second reason why political economists should concern themselves with the larger relationships is that ordinary people are aware of the problems involved and quite rightly expect the political economist to be able to make a sensible contribution. If political economists are not able to do so, outsiders will step in and provide answers which are often little more than pure speculation and ideological preconception. Economists should not forget the lesson they were taught when the population became interested in the overall relationship between economic growth, the environment and natural resources: the growth models being developed by economists at that time were wonders of mathematical rigour (see, for example, Stiglitz and Uzawa, 1969; Wan, 1971), but they had nothing at all to say about the problems in which the people were interested, which resulted in outsiders stepping in to offer models such as *The Limits to Growth* (Meadows, 1972) about which the economists were (rightly) rather horrified. Only afterwards did some economists find out that economics *is* able to say interesting things about the topic.

Schumpeter's type of thinking shows that it is possible to deal with the larger questions in political economy in an interesting way. What matters is not so much the answers that result, but rather the fact that such an endeavour is successfully undertaken.

---

[5] One of the few examples is Brittan (1975), a financial journalist.

Scientific thinking along his lines will only be possible if the institutions of scientific research are changed. A scholar writing articles in the Schumpeterian tradition—or even Schumpeter himself—would have very little chance today of having a paper published in a respectable journal. It is thus not sufficient to mourn the often unsatisfactory kind of theorizing done in political (and general) economy and to call for Schumpeterian thinking; one must suggest the institutional changes in scientific research necessary to lead to a demand for such thinking.[6]

Thesis 3

Some of Schumpeter's ideas have not been adequately introduced into modern political economy.

This thesis will be dealt with by way of examples. Five of Schumpeter's ideas which could be fruitfully introduced into public choice will be briefly described.

WAVES OF 'IRRATIONALITY'

Everybody knows that people may under certain circumstances behave quite differently from normal. Moral constraints and civilized modes of thinking, feeling and behaving disappear, and primitive, infantile and criminal propensities take over (*CSD*, pp. 256–57). This is often the case in revolutionary periods, for example in France after 1789 and recently in Iran. Even if the 'waves' are not immoral, but rather ideological, it is of great importance to take account of them in order to understand the political economy. Recent examples would be the rise of radical left-wing political thinking after 1968, and the current conservative movement. It may well be that the final origin of such waves are beyond the grasp of political economists, but certainly their propagation and the reaction to it by the establishment (whether right or left) could be studied. Schumpeter has given some clues in this direction which should be worked out further.

ADVERTISING AS THE ESSENCE OF POLITICS

According to Schumpeter, advertising of parties and interest groups is at the core of the competitive struggle for votes (e.g. *CSD*, pp. 263–64, 283). The

[6] The newly founded *Journal of Economic Letters* is hardly a step in the right direction as it publishes nice little theorems rather than new ideas.

'pure' models of party competition developed in public choice have, however, excluded political advertising. Thus the analogy of political and economic competition used in model-building has been taken so far that an essential part of politics has been thrown out. The analysis would be much more realistic if the models contained the element of advertising from the very beginning, which would result in a more interesting study of the role of information in political economy.[7]

FRAUDULENT POLITICAL COMPETITION

Schumpeter argues that unfair and fraudulent competition between parties and interest groups cannot be excluded if the analysis is not to end up as an unrealistic ideal (*CSD*, p. 271). But this is exactly where the axiomatic public choice theory of party competition has come to! The models are based on assumptions which set the stage for 'perfect' competition and which exclude fraudulent elements. As a result, most governments which have ever existed anywhere in the world are excluded from application of the models. Again the difference in thinking between Schumpeter and current public choice is sharp: Schumpeter develops a brilliant thesis (democracy as the competition for votes), but immediately sees that much of reality does not conform to it and that one must study other types of regimes too. Public choice, on the other hand, has taken up the idea and has stuck with it without being much concerned about its reality.

POLITICIANS' GROUP INTERESTS

In *Capitalism, Socialism and Democracy* Schumpeter stresses that politicians have become professionals, and they have evolved as a caste of their own. Though they are involved in a game of competition for votes in a democracy, they are at the same time an interest group which fights for *its* own interests *against* the rest of the electorate. Looking at political reality it is evident that he has a good point which would be well worth exploring in modern political economy.[8]

DYNAMIC PARTY COMPETITION

Schumpeter looks at political competition in the same dynamic framework that he applies to economic competition, namely as an evolutionary process.

---

[7] Some attempts are being undertaken within politicoeconomic modelling (see, for example, Palda, 1973).

[8] The only, but quite preliminary, attempt seems to have been made by Wittman (1973).

This aspect has been lost in the models of party competition as developed in public choice; it is not unfair to say that all that which is dynamic in the Schumpeterian sense has been thrown out exactly as was done in the economic general equilibrium models of the Walrasian tradition.[9] Accordingly there is no role accorded to the political entrepreneur in the existing formal models of party competition.[10] This disregard of Schumpeterian dynamics is certainly a great loss for political economy.

Thesis 4

> *Some of Schumpeter's ideas that are rejected by public choice are nevertheless of great interest.*

In the second section of this paper two ideas which were advanced by Schumpeter but which are at variance with the neoclassical public choice view were presented by way of example. The first was Schumpeter's idea that people may have an incorrect concept of reality and thus wrong expectations in the long term; the second was that public bureaucracy, due to a long tradition (at least in Europe), is a well functioning and stabilizing force *vis-à-vis* sometimes amateurish democratic politicians. It may well be argued that his views should be taken much more seriously than they are today, and that his ideas are at least partly correct. Concerning wrong conceptions in the politicoeconomic field, it may be pointed out that often the clues 'in the small' may strengthen conceptions which from a 'large' point of view are mistaken. An example may clarify what is hinted at. If in a planned economy the plans are not fulfilled and the economic performance is disappointing, the adherents of planning will immediately say that such a result is not surprising because the planning has not been strict enough. This will lead to the planning being intensified. If the economic performance continues to be disappointing, the same arguments will be offered again and planning again strengthened, etc. Such a process may go on for a very long time, as is evidenced by many planned economies. An outside, more objective observer might however draw a quite different conclusion from the weak economic performance. She or he may well attribute it to planning and suggest that it be reduced. The same kind of difference between observation 'in the small' and 'in the large'

[9] An aside: It is difficult to understand why Schumpeter, whose main contribution to economics may well be considered to be his discussion of the innovating entrepreneur, 'always referred to Léon Walras as by far the greatest economist of all time' (Samuelson, 1951, p. 53).

[10] Kramer's paper (1977) deals with the movement to an equilibrium of the programme of two competitive parties faced with the Arrow impossibility theorem, but not with dynamics in an evolutionary sense.

leading to conceptions and expectations which remain wrong in the long run may also hold for a market economy. If its performance is weak, the adherents of the free market ideology immediately argue that this is due to the fact that the natural market forces are not being used enough. If economic competition is then strengthened but the results remain disappointing, they will argue that it is still due to insufficient market competition. A more objective observer, on the other hand, may well come to the conclusion that the weak results may be due to overusing the market and that a certain amount of planning would improve the economic performance. In both the 'planned' and the 'market' economies there are thus forces at work which may for a long time *reinforce* wrong conceptions, leading to increasingly wrong expectations.

Schumpeter's refusal to reject public bureaucracy completely as is currently *en vogue* in public choice is certainly correct. In many instances there is no substitute for hierarchical decision-making and bureaucracy's performance is viewed in too negative terms. Though there are certainly problems with respect to the incentive structure—which he deals with at length (*CSD*, pp. 205–10)—it should not be overlooked that similar problems exist elsewhere in the real world. Bureaucracies in private firms larger than atomistic size are confronted with very similar problems as the public bureaucracy. This is acknowledged by public choice, but it is often seen that one is following the 'nirvana approach' by comparing public bureaucracy with a perfectly functioning atomistic firm under conditions of perfect competition. The actual alternatives in today's world are often various kinds of bureaucracies.

The almost panic fear of some American economists about 'shirking' on the part of public officials seems to be unfounded. Schumpeter rightly points out that the long tradition in European bureaucracies of taking pride in fulfilling one's assigned task is a strong counterweight to the tendencies to be lazy and to shirk. There are moreover many possibilities for reconciling individual interests with the goals of bureaucracy such as the dispensing of titles, orders and decorations, and indirect payments in the form of official residences, the use of yachts, etc. (*CSD*, p. 209).

The arguments advanced in this section are easy to summarize. Schumpeter can still give political economy many fruitful impulses with respect to both his style of thinking and content.

CONCLUDING REMARKS

Reading Schumpeter, one is at first thrilled by how many ideas that are now part of modern political economy are already contained in his writings (especially in *Capitalism, Socialism and Democracy*). On further enquiry, however, it turns out that he had no direct influence on the subsequent development of public choice and that today's state of the analysis has advanced a great deal beyond him, both theoretically and empirically. Thus he would seem to be quite outdated from today's point of view. If however the straightjacket of neoclassical public choice is left behind and a more open view of political economy is adopted, it becomes clear that Schumpeter's writings still have very much to offer. Modern political economy could benefit a great deal if his style of thinking were to be adopted complementarily to the others employed, and if some of his ideas about the workings of the politicoeconomic system were to be considered and extended further.

'Read Schumpeter and take up his ideas': this seems to be the logical but quite hopeless battle cry. What matters is that scientific institutions be developed which make it worthwhile for scholars to work and publish in Schumpeter's direction. This is not presently the case—a Schumpeterian innovator is needed.

REFERENCES

Arrow, K. J. (1951) *Social Choice and Individual Values*. New York: Wiley.

Beckerath, E. von (1950) Grösse und Verfall des Kapitalismus. *Zeitschrift für die gesamte Staatswissenschaft*, **106**, 193–222.

Brittan, S. (1975) The economic contradictions of democracy. *British Journal of Political Science*, **5** (April), 129–59.

Buchanan, J. M. (1975a) A contractarian paradigm for applying economic theory. *American Economic Review, Papers and Proceedings*, **65** (May), 225–30.

Buchanan, J. M. (1975b) Public finance and public choice. *National Tax Journal*, **29** (December), 383–94.

Buchanan, J. M. (1977) *Freedom in Constitutional Contract. Perspectives of a Political Economist*. College Station, TX, and London: Texas A. and M. University Press.

Buchanan, J. M. and Tullock, G. (1962) *The Calculus of Consent*. Ann Arbor: University of Michigan Press.

Downs, A. (1957) *An Economic Theory of Democracy*. New York: Harper.

Esteve Serrano, T. A. (1978) Un análisis económico de las elecciónes colectivas y de la democracia: introducción y selección de artículos. *Revista Española de Economia* (May–August and September–December), 245–70.

Frey, B. S. (1978a) Politico-economic models and cycles. *Journal of Public Economics*, **9** (April), 203–220.

Frey, B. S. (1978b) *Modern Political Economy*. Oxford: Martin Robertson.

Frey, B. S. (1982) *Theory of Democratic Economic Policy*. Oxford: Martin Robertson (forthcoming).

Frohlich, N. and Oppenheimer, J. A. (1978) *Modern Political Economy*. Englewood Cliffs, NJ: Prentice-Hall.

Haberler, G. (1951) Joseph Alois Schumpeter, 1883–1950. In *Schumpeter, Social Scientist* (Ed.) Harris, S. E. Cambridge, MA: Harvard University Press, 24–47.

Kantor, B. (1979) Rational expectations and economic thought. *Journal of Economic Literature*, **17** (December), 1422–75.

Kramer, G. H. (1977) A dynamical model of political equilibrium. *Journal of Economic Theory*, **16** (No. 2), 310–34.
Krueger, A. O. (1974) The political economy of the rent-seeking society. *American Economic Review*, **64** (June), 291–303.
Leontief, W. (1950) Joseph A. Schumpeter (1883–1950). *Econometrica*, **18** (April), 103–110.
McCallum, B. T. (1980) The significance of rational expectations theory. *Challenge*, **22** (January), 37–43.
Meadows, D., *et al.* (1972) *The Limits of Growth*. New York: Universe Books.
Mueller, D. C. (1978) Voting by veto. *Journal of Public Economics*, **10** (August), 57–76.
Mueller, D. C. (1979) *Public Choice*. Cambridge, England: Cambridge University Press.
Niskanen, W. A. (1975) Bureaucrats and politicians. *Journal of Law and Economics*, **18** (December), 617–43.
Niskanen, W. A. (1978) Competition among government bureaus. *The Economics of Politics*, Institute of Economic Affairs Readings No. 18, Institute of Economic Affairs, London, 161–69.
Niskanen, W. A. (1980) Bureaucrats between self interest and public interest. Paper contributed to the *Int. Symp. on Anatomy of Government Deficiencies*, Diessen am Ammersee, July 22–25.
Nordhaus, W. D. (1975) The political business cycle. *Review of Economic Studies*, **42** (April), 169–90.
Oates, W. E. (Ed.) (1977) *The Political Economy of Fiscal Federalism*. Lexington and Toronto: Lexington Books.
Olson, M. (1965) *The Logic of Collective Action*. Cambridge, MA: Harvard University Press.
Ostrom, V. and Ostrom, E. (1971) Public choice: a different approach to the study of public administration. *Public Administration Review*, **31** (April), 203–16.
Palda, K. S. (1973) Does advertising influence votes? An analysis of the 66 and 70 Quebec elections. *Canadian Journal of Political Science*, **6**, 638–55.
Posner, R. A. (1975) The social cost of monopoly and regulation. *Journal of Political Economy*, **83** (August), 807–27.
Riker, W. H. and Ordeshook, P. (1973) *An Introduction to Positive Political Theory*. Englewood Cliffs, NJ: Prentice-Hall.
Samuelson, P. A. (1951) Schumpeter as a teacher and economic theorist. In *Schumpeter, Social Scientist* (Ed.) Harris, S. E. pp. 48–53. Cambridge, MA: Harvard University Press.
Schäder, R. (1956) Schumpeter, Joseph A(lois). *Handwörterbuch der Wirtschafts- und Sozialwissenschaften*. Fischer, Mohr und Vandenhoeck und Ruprecht, Vol. 9, 151–58.
Schumpeter, J. A. (1918) *Die Krise des Steuerstaates*. Graz und Leipzig. Reprinted 1976 in *Rudolf Goldscheid, Joseph Schumpeter. Die Finanzkrise des Steuerstaates. Beiträge zur politischen Oekonomie der Staatsfinanzen*. (Ed.) Hickel, R. pp. 329–79. Frankfurt: Suhrkamp.
Schumpeter, J. A. (1918–19) Zur Soziologie der Imperialismen. *Archiv für Sozialwissenschaft und Sozialpolitik*, **46**, 1–39, 275–310. English translation 1951 as *Imperialism and Social Classes*. New York: Kelley.
Schumpeter, J. A. (1927) Die sozialen Klassen im ethnisch homogenen Milieu. *Archiv für Sozialwissenschaften und Sozialpolitik*, **57**, 1–67.
Schumpeter, J. A. (1976) *Capitalism, Socialism and Democracy* (First published 1942). 5th Edition with an introduction by Tom Bottomore. London: Allen & Unwin.
Spiethoff, A. (1949) Josef Schumpeter. *Kyklos*, **3**, 289–93.
Stiglitz, J. E. and Uzawa, H. (1969) *Readings in the Modern Theory of Economic Growth*. Cambridge, MA: MIT Press.
Stolper, W. F. (1968) Schumpeter, Joseph A. *International Encyclopedia of the Social Sciences*. pp. 67–72. New York: Macmillan and Free Press.
Taylor, M. (1971) Mathematical political theory: a survey. *British Journal of Political Science*, **1**, 339–82.

Tidemann, N. T. and Tullock, G. (1976) A new and superior process for making social choices. *Journal of Political Economy*, **84** (December), 1145–60.
Tullock, G. (1965) *The Politics of Bureaucracy*. Washington, DC: Public Affairs Press.
Tullock, G. (1967) The welfare costs of tariffs, monopolies, and theft. *Western Economic Journal*, **5** (June), 224–32.
van den Doel, H. (1979) *Democracy and Welfare Economics*. Cambridge, England: Cambridge University Press.
Wagner, R. E. (1966) Pressure groups and political enterpreneurs: a review article. In *Papers on Non-Market Decision-Making* (Ed.) Tullock, G. pp. 161–70. Charlottesville: Thomas Jefferson Center in Political Economy.
Wan, H. Y. (1971) *Economic Growth*. New York: Harcourt, Brace, Jovanovich.
Wittman, D. A. (1973) Parties as utility maximizers. *American Political Science Review*, **67** (June), 490–98.
Wright, D. McĊ. (1951) Schumpeter's political philosophy. In *Schumpeter—Social Scientist* (Ed.) Harris, S. E. pp. 54–63. Cambridge, MA: Harvard University Press.

Chapter Nine

Schumpeter as a Historian of Economic Thought

MARK PERLMAN

THIS opportunity to participate in the honouring of Joseph A. Schumpeter, generally, and to discuss specifically his work as a historian of economic thought provides simultaneously a welcome opportunity and a far-from-easy intellectual exercise. It is a welcome opportunity because it results in the necessary pressure for me to try to resolve, on a better level, many conflicting thoughts I have had about the history of economic thought. It is a far-from-easy intellectual exercise because Professor Schumpeter's writings, perhaps even more than most industrious scholars', contain intuitively stimulating but nevertheless ambiguous theses. Perhaps such confusions are inevitable, particularly when one's interest in so complex a topic lasts throughout a very long career, a career itself affected violently both by a series of personal experiences and also by a limited willingness to absorb the research work undertaken by others.

Schumpeter's work in the history of economic thought may be found in four places. There is the early work, *Epochen der Dogmen- und Methoden-geschichte*, entitled in English *Economic Doctrine and Method*, first published in 1914, republished in 1924, and translated into English in 1954. Secondly, there were a great many book reviews and memorial essays; some, but only a minor proportion of these (apparently selected by his widow, Mrs Elizabeth Boody Schumpeter), appeared in two posthumously published books, *The Essays of J. A. Schumpeter*, edited by Richard V. Clemence, and *Ten Great Economists: From Marx to Keynes*. Both were published as collected volumes (although in both cases written long beforehand) in 1951. The third source of Professor Schumpeter's work in the area is clearly his 'half course in the history of economic thought', which he gave at Harvard between the autumn term 1939 and the spring term 1948. And finally there is his 1954 massive *History of Economic Analysis*, which he did not live to complete, but his widow and others contributed to filling in some lacunae existent at the time of his death in 1950. Because of time, space and data limitations, this paper is principally based on the first and the last of these four. The second can, I think, be subsumed by the final effort. I regret that I have not had access to written students' notes on his course, but the stories about it are not only legion but also suggest that the lectures varied in tone and content as they were delivered. Thus what I am offering is my interpretation of his two principal works in the History of Economic Thought plus some additional material brought in for comparative purposes. The first section copes with Schumpeter's definition of the topic; section two is an effort to provide a 'reader's guide' to Schumpeter's aforementioned two major works on the History of Economic Thought; the third section compares Schumpeter's approach to the history of thought with Wesley Clair Mitchell's; and the final section is full of explicit judgements.

SCHUMPETER'S DEFINITION OF THE TOPIC

Let me start by admitting that I am unable to present a clear delimitation or definition of Schumpeter's perception of the history of economic thinking. In his 1914 essay Schumpeter described the topic as 'The development of economics as a science'[1] and suggested that it had two halves—one was purely philosophical learning for its own sake and, as such, was intellectually integrated and coherent; the other centred on the 'scribblings', to paraphrase Gibbon's potential patron, of the intellectual servants or hirelings of special-economic interest groups. Yet, once having identified these two approaches or sets of products, Schumpeter, I believe, backed away from the implications of the distinction. But he did not abandon this early division, perhaps because of the pedagogical neatness of what he was proposing; and even if in practice this division does not work out perfectly, its pedagogical utility remains. After all, the pragmatic is not the only test, much less necessarily a legitimate one.

In Chapter 1 of his posthumous *History of Economic Analysis*[2] there is a rather brilliant if unsuccessful effort at reconfirming his 1914 approach to the development of economics as a science:

> By History of Economic Analysis I mean the history of the intellectual efforts that men have made in order to *understand* economic phenomena or, which comes to the same thing, the history of the analytic or specific aspects of economic thought (*HEA*, p. 3).

---

[1] Schumpeter (1914) *Economic Doctrine and Method* will henceforth be referred to as *EDM*.

[2] Schumpeter (1954) *History of Economic Analysis* will henceforth be referred to as *HEA*.

However, the older Schumpeter then explains why he pursued the study of the 'history of economics' (*sic*); and in so styling the topic, he has already moved from discussing the history of a science to the more pedestrian 'history of economics'. How does he justify this sleight-of-hand? He suggests that virtually all modern work combines some current institutional overtones, which must be compared to earlier manifestations of the same idea in order to be purged of their time-limited characteristics. Thus, it is already clear that the cosmopolitan Schumpeter seems to have assured his readers and his students that there was a *wertfrei* and a *zeitfrei* goal for economic science, but he really did not completely believe that he could lead them to it.

What he seems to have wanted most was to treat his topic as an exercise in epistemics, that is an exercise in the theory of theories, using economic thought as exemplar material, while admitting that in its details it differs from the 'purer' sciences:

> It is in fact our main purpose to describe what may be called the process of the Filiation of Scientific Ideas—the process by which men's efforts to understand economic phenomena produce, improve, and pull down analytic structures in an unending sequence. It is one of the main theses to be established in this book that *fundamentally* this process does not differ from the analogous process in other fields of knowledge (*HEA*, p. 6).

What I am saying is that there is something of a contradiction between the simplicity of outline that Schumpeter originally suggested as his topic (the discovery of straightforward, universal, scientific economic principles), and what he then went on to present, namely, a more conventional circuitry, full of the interactions of men, ideas, and events. Thus I conclude that the differences between Schumpeter's approach to the topic of the history of our discipline and the approach of many others are not as startling as he seems to suggest they were. But if I mark him down on the score of originality, I mark him up on the score of qualitative execution. What he did was not so different from other's efforts, it was just better. And who would not be delighted to be so adjudged?

A 'READER'S GUIDE' TO SCHUMPETER'S THINKING ON THE HISTORY OF ECONOMICS

At some unspecified time in his career, Professor Schumpeter wrote a brief piece he called 'A reader's guide to Adam Smith' (*HEA*, pp. 186–93). I intend as the 'heart' of this paper to provide a rather general 'reader's guide' to Schumpeter as a historian of economics thinking.

From the panoramic standpoint, Schumpeter relied only in the first approximation sense on a chronological presentation of ideas and writings. But he tended to depart from the purely chronological in order to pursue the evolution of ideas. Moreover, Schumpeter seemed not only unable to resist the temptation, but also to be actually eager to include discursions into other disciplines—mostly these discursions were in the disciplines of moral, ethical, and historical philosophy; they did not consciously focus on the relationship of historical events (as Wesley Clair Mitchell preferred to do) or on the pleasurable, if not actually Elysian, fields of aesthetics.

Schumpeter was a great name-, title-, and adjective-dropper. The vastness of his bibliographic recall all but boggles the mind. The quick metaphor and the studied simile brighten up the page; on many occasions they were also used to blacken the character. Whatever the relation of the intent to the result, it seems to give his writing a highly personal flavour.

To my way of thinking, one of the most interesting aspects of Schumpeter's work was his decision to divide the history of developments in economics into four basic parts, which although presented chronologically nonetheless carry initial overtones, which ultimately transcend time-frames and point to a universal goal.

1. An era of original philosophical dominance, including not only most everything up to the *Wealth of Nations* but also the *Wealth of Nations*. Smith thus is separated from the classical tradition and is consequently compared to such cosmic system builders as Aristotle, the Church Fathers, Aquinas, and Pufendorf. Such a separation and such a comparison, of course, make Smith appear less of a giant.
2. The era of the classical system, running from approximately 1790 until approximately 1870.
3. The period of the schools (and this is my term); these include the German historical, the marginal utility and marginal product, the Marxian, the American historical, the Marshallian neoclassical, and the general static equilibrium schools. It also includes the era of the development of such subdisciplinary centres as business cycles, labour economics, fiscal economics, and public utilities.
4. The era of modern macroeconomics, an era when there are as yet no more than unsuccessful attempts to develop a coherent, broad-scale economics, related to other cognate disciplines including philosophy, and which embrace not only an empirical (statistical and econometric) effort but also a more purely *a priori* theory. But this is the era when the majesty of the earliest phase, the one devoted to grand system building, will be regained.

Essentially I think that Schumpeter's two books, the 1914 *Epochen* and his posthumous *History of Economic Analysis*, really tried to do three things. They tried to show how the history of economists' serious thinking should lead to a dynamic general equilibrium system, that is, to a general system which if it does not have a precise teleological goal, does have an identifiable dialectical pattern. Secondly, they show that the rhythm of thought and the academic life serve to shape a more stable understanding of the future than does the compilation of a record of partisans' rationalizations. The goal of the 'consultant administrator' (his version of Plato's golden man) is in several senses superior to particularistic 'pamphleteers'—clearly an anti-Mandeville kind of view towards the conflicts or the competition among ideas. And finally, the books suggest that economics as a discipline is a subset of epistemology, not a simple interdisciplinary exercise in social studies. This point is worth repeating.

To my mind the most important thing to grasp in Schumpeter is the locus of his thinking. In *EDM* he starts by contrasting the consultant administrator with the pamphleteer. Or to concretize, he contrasts thinkers of the calibre of Aristotle and Pufendorf and Turgot against mere pamphleteers like Barbon, North, and Misselden. Even more so the case is the comparison of the latter's compiler, Adam Smith, who is contrasted unfavourably with the physiocrats, whose virtue was their perception of economics as a circular system (that is, as a self-contained or balanced aquarium). Smith's *Wealth of Nations* (1776), he suggests, contains not only no new perceptions; worse yet, it was a politician's cookbook, no less and no more. In this sense, it was not inspired; he was not taken with the aesthetics or style of the *Wealth of Nations*.

From there, Schumpeter goes on to discuss the classical system which he believed was at its creative peak for 'ten to fifteen years' after the 1817 appearance of Ricardo's *Principles* and which ended with a final burst of splendour with the work of John Stuart Mill (1848). Here he lays out his thinking in 12 numbered points. The first deals with the identification of the period. The second suggests that doctrines, not persons, are the heroes. The third observes that the initial success of the classicists with regard to policies led them to fractionate, and in so doing they tended to lose sight of the 'grand scheme' and to become somewhat less impressive, to become pamphleteers. This transformation from philosophers to pamphleteers (many in the form of textbooks and catechisms) led to a further narrowing of vision and, in sum, to a loss of any tie to an epistemological grand scheme. The fifth point discusses who dominated the profession in various countries—in Germany it was the professors, in France the merchants, in the United Kingdom the Benthamite utilitarians. He was particularly fascinated with these Benthamite utilitarians because while they were very versatile they relied principally on a provincial knowledge of British history. I infer that he was disturbed that they were not particularly well versed in moral philosophy. The sixth point stresses that the classicists preferred an *a priori* method; however, they really were ignorant of its limitations. The seventh point tried to come to grips with the cultural economic sociology, which had over time diluted much of the initial scientific thrust of the classical tradition. The eighth point relates to the peculiar sociological attitude of the classical economists, who viewed nations as hierarchically organized and having three classes (the landowners, the workers, and the capitalists). This attitude was presented as an immutable and inevitable social structure with each of these classes basing its actions on a rather narrowly defined self-interest. The implication is that the particularistic pamphleteer mentality replaced the wiser general philosophical one. The ninth point was that the classicists' perceptions of what economic theory was supposed to be about were largely circumscribed by the first and second books of the *Wealth of Nations*. The tenth point was that price determination was at the centre of their thinking. The eleventh point was that their best work was done on the theory of distribution, where they did a good but not complete job. And the twelfth point was that as a group they tended to eschew discussion of the theory of money, although John Stuart Mill himself did have a quantity theory of money. This treatment of the classical economists amounts to approximately three-eighths of the early book.

Schumpeter then goes on to the era of schools and of the subdisciplines, where his concern centres on the dangers of slogans, easy formulas, and with an excessive fascination with 'policy implications'.[3] His treatment of the early German historical school is comprehensive, although he believes that a historical element must be balanced by a theoretical element. But if he was no 'Austrian' in terms of the line-up associated with the famous *Methodenstreit*, his identification of the British disciples of the German historical school (namely, Cliffe Leslie, J. K. Ingram, and Sir William Ashley) as irrational says something very important too. What it says is that he condemned the roles they played in limiting epistemological growth. He also discusses the intellectual conflict the French economists had with the French sociological tradition. He then turns to the *Methodenstreit* itself, and notes that the issue was not really abstraction versus empirical fact, but was rather a conflict about the role of free trade and tariffs; in other words, it related not to a higher-order, nominally epistemological issue but to a lower-order, pamphleteering kind of thing. There follows a discussion of the mathematical method, an epistemologically high-order topic for which he has an obvious respect. He lists amongst the principal contributions those of Whewell, Cournot, Jevons, Marshall, Edgeworth, Fisher, Auspitz, and Lieben.

Not content to leave the historical school with a listing of names and intellectual ties, he returns to assess it. He believes that it gave economics a perception of reality, that it stressed the unity of social activities, and that

[3] Cf. Hutchison's work, *Knowledge and Ignorance in Economics* (1977).

it identified the place that antirationalism has in the development of societal organization. At its best it stressed evolution, while the more traditional classical economists focused on statics. And he is particularly careful to point out the historical school's interest in correlations (suggesting relationships without identifiable cause–effect sequences). And finally influenced as he was by Marxism, he stresses the organic point of view that the historical school also emphasized.

From there he turns to the burst of theorizing after 1870. He mentions the earlier precursors of this group (in his later work he was to call them 'men who wrote beyond their time') and he identifies specifically the contributions of Menger, Jevons, Walras, von Böhm-Bawerk, and von Wieser. He notes how freely and widely the marginal method was employed and he particularly notes the development of a new theory of price.

Many years later when writing the *History of Economic Analysis*, he generally followed the pattern suggested in *Economic Doctrine and Method*. The *HEA* is organized in five parts. Part 1 (3.7 per cent of the book) is the imperfect delineation of what Schumpeter thought he was doing, to which I have referred at the beginning of this paper. It reflects the conflict between 'science and ideology', where he tries to establish a distinction, but does not succeed. In the four chapters of this part, there are 22 sections, with each section being a separate and, if related, not smoothly flowing, set of observations. My own judgement is that his approach reflected a desire to develop a sense of cause and effect as seen by the physicists of his time, but that he realized that perceptions are grasped by ideologically conditioned minds. In other words, nothing starts really *tabula rasa*, and the best that we can do is to examine continuously our conclusions and to see whether we have unconscious or, better yet, unarticulated premises that shape them. But I am somewhat at a loss to understand what one can do even if one can identify the unarticulated or emotional premises—certainly one may do something for others, but can one 'correct' for oneself these perceptions? If so, how?

Part 2 of the *History of Economic Analysis* is slightly more than a quarter of the book. It is the summary of the struggle between the consultant administrators (those aspiring to a broad-gauge view) and the particularistic advocates, still rather sneeringly referred to as 'pamphleteers'. Truth, or better yet scientific truth, stretches to the horizons in all directions—the historical, the spectrum of disciplines, and the multidimensions (up, down, right, left, the progressive and the traditional spheres of culture). Pamphleteers, by way of contrast, want only to fight tactical and not strategic battles.

As before, Schumpeter's approach seemingly employs chronological sequence but only as a first approximation; the sequence is Aristotle, the Church Fathers, natural law and those who apply it to problems of production, distribution, and exchange (the latter being the economists). In

Schumpeter's view the great philosophical breakthrough for economists remains the physiocrats' perception of circularity. They key names were Boisguillebert, Cantillon, Quesnay, and Turgot. Smith's name then tags along!

Money and value were studied as topics and were quite well understood, even by modern standards. Smith lost this thread when he came to weaving the *Wealth of Nations* and the classical rug merchants thought it might be done without. Schumpeter dissented.

Part 2 concludes with a grudging review of the truths employed and presumably in some senses discovered by the pamphleteers. I would say that, in this sense, Schumpeter differs very markedly from Jacob Viner and in a major sense from Lionel Robbins, who saw in the pamphleteers the basis of a truly competitive market of ideas.

Part 3 covers the classical period but also identifies those who transcended it. It is almost a third of the book and provides a very concise statement of an important era. It ties classical economics to other partial intellectual systems prevalent at the time. While it does so in something of a chronological order, the stress is on breadth rather than on the historical order; he mentions the romantic movement, developments in sociology, an enthusiasm for evolutionism, concern with human psychology, development of logic and epistemology, and a new 'theology' (pre-Marxian socialism). It balances the darker Ricardian beginnings of the classical era with a rather admiring view of John Stuart Mill's culminatory contribution. Given Schumpeter's essential belief that the classicists were only talented specialists, I find it a balanced evaluation of them. The treatment focuses mostly on England and its English intellectual experiences, but it does include other topics: there is a particularly fine discussion of the Marxian system, even though Marx himself is relegated to something less than the heroic role.

The fourth part of the book (eight chapters and an appendix on 'The theory of utility') is on the era of schools. It is again about a third of the book. I think it is the best of the various parts. It starts with long sections (about 18 per cent of the whole) on what was going on in other areas—social policy formation, other disciplines (history, sociology, psychology) and how these activities affected the mainstream economists (i.e. the consultant administrators).

Schumpeter then goes on to his three 'greats'—Jevons, Menger, and Walras. His lesser greats, including the Marshallians (certain key inventors and their discoveries) and such as Pareto, certain Americans and some Marxians, each of whom are mentioned rather superficially.

The consultant administrators of this era are generally of a historically lesser calibre—of them Marshall is the best but with a personal perception of dynamics as being no more than a commitment to progress. Marshall's vision was essentially inherited from John Stuart Mill. Schumpeter's appreciation of the younger Mill, who by historical standards was one of Britain's broader-gauge statesmen–philosophers (hence a consulting administrator), reveals a great deal about Schumpeter and his value scheme. Mill was hardly an innovator of analytical technique, although there was a streak of originality in some of his expository material (e.g. the stationary state). But he was a philosopher with breadth, and that is what counted most. If to Schumpeter, John Stuart Mill was cultured, Marshall was to him at best only a mathematician with some historical interests. Schumpeter sees the period as full of progress, but most of the progress was in the perfection of technique and in the specialization in subfields.

The important part of this section is Chapter 7 and its appendix on equilibrium analysis. Although only one-eighth of the book, it contains Schumpeter's assessment of the accomplishments of the period. These are placed in the perspective of the problems of the era and the practical type of work carried out in attempts to solve them—work on credit and business cycles. This chapter and its appendix summarize the greatest advances—advances in concepts and application. But eschewed completely are the contributions of Wesley Clair Mitchell and Frank Knight, however. I find these omissions intellectually inexplicable.

The book concludes with a fifth part, which traces the breakdown of the Marshallian tradition and identifies the unfulfilled quest for a dynamic theory of general equilibrium, or to put it explicitly, the Holy Grail which is as yet undiscovered. It does mention, but only briefly, research on statistical material with some attention being paid to business cycles. There is a full-scale and rather ill-focused attack on Keynes's *General Theory*. In my view G. L. S. Shackle's *The Years of High Theory* (1967) is better with regard to the breakdown of the Marshallian hegemony. Shackle's own work on the complexity of uncertainty in a dynamic general equilibrium theory suggests that the new plane of understanding has not yet been identified, much less rigorously surveyed. Schumpeter, as one of the founders of the Econometric Society, must have been quite aware of what Tinbergen, Frisch, Koopmans, and Marschak were up to.

At best, the book ends in speculation. Yet it must be remembered that Schumpeter was writing prior to the era of the high-speed computer, that this portion of the book (being the last) may have been given less attention because it was so difficult, and that the book itself was truly unfinished before he died.

COMPARISON OF SCHUMPETER'S APPROACH WITH THAT OF MITCHELL

While there are only a few people in Schumpeter's time, or any other period, who have had an interest in developing a general interpretation of the development of the history of economic thought, there were, nonetheless, some. For students of my generation there was the general textbook by Charles Gide and Charles Rist (1915). Erich Roll (1938) published a most interesting text on the subject—a text since revised but never overcoming a curious dichotomy between the earlier part, which was written while Roll was clearly an ardent Marxist, and the latter part, when he clearly was not. Even briefer were interpretative surveys, such as the one by Professor of Economics at the University of Edinburgh, Alexander Gray, which incidentally remains in print.

In addition, there were a great many other figures who did substantial work in trying to deepen our perception of particular schools of economics or particular individuals. Names in this group are really too numerous to mention, but certainly those of Jacob Hollander, Edwin R. A. Seligman, Lionel Robbins, Jacob Viner, Frank Fetter, Joseph Spengler, and William Jaffé are only a few that could appear on most persons' lists of the 'five leading names'.

However, to my mind the outstanding synthesis of the topic, the only one with which the Schumpeter synthesis should expect to be compared, is the one presented by Wesley Clair Mitchell (1967–69), long-time Professor of Economics at Columbia University and perhaps even now best remembered as the founder and director of the National Bureau of Economic Research.

I feel that a comparison with Mitchell is particularly relevant because he and Schumpeter were contemporaries working in the American scene; had some other common areas of scholarly activity, namely business cycles; and basically had very different views of the role of the history of economics. Mitchell started lecturing on this topic by the midst of World War One and continued until 1937, which is about the time he retired from Columbia University. Professor Mitchell died in 1948; indeed, one of my more vivid personal memories is the rather discursive, not purely complimentary, and somewhat self-projecting eulogy that Schumpeter gave on the occasion of the Mitchell memorial service at Columbia University late in 1948. My point is that the comparison between the two is not ingenuous; indeed Schumpeter, himself, doubtless had it in mind and, as we shall see, so did Mitchell.

As was the case with Schumpeter, Mitchell never completed the job of editing his notes on the history of thought. I have been told by Arthur F. Burns and others that he intended to turn to this task after he completed other duties, particularly work that hung over from his monumental *Measuring Business Cycles* (Mitchell and Burns, 1946).

However, we do have pretty good records of what Mitchell covered in his lectures. There was a mimeographed version prepared by John Meyers (a student) from stenographic notes taken during the lectures of academic year 1926–27. And shortly after Professor Mitchell's death his widow authorized mimeographing of a 1935 version of the lectures. Ultimately she gave permission to Joseph Dorfman, Mitchell's student and later colleague, to edit (through expansion) the set of notes. The Dorfman version, published in 1967 by Augustus M. Kelley, and carrying the title *Types of Economic Theory: From Mercantilism to Institutionalism*, runs to a massive 1447 pages.

It consists of no 'parts' or 'sections', only 22 chapters, each focused on one or more topics. In the Dorfman version, 34 pages are devoted to a general orientation to the subject, in marked contrast to Schumpeter.

Mitchell's opening discussion is of 'Adam Smith and how political economy came to be systematized in England', and covers about 136 pages. It leans very heavily on Smith's own writing and very little on Smith's natural law and physiocratic precursors. It is very 'United Kingdom-oriented', and although it does mention Smith's earlier book, the *Theory of Moral Sentiments* (1759). it does not do so in great detail. On p. 145 Mitchell says:

> Economists like to speak of economics as a science, and of Adam Smith as the father of political economy. In their more careful moments, they have perhaps some reservations about both remarks. They know that Adam Smith was preceded by Quesnay; that Quesnay was preceded by Cantillon; that Cantillon was preceded by a whole group of at least half-enlightened mercantilist writers upon public policy. Yet when all these deductions are made, it remains a fact that the *Wealth of Nations* was, in a genuine sense the start, the foundation of modern economics.

Such was the view of Mitchell; such clearly could not have been the view of Schumpeter, who identified the beginning of economics with Aristotle and had a very different view of Smith.

The next section (4.4 per cent of the whole) of Mitchell's treatment focuses on Bentham and utilitarianism. There then follows a very short, only 26 pages, discussion of 'Malthus and the empirical trend'. Much of this discussion is on Population Malthus. However, with reference to Malthus's *Principles of Political Economy* (1820), Mitchell was mainly impressed by the theory of 'general overproduction' or underconsumption.

Not surprisingly there follows a lengthy 120 page chapter on 'David Ricardo and the making of classical political economy', containing not only an explanation of what Ricardo thought, including some of his changes in thinking, but also a good deal of economic history. It also contains several rather interesting assessments of Ricardo by others, e.g. Walter Bagehot. Most of all it tries to put Ricardo's own views, particularly with regard to his intellectual relationship with Malthus, into a context easily grasped by American students with some knowledge of Regency Britain. It is quite clear that Mitchell is not an avid admirer of Ricardo or classical economics. But if not a finder of essential truth or insight in the classical tradition, he certainly as a historian was ready to give the Ricardian group 'high marks' for reflecting as well as shaping events. The three chapters following the one on Ricardo run to a lengthy 223 pages and are entitled 'The new social sciences at work: the philosophical radicals', 'Political economy in the days of its triumph', and 'John Stuart Mill and the humanization of classical economics'. My reading of the last, the chapter on Mill, yields a judgement that Mitchell assesses Mill's conversion from Benthamite utilitarianism to ethical socialism to be an important development in the history of economic thought, not merely of one man's 'born again' revelation, because it reveals an insider's assessment of the heartlessness of the historical impact of classical economics. The quintessential personalness of this change is something I fancy Professor Schumpeter would have thought to be not epic but cloying or sentimental. Moreover, Mill was considered by Mitchell a great humanitarian as well as a scholar, but not very original; I read Schumpeter's verdict as something even more favourable—Mill was original and had that rare kind of grasp unknown to most Englishmen, the breadth of philosophical (as distinct from historical) vision reserved to those on the all-time international list of consultant administrators. My point, put bluntly, is that what Mitchell most admired in J. S. Mill left Schumpeter relatively cold, and what enthused Schumpeter, Mitchell did not value highly. Strange that both so admired contrasting sides of the same man.

Mitchell then turns to the great reformers: Jevons, Menger, and Walras. To them he devotes only 110 pages, with the largest share going to Jevons. Schumpeter put Jevons as the least of the three.

After that comes a chapter on Alfred Marshall, again another 110 pages. My reading of Mitchell's view is that Marshall, not J. S. Mill, is the wisest of the English contributors: Marshall's definition of economics suggests a realistic science (although all of his analyses rest on some simplifying assumptions), while Mill insists that political economy must be highly abstract. Marshall insists that he is talking about real men, while Mill explicitly uses an artificial definition of man—a being animated solely by desire of wealth, aversion to labour, and a preference for present to future enjoyment. Marshall agrees with Schmoller that the economist must use both deduction and induction, while Mill insists that political economy must rely upon the concrete deductive method, although conclusions should be verified by 'specific experience'. Marshall holds that money is the centre around which economic science clusters, while Mill holds that 'money is a thing of indifference' that exercises no influence upon human behaviour except when 'it gets out of order' (Mitchell, 1967–69, p. 217). As I have indicated previously, Schumpeter had rather mixed judgements about Marshall; my inference is that Mitchell did not. Again a major distinguishing difference.

At this point in the text, Mitchell turns to discussion of American economists with a 30 page chapter on 'The development of American economics and the role of J. B. Clark'. Then follows a larger (50 page) chapter on 'Frank A. Fetter and the American psychological school'. Fetter was influenced by J. B. Clark, by Simon Patten (University of Pennsylvania) and, of course, by the Austrians, particularly von Böhm-Bawerk. After, there is a reasonably long chapter on Herbert J. Davenport, whose rather abstract, price-oriented economics was the subject of a fair amount of evaluational disparagement:

> In other words, [Davenport] supposes prices to exist for other articles in indefinite number in the very process of explaining the price at which any given article will be supplied. To repeat what I said at the beginning, the theorist finds his price analysis is itself circuitous—he explains prices by prices. The price of one thing is in very large measure explained by the prices of other things. If his pecuniary analysis is both superficial and circuitous, where does he stand? (Mitchell, 1967–69, p. 341).

And the answer tends to be, human desires, productive capacity, and instrumental equipment (technology).

After that comes a brief chapter on von Wieser and a slightly longer chapter (41 pages) on 'The pure economics of Joseph Alois Schumpeter and Vilfredo Pareto'. His work on Schumpeter does not mention Schumpeter's interest in history of economic thought; rather it focuses on Schumpeter's *The Nature and Main Content of Theoretical Economics* (1908) and Schumpeter's *Theory of Economic Development* (1912). Pareto is treated somewhat more briefly than Schumpeter, but not necessarily any more gently. In many senses Mitchell apparently believes that Schumpeter's theoretical ideal was better handled by Pareto than by Schumpeter (Mitchell, 1967–69, p. 412).

The next chapter, 'The mathematical approach of Gustav Cassel' is very short, only 31 pages. There is then a chapter on the American monetary economist, Benjamin McAlester Anderson, Jr. After that a short chapter on John A. Hobson and the rise of British welfare economics.

Mitchell was, himself, an American institutionalist. Part of the origins of American institutionalism are to be found in the German historical school, and the nineteenth chapter is on von Schmoller. It is principally in this context that Mitchell reveals his judgements of Marx. He compares Schmoller adversely to Marx as an economic historian. Following, there is a very long chapter on Mitchell's own teacher, Thorstein Veblen. To Mitchell, Veblen was the basic American institutionalist, and although Mitchell was appropriately respectful to Veblen and certainly intrigued by the originality of Veblen's interpretations, I do not think that Mitchell felt constrained by any of the limits that Veblen's approach involved. Indeed, Mitchell immediately turned to Professor John R. Commons as another American institutionalist, indeed one who was 'self-proclaimed'.

The volume then ends with almost 60 pages of retrospective and then prospective conclusions.

It is plain that Mitchell's plan was to paint a narrower panorama than Schumpeter set out to do. It is also clear that Mitchell was far more oriented to English-speaking economists, with an occasional sidestep towards German and French economists, than was Schumpeter. I should mention, of course, that the two men were competitive with regard to their perceptions of the nature, origin, and impact of business cycles. But their work on business cycles is not an essential part of my story, and for reasons of time and space I must eschew it.

If I were to compare Schumpeter and Mitchell I would probably conclude the following four principal things:

1. Schumpeter thought the proper approach was to consider the history of economic analysis as essentially an organic subset of epistemology; Mitchell's view was to emphasize that economic thinking was dominated by historical events. In this sense, Mitchell accorded pamphleteers much greater respectability than did Schumpeter. Mitchell was reasonably distrustful of all who believe they were 'consultant administrators'; one tends to think that Mitchell shares the American cultural preference for men turned bronze by hard labour in the sun, rather than for men 'born gold' by an inherited combination of family advantages and brilliant tutors.
2. Mitchell thought it was sufficient for economists to have a grounding in recent modern history; for that reason he started with Smith's *Wealth of Nations*. Schumpeter thought any knowledge of modern intellectual systems had to be grounded on the perception of the natural rights philosophical system, and beyond that its precursors. I doubt that Mitchell could be said to have had as a high-school student the equivalent of a *Gymnasium* education, while Schumpeter had not only that but he probably could have been graduated from the *École Polytechnique* as well.
3. Mitchell was much more cautious than Schumpeter about predicting current goals and current trends. This caution is inherent in his perception of institutionalism, which after all was his school. The very nature of institutionalism, as one of its practitioners has observed, was that it dated itself; as institutions matured and declined, the ideas that prompted their growth would by the nature of any kind of dialectical process (to say nothing of more abrupt changes) become valueless.
4. Mitchell was essentially English-material oriented—not only because of language limitations, but probably also because he was rather sceptical of the likelihood of, much less the need for, discovering economic universals. Schumpeter, on the other hand, moved in several cultures and in at least

two of them (the German/Austrian and the American) became something of an interpreter of other cultures as well.

This comparison between two of the most eminent and sophisticated professors in American universities should not be taken to suggest that we have exhausted the ranks of such broad-gauge historians of economic thought. The history of economic analysis was taught during much of this time at the University of Chicago by Professor Frank Knight and there and particularly at Princeton University a little later on by Professor Jacob Viner. It was taught at Duke University by Professor Joseph J. Spengler and at the University of California at Berkeley by Professor Leo Rogin. And there are many other names, certainly too numerous to mention, to suggest that either Mitchell or Schumpeter (or a combination of the two of them) had dominated the sub-discipline of the history of economic analysis. And what was true of America was, of course, no less true in London where Professor Lionel Robbins lectured. But the comparison between Mitchell and Schumpeter is important because both men, leading practitioners in the development of economic analysis, were interested in giving their students not only some details of the history of their discipline, but also they tried to identify for their students what they thought was the quintessential background. That quintessential background was, in the case of Schumpeter, epistemology; in the case of Mitchell, it was a detailed knowledge of reasonably recent historical events. And it is that distinction which I think illuminates both the strengths of each man's approach as well as some inherent weaknesses—for the study of background material is resource-consuming and to study the more of one suggests (but does not completely preclude) the less of the other.

CONCLUSIONS

A modicum of good sense, if not of modesty, leads me to conclude this assessment of Schumpeter as a historian of economic thought principally by referring to the various judgements of those who reviewed his posthumous *History of Economic Analysis*.

Before doing so, however, I want to mention two unrelated points. The first is to note that no one has yet, to my knowledge, compared Schumpeter's work to that of Luigi Cossa, whose 1891 survey, *An Introduction to the Study of Political Economy*, may well have been the lodestar that set Schumpeter on his course. The similarity of organization and of thought seems to me to be too great to be a result of chance.

The second point is that *EDM* seems never to have been seriously reviewed—at least not in the American or English materials available to me. Yet it clearly was read and was appreciated. No less an authority and great teacher than Lionel Robbins (1955, p. 1) much later says that *EDM* 'had at once taken its place as incontestably the best short introduction to its subject'. It seems to me to be a fact that by the mid-1920s everyone counted Schumpeter as one of the great figures in the history of thought, yet no one reviewed or summarized this version of his grand scheme—strange.

These assessments of *HEA* are taken from only a few of the many reviews the book received, F. L. Nussbaum (1954, pp. 62–64), a professor who did important work in the Schmoller tradition, wrote

> This great work is too monumental to be disposed of in a limited review, but as cats may look at kings it may be proper to examine it casually somewhat as Schumpeter did his subjects, less with regard to its general virtue than regard to its virtue as history. . . . The book remains a superb scrics of analyses of the analyzers, but it becomes a rationally organized biographical dictionary of the economists.

He found appealing the 'reader's guide' to Adam Smith and others; although he regretted the omission of a similar service for Karl Marx. George Stigler comments that 'the quality of the performance is not rivaled by any other work of comparable scope'. Stigler wonders why anybody wants to write in such a large scale, and he worries about the uneven quality of the analysis. But, as he wrote,

> This is, of course, a criticism of what Schumpeter set out to do, not of the manner in which he did it. His comments are, as ever, supremely sophisticated, and, as usual, full of shrewd insight. He had an almost other worldly detachment with respect to theories and policies, and it was reinforced by the mischievous pleasure he got from keeping out of step with the crowd. . . . The only general dissent I would make from them is that his admiration for the superior formal theorist leads him to put this genre on too high a pedestal. . . . This excessive praise carries with it an underestimate of the English tradition of substantive generalization, and especially of its greatest exponent, Adam Smith (Stigler, 1954, pp. 344–5).

Professor Simon Kuznets (1955) opened his review,

> This is a grand and grandiose book: grand because it was written by a scholar of great erudition, wide interest, brilliant insight, and perceptive, if erratic, judgement; grandiose because the design is of such vast proportion that even a long lifetime's effort was bound to leave wide gaps and hasty patches. . . . This is an important and valuable book—not as a standard guide to the uninitiated nor as a collection of definitive and balanced accounts for the technically trained. The flavor of it may best be conveyed by a brief quotation. Here is Schumpeter discussing Petty's appeal to replace verbal slogans by measurement: 'It was the inspiring message, the

suggestive program, which wilted in the wooden hands of the Scottish professor and was practically lost to most economists for two hundred and fifty years. A. Smith took the safe side that was so congenial to him when he declared . . . that he placed that much faith in Politickal Arithmetick' (p. 212). The quotation is typical both in its emphasis on a phase in the history of economic thinking unfamiliar to many economists and in this partially defensible and partially biased judgment of Adam Smith (Kuznets, 1955, pp. 323–34).

And there is the lengthy *American Economic Review* article by Jacob Viner, who says on the positive side,

> . . . The fact remains, nonetheless, that Schumpeter did possess learning and skills manifestly exceeding in range those displayed by any other economist of his or our time, and that in this book he applied these endowments to the enlightenment of his readers with a brilliance and virtuosity which excite and dazzle even when they fail wholly to persuade. When all [the irrelevance, the cryptic, the strongly biased, the paradoxical] is set aside, there still remains enough to constitute by a wide margin the most constructive, the most original, the most learned, and the most brilliant contribution to the history of the analytical phases of our discipline which has ever been made (Viner, 1954, pp. 894–5).

And as I have noted earlier, Viner was not a man given to flattery.

On the negative side he says that the book is 'badly name-ridden' and that there is excessive grading of people and contributions, unfair assessment, bias against many, if not most, English contributors.

And finally, Lionel Robbins wrote a lengthy review article which appeared in the *Quarterly Journal of Economics* in February 1955:

> Let it be said at once that the result, slightly unfinished as it is, is something which is without serious rival. . . . *The History of Economic Analysis* has attracted some very first class talents: some of the contributions—such works, for instance as Professor Viner's *Studies* or Mr Sraffa's *Ricardo*—are outstanding in the scholarship of historical studies in general. But for the most part the work of high excellence here has taken the form of special studies rather than general history. There is very little that is absolutely first class in this sphere and nothing that will stand the comparison, either in respect of scale or insight, with this work of Schumpeter's (Robbins, 1955, pp. 3–4).

Yet Robbins is all but appalled by some of Schumpeter's principal judgements; amongst these are a ranking of Cournot above Ricardo. As Robbins puts it,

> . . . *let us apply the good Austrian test of the so-called loss principle.* Suppose the theoretical contributions of Ricardo and Cournot to be alternately withdrawn—which would involve the greater impoverishment? Can there really be any hesitation about the answer? . . . Similarly, later on in the book, we find pre-eminence in his period assigned to Walras rather than to Marshall—although it must be said at once that Schumpeter has many fine things to say about the latter. . . . Undoubtedly Walras was a great economist, perhaps among the greatest. But is it really to be argued that the loss of his contribution, outstanding though it was, could outweigh the loss of Marshall's? . . . But I submit it is to get our perspective wrong if, in the laudable effort to rehabilitate . . . [Walras], we rate him as high as all that (Robbins, 1955, pp. 5–6).

This quotation is typical. Robbins sees brilliance in Schumpeter's handling of the English classicists, '. . . It was a stroke of expository genius . . . to make Senior's fundamental propositions the peg on which to hang his central analysis of the Classical position . . .' (Robbins, 1955, p. 10). But genius and brilliance are not the same as good judgement and discretion.

After such judgements, what can we say? What we can say is the obvious; Schumpeter's *tours de horizon* are monumental because they are epistemological rather than social sciences oriented. And if his forest overwhelms and at times his trees are only suggested in a vague romantic or Wagnerian way, the record shows that when he wanted to he could get down to specific cases. When he was at his best he was a Renaissance man turned economist.

Chairs are ultimately named for men rich in fortune or vision. As for the latter, if after time has lapsed and the errors of judgement and the small elements of the human personality have been forgotten, if the cruelties intentional and otherwise have been forgiven, and if there remains something in the form of a large intellectual pyramid and something that manifests repeatedly brilliance in several of its many forms, then Chairs like this one are endowed. And it was because Schumpeter had these qualities that we are here today.

REFERENCES

Cossa, L. (1891) *An Introduction to the Study of Political Economy*. Revised by the author and translated from the Italian by Dyer, L. London and New York: Macmillan.

Gide, P. H. C. and Rist, C. (1915) *A History of Economic Doctrines from the Time of the Physiocrats to the Present Day*. Translated from the second French edition by Richards, R. Boston and London.

Hutchison, T. (1977) *Knowledge and Ignorance in Economics*. Chicago: University of Chicago Press.
Kuznets, S. (1955) *History of Economic Analysis:* a review article. *History of Economic Thought*, **15**, 323–34.
Malthus, T. R. (1820) *Principles of Political Economy*. Paris and London.
Mill, J. S. (1848) *Principles of Political Economy*.
Mitchell, W. C. (1967–69) *Types of Economic Theory: From Mercantilism to Institutionalism* (Ed.) Dorfman, J. New York: Kelley.
Mitchell, W. C. and Burns, A. F. (1946) *Measuring Business Cycles*. New York: National Bureau of Economic Research.
Nussbaum, F. L. (1954) Review of *History of Economic Analysis*. *American Economic Review*, **60** (October), 62–64.
Ricardo, D. (1817) *Principles of Political Economy and Taxation*. London.
Robbins, L. (1955) Schumpeter's *History of Economic Analysis*. *Quarterly Journal of Economics*, **69** (February), 1–22.
Roll, E. (1938) *A History of Economic Thought*. London: Faber and Faber.
Schumpeter, J. A. (1908) *The Nature and Main Content of Theoretical Economics. (Das Wesen und der Hauptinhalt der Theoretischen Nationalökonomie)*. Leipzig.
Schumpeter, J. A. (1912) *The Theory of Economic Development*. English translation, 1934. Cambridge, MA: Harvard University Press.
Schumpeter, J. A. (1914) *Epochen der Dogmen- und Methodengeschichte*. Tübingen. 2nd Edition, 1924. Tübingen. Translated into English, 1954, by Aris, R. as *Economic Doctrine and Method: A Historical Sketch*. New York: Oxford University Press.
Schumpeter, J. A. (1951) *The Essays of J. A. Schumpeter* (Ed.) Clemence, R. V. Cambridge, MA: Addison-Wesley.
Schumpeter, J. A. (1951) *Ten Great Economists: From Marx to Keynes*. New York: Oxford University Press.
Schumpeter, J. A. (1954) *History of Economic Analysis* (Ed. from manuscript) Schumpeter, E. B. New York: Oxford University Press.
Shackle, G. L. S. (1967) *The Years of High Theory: Invention and Tradition in Economic Thought, 1926–1939*. Cambridge: Cambridge University Press.
Smith, A. (1759) *The Theory of Moral Sentiments*. London.
Smith, A. (1776) *An Inquiry into the Nature and Causes of the Wealth of Nations*. London.
Stigler, G. J. (1954) Schumpeter's *History of Economic Analysis*. *Journal of Political Economy*, **62** (August), 344–45.
Viner, J. (1954) Schumpeter's *History of Economic Analysis:* a review article. *American Economic Review*, **44** (December), 894–910.

Chapter Ten

Joseph A. Schumpeter as Minister of Finance of the First Republic of Austria, March 1919–October 1919

EDUARD MÄRZ

JOSEPH A. Schumpeter held in 1919, for little more than half a year, the post of the Austrian Minister of Finance or, as it was called at that time, the State Secretary of Finance. It can be safely stated that the young professor of economics was excellently prepared for assuming this position. Shortly before the outbreak of war, before he had reached the age of 30—the 'age of sacred fertility', as he was to call it later—he had written two of his most brilliant works that demonstrated his profound knowledge of economic theory as well as his talent for opening up as yet unexplored theoretical territory.[1] During the war years he studied the sociological and financial problems of the conflict between the great powers which sapped to the utmost their material as well as their moral powers of resistance. He summarized his conclusions in two essays which, I believe, were largely responsible for his nomination as minister of the Renner government in the spring of 1919 (Schumpeter, 1918, 1919).

The desperate economic and financial plight of the Republic of Austria during her first years of existence has been extensively recorded.[2] Here, I can confine myself to a few salient facts. In the first few months of 1919 weekly meat consumption in Vienna amounted to no more than 400 000 kg, which

[1] Schumpeter's early theoretical works are *Das Wesen und der Hauptinhalt der theoretischen Nationalökonomie* (1908) and *Theorie der wirtschaftlichen Entwicklung* (1912).

[2] Some of the relevant works are Bauer (1923), Gulick (1948), Cratz and Schüller (1930), Kreissler (1970) and Strong (1939).

constituted a bare 10 per cent of the average consumption of the last pre-war year (see Goode, 1920, p. 4).[3] The daily bread ration of 165 g, i.e. approximately six ounces, which the Viennese people were apportioned during the last war year, was gradually increased until it reached in August 1919 the substantially higher but still insufficient quantity of 235 g per day. In the autumn the bread ration had to be reduced, once again, and varied in December of the same year between 100 and 170 g (Goode, 1920, p. 6). The Allied Relief Administration estimated that the Viennese derived from their daily food rations during the critical period of spring and summer 1919 no more than 1270 calories instead of the required minimim of 2300 calories (Goode, 1920, p. 7). The situation in the provinces was somewhat more favourable than in Vienna.

The critical situation of the year 1919 resulted from several causes. The harvest of the last war year was even more inadequate than the notoriously poor harvests of the previous years. The difficulties arising from low grain stocks were aggravated by the fact that the new national states, soon after coming into existence, put exports of foodstuffs and coal under severe restrictions. Again, the blockade of the Allied Powers which had generally been expected to be lifted after the end of hostilities remained in force until well into the spring of 1919. Lastly, there was the suddenly asserted aversion of the agrarian provinces *vis-à-vis* Vienna which were only disposed to supply the capital city with foodstuffs on the basis of strict reciprocity.[4]

The severe shortage of coal not only augmented the suffering of the urban population, but led to the stoppage of the great majority of the industrial and transport enterprises of the country. The curtailment of production due to the scarcity of coal, the sudden halt of the manufacture of arms, and the influx of war veterans into the labour market caused a steady increase of unemployment. In December 1918, according to an official count, unemployment stood at 46 203 persons. Two months later the corresponding figure was well above 162 000 persons, of whom two-thirds lived in Vienna. In May 1919 unemployment attained the unprecedented level of more than 186 000 persons (Palla, 1920).

Suffering on such an enormous scale soon undermined the faith of the people in the viability of the new state. Thus discussion got under way which divided the country in two hostile camps and weakened the moral resistance

[3] The turnover of the black market is not included in the above figure. It must have been quite considerable in certain periods. In the spring of 1919, Walther Federn estimated that one-quarter of the meat consumption was met from illegal sources (see Federn, 1919a).

[4] There were frequent references in the newspapers to these incidents. To cite one characteristic instance: in its issue of 7 February 1919 the *Volkswirt* reported that the Province of Oberösterreich had stopped all exports of foodstuffs to other provinces including Vienna.

of its inhabitants against foreign influences. Closely associated with the problem of viability was another, and hardly less important problem, viz. the socioeconomic orientation of the country. Under the influence of the October Revolution in Russia and the social upheaval in neighbouring Hungary, large segments of the Austrian working class clamoured for a fundamental reform of the existing social order. The Social Democratic members of the government took account of these demands by instituting a so-called 'Socialization Commission', which was composed in equal parts of socialist as well as conservative politicians. The Commission was to make a thorough study of the conditions, possibilities and perspectives of socializing the Austrian economy. After the revolutionary emotions had calmed down in the summer and autumn of 1919, the Socialization Commission vanished from the political scene without having made a visible impact upon the prevailing economic order.[5]

The desperate financial plight of the Austrian state during World War I had inspired Schumpeter to make the following comment:

> . . . The financial history of a nation must be seen as an essential part of its general history: The destiny of nations is decisively affected by the economic blood-letting, which the public needs require, and by the way in which the results of this procedure are employed. The immediate impact of the financial requirements and of the financial policies of the state upon the further development of the economy and thereby upon all social and cultural modes of life is in certain periods of history the key to the understanding of all principal social trends. . . . (Schumpeter, 1918, p. 6).

The acute emergency of the year 1919 was reflected, of course, in the key figures of the state budget. During the first six months of 1919 only two-thirds of total expenditures could be covered by tax revenue. The ensuing deficit had to be financed through the issue of fiduciary central bank money, a practice initiated during the war and largely responsible for the ever-accelerating pace of inflation. In 1919 and the following three years the Austrian government continued to rely on the printing presses for the financing of its principal needs.

The unbalanced state of the budget was due primarily to four items: first, the interest and amortization requirements of the Austro–Hungarian war debt; secondly, the funds needed for the support of the unemployed; thirdly, the food subsidies which resulted from the difference between the price for food when acquired by the government and the price actually paid for by the

[5] The 'Socialization Commission' was created by an act of parliament, 14 March 1919. It was composed equally of socialist and conservative members of parliament.

consumer; fourthly, the financial means for the maintenance of a state bureaucracy tailored to the needs of a great empire as well as to the enormous duties accruing from four years of total war.

It seemed at first that the financial obligations which the new Austria had inherited from its imperial predecessor were far more onerous than the emergency expenditures for food and for the unemployed. In the spring of 1919 the Finance Ministry had to appropriate the amount of 530 million crowns to meet interest and amortization payments (Federn, 1919b). The burden grew, however, progressively lighter as a result of a long drawn-out inflationary process, especially since the authorities refused to consider the full or partial valorization of all war and pre-war debts by proclaiming the principle 'crown remains crown'. Again, expenditures for the state bureaucracy constituted a continually shrinking part of total budgetary outlays, for unlike other professional groups government employees were unable to raise their incomes in line with the steadily rising price level.

Expenditures arising out of the financial assistance of the unemployed were at first no less onerous than interest and amortization payments. An amount of 500 million crowns had to be spent on the unemployed from the middle of November 1918 until the beginning of May 1920, i.e. for a period of roughly one and a half years. However, an amount of similar magnitude was required to meet the food subsidies for the comparatively short period from July to December 1919 (Pribram, 1921). Thus it became evident at a rather early date that the food subsidies constituted by far the heaviest fiscal burden. To preserve or abolish this expensive method of subsidizing the standard of life of the great masses became one of the most explosive policy issues.

The provisional government which ruled Austria after the collapse of the monarchy was hopeful at first that it could cope with the financial crisis by traditional fiscal measures especially in regard to expenditures such as food subsidies and unemployment insurance which were considered to be of an emergency nature. As far as the public debt was concerned, which had assumed astronomic proportions towards the end of the war,[6] unorthodox methods of redemption were increasingly ventilated. During the war years proposals had been made by both conservative and progressive economists which provided for the most far-reaching encroachment upon existing property relationships. On the right, two finance ministers, Dr Alexander Spitzmüller and his successor, Dr Wimmer, advocated the imposition of a

[6] The war debt of the Western half of the monarchy amounted to 58 billion crowns. After making allowance for additional obligations of the Austrian government resulting from purchases of war materials and other war-related expenditures, Paul Grünwald (1919) arrived at the much higher figure of 65 billion crowns.

broadly conceived levy on property. On the left, Dr Rudolf Goldscheid, sometimes referred to as the first sociologist in the fields of financial administration and policy-making, insisted that the public debt, the greatest liability of the nation, be transformed into its greatest asset by using it as a key to socialization. By the transfer of a considerable part of the productive capital into public property the state could become the greatest share-owner of the nation, whereby two objectives could be achieved: first, the financial position of the state could be consolidated; and secondly, political control by its democratic organs could be expanded into economic control. An important step in extending democracy could thereby be taken. Goldscheid was thus the only leading financial theorist who intended to use the great, once-and-for-all levy on property for ambitious objectives of social engineering (see Goldscheid, 1976).

Schumpeter, too, had published in the last year of the war a widely read essay in which he advocated a rigorous capital levy. In contrast to Goldscheid, he did not aim, however, at any change in existing property relations. What he did want to accomplish through such a radical measure was somewhat less ambitious, but still vitally important: the balancing of the budget by eliminating the greater part of the public debt. Schumpeter added after analysing the merits of a capital levy somewhat wistfully that no matter how desirable such a course might be, it could nevertheless prove futile unless pursued by a popular government capable of overcoming the predictably strong forces of resistance. In concluding his article, Schumpeter (1918, p. 45) spelled out the characteristics of the political leader who would be called upon to conceive and put into operation a programme of such scope: 'A man who is to cope with such a task requires genuine political as well as financial talent—and that glamour of word and action which commands the trust of the people'. It must be assumed that Schumpeter included among the candidates for the position of the finance minister of the first post-war cabinet his own person who indeed exhibited some of the characteristics enumerated in the article.

The State Secretary of Finance of the first Renner cabinet was, however, Mr Steinwender, a member of the Pan-German Party, who had little professional training and less experience, and consequently attempted to resolve the singular financial crisis by traditional fiscal means. Schumpeter became a member of the second Renner cabinet which was formed in March 1919 after an impressive victory of the Social Democratic Party at the national election in the preceding month. His main sponsor was Otto Bauer, the prominent socialist politician and theorist, who had met him as a student at Vienna University, and had regarded him since then as a competent, creative economist, thoroughly conversant with the ideas of socialism. Moreover, the public advocacy of a capital levy by Schumpeter had undoubtedly won him the sympathies of Bauer and other prominent socialist leaders.

Soon after assuming his new duties, Schumpeter informed the public of the main features of his reform programme. Its principal points were: first, the great capital levy, which was mainly designed to eliminate the war debt;[7] second, the stabilization of the exchange rate of the Austrian crown[8] (Schumpeter took, however, pains to emphasize in this context that he had no intention of re-establishing the old parity of the crown); third, the founding of a new central bank which was to pursue a lending policy independent of the state;[9] fourth, a stronger reliance on indirect taxation so that large strata of the population be given the opportunity to make an adequate contribution towards balancing the budget; fifth, though by no means last, the re-establishment of conditions under which Austrian industry could become creditworthy, once again. In a speech before a select audience at the University of Vienna the new minister pointed out that 'the provision of foreign credits for Austrian industry was a task that the state must assume in the most resolute fashion'.[10]

The problem of procuring credits, especially abroad, made it necessary, for obvious reasons, to take a clear decision about the extent of the socialization measures which had been debated with increasing intensity since the beginning of the year. As far as the socialization issue was concerned, Schumpeter underwent an amazingly rapid change of mind. On 20 March, i.e. shortly after assuming office, the minister made a public statement before the press, which largely reflected the point of view adopted by the Social Democratic Party. 'We shall have to intervene on a massive scale in the private economy. Socialization is the decisive issue of our time. It is quite hopeless to believe that this idea will be a passing fad. We shall have to make efforts to realize it, and we shall have to travel sufficiently far in this direction so that left of us there remains little to be socialized. Whatever remains outside the scope of socialization should be administered freely by the private economy'.[11] On 26 April, five weeks after his peremptory statement on socialization, Schumpeter explained to an audience at the University of Vienna, in the speech referred to above, that it might prove necessary in the interest of

[7] Das Programm des Staatssekretärs Schumpeter, *Neue Freie Presse, Der Economist*, 20 March 1919.

[8] Das Programm des neuen Staatssekretärs für Finanzen (from an interview), *Neue Freie Presse*, 16 March 1919.

[9] *Neue Freie Presse*, 19 March 1919.

[10] *Neue Freie Presse*, 27 April 1919.

[11] Staatssekretär Schumpeter über die wirtschaftlichen Aufgaben der Zukunft, *Neue Freie Presse, Der Economist*, 21 March 1919.

opening up avenues of capital import to steer a more moderate course in matters of socialization. The relevant passage reads as follows:

> We are confronted with the task of reconstruction. It would be possible, if only at a considerable cost in terms of social friction and unrest, to socialize the whole economy. I have to admit that from a professional point of view I regard such a step with a good deal of sympathy. The other option open to us is a radical, decisive, but *limited* socialization measure affecting certain industries and enterprises but permitting the rest of the economy to operate in its usual manner. For the latter alternative a number of arguments can be marshalled which, one is inclined to believe, must be considered compelling, especially the necessity of important capital from abroad, which would not be available—or not available in sufficient quantity—to a socialized economy.[12]

With his plea for 'limited socialization measures' Schumpeter made it clear that his views on socialization ought not to be identified with those of Otto Bauer—and his audience, it is known, was quick to recognize the defiant undertone in his plea (see Fellner, 1954).

While the principle of the capital levy for the purpose of the redemption of the public debt was generally accepted, the question of its extent and of its social significance remained highly controversial. Another factor which delayed the formulation of its definite version was the total lack of information concerning the economic clauses of the peace treaty which were still hotly disputed in a Paris suburb. There was also much internal opposition to the capital levy especially among the representatives of the peasantry, who were determined to defend their followers against any and all encroachment on their property.

In the meantime the major part of current expenditures had to be covered by short-term treasury bonds which were placed with the commercial banks, but eventually discounted by the Central Bank. The funding of this quickly growing debt according to well established wartime practices proved impossible in view of the unsettled political situation. But the Austro-Hungarian Bank which had survived the collapse of the monarchy encountered growing resistance in pursuing its inflationary course. It had been forced—under pressure of the new national states—to widen the composition of its leading organ by members from all parts of the defunct monarchy. The representatives of the new states demanded that the Bank introduce a rigorously anti-inflationary course, above all that it cease to make advances on imperial war bonds as had been the practice during the war years (cf. Rasin, 1923). It may appear strange that the Austro-Hungarian Bank insisted

[12] *Neue Freie Presse*, 27 April 1919.

on honouring its obligations *vis-à-vis* the owners of war bonds. On the whole this was not a time when public authorities put particular emphasis on redeeming the promises of their predecessors. The policy of the Bank becomes more intelligible, however, if one considers the special interests of the new Austria. As was generally known, the German-speaking people of the monarchy held a disproportionately high proportion of the Austro–Hungarian war debt, whereas most of the other peoples held small amounts of war debt, and had preferred to accumulate bank notes instead. By insisting that the Bank continue to make advances on the war debt, whose value seemed increasingly dubious with each passing day, the Governor protected of course the interests of his Austrian compatriots. On the other hand, when the representatives of the new national states attempted to prevent the Bank from following an inflationary policy by generously lending money against Austro–Hungarian bonds, they had the interests of their fellow-citizens at heart (see von Mises, 1919).

The inflationary policy of the Austro–Hungarian Bank left the national states little choice but to take a course towards an early separation of their currency from the Austrian crown. There can be little doubt, however, that they would have done this in any event, since none of the new states would have considered itself as independent of the financial domination of Vienna as long as the former capital of the monarchy remained responsible for the monetary policy of the Danube basin. The first state which turned its back on the Austro–Hungarian Bank was Yugoslavia. Between 8 and 20 January 1919 the banknotes of the Bank, circulating on Yugoslav territory, were officially counted and stamped. Czechoslovakia followed suit between 3 and 7 March 1919. With the Czechs and the Yugoslavs seceding from the Austro–Hungarian Bank, economic cooperation among the Danubian peoples within the framework of a currency union came to a definite close. Austria, which had shown a genuine interest in the preservation of the union, now had no other option than to follow the example of Yugoslavia and Czechoslovakia. The separation of the Austrian currency was effected between 12 and 24 March 1919.[13]

Otto Bauer, who held the post of State Secretary for Foreign Affairs, was the principal exponent of 'Anschluss' both within the cabinet and the top échelons of the Socialist Party. He considered the break-up of the currency union, the last economic link between the one-time Danubian partners, a suitable occasion for taking the first step towards Anschluss. In March 1919, when Austria severed its links to the currency union, Bauer visited Berlin, and proposed to the German government that the two countries establish a

[13] For a brief account of the various phases of the currency separation, see Kerschagl (1920). For a review of the Czech separation measures, see Federn (1919c).

common currency at the earliest possible moment. The Reichsbank, so Bauer suggested, should grant a loan to a new central bank in Austria which would enable it to exchange German marks for Austrian crowns at a fixed rate. The German government declined Bauer's offer by pointing out that it was not advisable to saddle the Reichsbank with a burden of unknown proportions before the conditions of the peace treaty became known (Bauer, 1923, p. 144). It appears likely, however, that the reasons why the German negotiators took a negative attitude towards plans aiming at Anschluss at this critical moment were primarily political (Schausberger, 1978).

The idea of a currency union between Germany and Austria was, however, not entirely dropped, but received further attention at meetings of a bilateral financial committee which, on 19 April 1919, took the solemn decision that Austria introduce the German mark as its sole standard of value on 1 January of next year.[14] The plan, which was kept secret at first, but soon leaked out to the press, revealed a state of mind on the part of its sponsors strangely remote from the world of 'Realpolitik'. Schumpeter, who during the war years had sceptically viewed all efforts to form a closely knit economic union between Germany and the Habsburg monarchy (see Verosta, 1976, p. 373ff.), showed little sympathy for similar plans, even though circumstances had since then drastically changed. Soon after taking office as Minister of Finance he argued, if only indirectly, against Anschluss by pleading for the preservation of Vienna as a financial centre of the Danube basin and for close economic cooperation among the successor states. In a speech before the Austrian press, Schumpeter addressed himself particularly to the Czechs:

> Austria and especially Vienna shall have to remain financial centres for a considerable period of time . . . To make a national economy self-sufficient is only feasible within rather narrow limits; it is far easier to accomplish this politically than economically. We shall have to find eventually a *modus vivendi*. The frontiers of future development can be recognized even today with great clarity. In the new organism Vienna will continue to function as the financial centre, and political separation will affect the purely economic relations only marginally.[15]

Ignaz Seipel, a leading conservative politician, who, as the evidence indicates, used the pro-Anschluss agitation as a ploy with which the Allied Powers could be manoeuvred into granting concessions at the peace conference, had established close contacts with the Finance Minister in the spring of 1919, as Professor Verosta reports in an interesting article. Seipel made the following revealing commentary in a letter to Heinrich Lammasch, the one-time Prime

[14] Finanzarchiv Vienna, Zl. 691/Präs. 1919.

[15] Staatssekretär Schumpeter über die wirtschaftlichen Aufgaben der Zukunft, *Neue Freie Presse*, 21 March 1919.

Minister of Austria–Hungary, who is likely to have introduced his young admirer Schumpeter to Seipel: 'I am in close contact with Schumpeter, who is very brave . . . The policies of Otto Bauer have been shown to be absurd. In the whole of Austria there is an undercurrent of opinion that Anschluss will come to naught' (Verosta, 1976, p. 401).

Seipel's letter is dated 1 May 1919. His moral support must have encouraged Schumpeter to question ever more openly the wisdom of Bauer's Anschluss strategy. On 8 May Schumpeter gave an interview to an evening paper, the *Neues 8-Uhr-Blatt*, in which he conceded that Anschluss could not be prevented indefinitely; at the same time, he pronounced the warning that Anschluss, if carried out, would require great sacrifices, and that as a consequence one would have to demand from Germany 'far-reaching concessions'. The main point of the interview must be seen, however, in the statement: 'Our safety lies in our peaceful intercourse with all states, and especially with our immediate neighbours' (Verosta, 1976, p. 401ff.).

Bauer's reaction to Schumpeter's interview was a long letter which is reprinted in its entirety in the afore-mentioned article of Verosta. Here it will suffice to quote some of the key passages: Bauer reproached his colleague for having expressed opinions which were bound to weaken the bargaining position of the Austrian delegation at the peace conference. He then added, with some justification no doubt, that it had not been customary heretofore for statements about foreign policy to emanate from sources other than the competent ministry unless prior consultation had taken place between the foreign minister and his otherwise unauthorized colleague: 'If you believe my policy to be incorrect', so Bauer stated literally, 'the right method of procedure would be to submit the controversial subject to the cabinet for discussion'. In concluding his letter, Bauer held out an olive branch by emphasizing his readiness to resolve their differences through informal discussions (Verosta, 1976, p. 402ff.).[16]

It is not known whether such a discussion took place. At any rate, Schumpeter did not seem greatly impressed by Bauer's warnings. Around the middle of May he established contact with the British financial expert, Sir Francis Oppenheimer, who visited Vienna at the request of his government. According to Oppenheimer, Schumpeter acquainted him with an economic reform plan which provided for long-term credits from the West and gave the Allied nations sweeping powers of control over the Austrian economy. Above all, the management of the central bank, to be established in the near future, should be entrusted to the Western powers with the proviso that the sensibilities of the Austrian people be duly considered.[17]

[16] Otto Bauer's letter is dated 11 May 1919.

[17] Cable of Oppenheimer to Keynes, 18 May 1919, PRO FO 608229/10960 (cf. Hoffmann 1977).

Three weeks after his sensational statement to the *Neues 8-Uhr-Blatt* Schumpeter held a major speech before the Viennese Association of Commerce and Industry (*Weiner Handels- und Industrieverein*) in which he gave a detailed account of the economic policy to be followed in the coming years. There are some indications that Schumpeter had consulted beforehand with some of the leading experts of the City, since his speech reflected to a high degree the opinion of the financial community. In the beginning Schumpeter emphasized, once again, that the states of the Danube basin depended on close economic cooperation, whether they wanted it or not. He therefore advocated trade and currency agreements among them of one form or another. He then took up the hotly discussed subject of the viability of the Austrian state, and stressed that national independence, even though imposed from outside, did not mean economic catastrophe. 'One must not think', he said literally, 'that a country in order to survive economically must possess all essential raw materials within its own frontiers. True, we must have coal, but even if coal were available in Austrian territory, our industry would still have to purchase it, and this is all it has to do when importing it from Ostrava [the great Czech coal basin]'. The key passage of the speech is to be found in his reference to Vienna as a financial centre: 'Again, the neighbouring countries cannot exist without us or without our financial mediation. It will continue to be the function of Vienna to finance the commerce of the countries, formerly belonging to the Monarchy, with the rest of the world . . . Only the Viennese banks can act as reliable depositories of foreign capital imports'. In the end, he reiterated that the socialization measures should be swiftly taken and limited in scope. Nationalization rather than socialization should be aimed at, for this sort of restructuring of the economy would be digestible by the capitalist system, and would not noticeably impede the rebuilding of the Austrian economy.[18]

Schumpeter's speech must be interpreted as an open challenge to Otto Bauer, whose conciliatory gesture was almost flippantly ignored. The defiant attitude resulted no doubt from the strong, and still growing support which Schumpeter had found among his conservative cabinet colleagues and some representatives of Western financial interests. Bauer, on the other hand, was now determined to bring about Schumpeter's political downfall at the first possible occasion. In a letter to Karl Renner dated 31 May Bauer evaluated the work of some prominent members of the government: 'Fink is loyal, as far as I can judge; Eldersch develops quite satisfactorily. Schumpeter, however, carries on with his intrigues, I shall do nothing for the time being, but after the conclusion of the peace treaty it will be inevitable to force his resigna-

[18] Staatssekretär Dr Schumpeter über die industrielle Zukunft Österreichs, *Neue Freie Presse*, 31 May 1919.

tion'.[19] Bauer was to realize quite soon that his conflict with the Finance Minister had not yet reached its climax.[20]

In the meantime the 'Socialization Commission' under the chairmanship of Otto Bauer continued with its deliberations without making much visible progress. On 22 May the government announced, under the prodding of Bauer, that it had decided to nationalize at an opportune moment the iron and steel works, the power stations, the mining industry, the great forests and certain sectors of the timber industry.[21] This programme of *partial* nationalization corresponded to Bauer's 'first step' of his long-term socialization strategy outlined in his famous pamphlet *The Road to Socialism*. Moreover, it did not contradict Schumpeter's repeatedly pronounced, more limited nationalization scheme.

Jodok Fink and other conservative members of the government could hardly dare to oppose the socialist nationalization plan openly at a moment when the Austrian working class was deeply agitated by the seizure of power by the Hungarian Communist Party led by Bela Kun. In this predicament they had to resort to dilatory tactics which were considerably facilitated by the resistance put forth by the provincial *diets* and other governing bodies to all initiatives and directives emanating from Vienna. But the final blow against the nationalization scheme of 22 May fell when the Alpine Montangesellschaft, the greatest Austrian enterprise, and the sole owner of its considerable iron ore reserves, was taken over by Italian industrial and banking interests.

There was a natural tendency towards the sale of industrial and other assets abroad at a time when the Austrian economy was deficient of foodstuffs and other vital necessities of life (Ausch, 1968). The influx of foreign capital was further enhanced when Austrian industrialists made great efforts to attract foreign partners in the certain knowledge that their government would not venture to nationalize enterprises which were owned to some extent by Western capital. Italy took a special interest in the Austrian iron industry for it seemed to provide the material basis for the iron-starved heavy industry of the Po region. In the spring and summer of 1919 the shares of the Alpine Montangesellschaft could be acquired very cheaply as a result of special circumstances besides the low exchange rate of the Austrian crown and the depressed atmosphere at the Vienna stock exchange: the Prager Eisenindustrie Gesellschaft, the leading steel manufacturer of Czechoslovakia, which

---

19 H.H.u.St.A.Vienna, NPA, Präs. K.261, Nachlass Bauer.

20 Renner, too, reacted negatively to the public utterances of the Finance Minister as is evident from a cable sent to Vienna from the Paris peace conference; cf. H.H.St.A., NPA, K.349, 8 June 1919.

21 *Volkswirt*, 31 May 1919, Kalendarium, p. 642.

had hitherto held substantial shares in Alpine, now disposed of its entire holdings and contributed thereby to the further decline of these formerly highly valued industrial assets.

The purchase of Alpine shares by Italian interests was negotiated by the Vienna banking firm of Richard Kola & Co. Kola, who specialized in foreign exchange dealings, had been commissioned by the Ministry of Finance to procure Western currency on behalf of the Austrian state. In the spring and summer of 1919 he was instrumental in the sale of 200 000 shares of the Alpine Montangesellschaft to a Milanese banking house which was backed by the well known Fiat works. The foreign currency yield resulting from the transaction was put at the disposal of the Ministry of Finance which required foreign exchange for the procurement of foodstuffs and raw materials (Kola, 1922). The repeated purchases of Alpine shares at the Vienna stock exchange did not remain unnoticed and resulted in a speculative boom which spread to other industrial values as well.

In its issue of 20 August 1919 the *Arbeiter-Zeitung*, the chief organ of the Social Democratic Party, accused the Minister of Finance of having indirectly supported the transactions of Mr Kola by an attitude of passive acceptance: 'The Ministry of Finance would have been in a position to stop this speculative orgy. And indeed, a circumspect and active financial administration would have found the means of preventing it'. And in another passage the author of the article (most probably the editor of the paper) implied that the transfer of Alpine shares to foreign interests might have been motivated by anti-socialist designs: 'We admit', so the author continued, 'that the sale of Austrian securities to foreigners may be inevitable under certain conditions. As long as we are incapable of paying for foodstuffs and raw materials from abroad with products of our own labour, we shall have no choice but to trade for them our industrial assets and natural resources. But even if one concedes that much, one remains doubtful whether Alpine shares had to be sold to foreigners since the Alpine Montangesellschaft figures among the first enterprises to be socialized'.

Otto Bauer underscored this charge some years later in his well known book *Die österreichische Revolution* (1923): 'Schumpeter supported this operation [of Richard Kola] although he knew that we had decided to socialize the Alpine Montangesellschaft. He supported it without consulting the other members of the cabinet . . . This action on the part of Schumpeter provoked a violent conflict inside the coalition government during which Schumpeter solicited and obtained the support of the Viennese Christian Social Party members' (Bauer, 1923, p. 178ff.). Schumpeter's reply to this charge came many years later in two letters addressed to Professor Gulick, wherein he categorically declared that he had neither authorized nor sanctioned the sale of the Alpine shares. In a further remark he made it clear, however, that socialization measures under the prevailing circumstances would have only increased the difficulties of a difficult situation, and that their prevention would have been a service to the country, the government and, above all, to the Social Democratic Party (Gulick, 1948, p. 141).

Bauer's accusation that Schumpeter had supported Kola's transactions, in the restricted sense of having passively submitted to them, is, however, borne out by a letter of the Finance Minister addressed to the State Chancellor, Dr Renner, shortly after the publication of the denunciatory article in the *Arbeiter-Zeitung*, referred to above. I confine myself in the following to a few excerpts from the rather long-winded letter:

> At the end of June 1919 I received the surprising letter . . . from the banker Richard Kola that he could put at my disposal the amount of 15 million lira, which he had obtained from an Italian party for the purchase of Alpine stock. Although I was pleased at the repletion of our exchange reserves by this unexpected capital influx, I expressed the wish that the purchases should not alter the majority position of our native shareholders. In the beginning of August Mr Kola provided me on two occasions with the amount of 5 million lira for similar transactions. Again, I prevailed on Mr Kola not to persist in the purchases . . . I wish to point out in this context that I consider it advantageous if there is some interest abroad in our securities, and if foreigners participate in our security trade. In the event that our securities were to meet with no interest abroad, and would cease to be an object of foreign transactions, the Austrian crown would be helplessly exposed to every attack from abroad.

Schumpeter concluded his long letter with a reference to his conservative programme of financial reform and with an appeal to the loyal attitude of the chancellor:

> I know my conservative programme of financial reform and of the smooth and steady reconstruction of our economy without disruption of the social order is being subjected to formidable, and I am ready to admit, deeply felt objections. I hold the opinion that our country can be led out of its impasse without the violent disturbance of its financial and economic foundations. If others do not deem it possible, the ensuing conflict should be fought in a realistic and political manner . . .[22]

After a careful reading of Schumpeter's letter to Renner one is left with the impression that his repeated pleas to Kola that he discontinue the sale of Alpine shares to Italian interests were stated with very little conviction, for it

[22] Undated letter of the Finance Minister, Schumpeter, to the State Chancellor, Renner; H.H.u.St.A., AVA, Bundeskanzleramt, Präs., Korrespondenz Renner, Karton 65a.

seems hardly possible that the foreign exchange dealer, who acted on the authority of the Finance Ministry, would have ignored explicit orders. Schumpeter may have even intimated in his occasional meetings with Kola that the nationalization of the Alpine Montangesellschaft would be likely to increase the difficulties of a difficult situation, as he expressed it in the letter to Gulick, and that the prevention of such a contingency may be considered a patriotic deed. It is only fair to add that in tolerating the transactions of Mr Kola, Schumpeter may have acted in conformity with the intentions of the moderate wing of the Social Democratic Party which, as Renner once stated, did not aspire at the 'socialization of debts'. Considering this alignment of political forces, the nationalization of key industries, as advocated by Otto Bauer and his left-wing adherents, seems to have been a rather unrealistic programme even in the turbulent spring days of 1919. Schumpeter, two years later, wrote the epitaph on this historical episode: 'Full socialization as an immediate program has been no more than political phraseology both in Germany and Austria' (Schumpeter, 1921).

The conservative programme of financial reform, which Schumpeter mentioned in his letter to Renner, had been submitted to the public—in its rough outlines—soon after the assumption of office by the new Finance Minister. In the following months he repeatedly announced the preparation of a definitive version without actually publishing it, which made it appear as if he was slow in making up his mind about the details of the plan. But even his opponents had to admit that 'before the conclusion of the peace treaty the activities of the financial administration were narrowly circumscribed'.[23] In an article in the *Arbeiter-Zeitung* of 10 October 1919 Schumpeter was especially criticized for having failed to prepare a financial plan for the time immediately after the publication of the peace treaty. This criticism proved erroneous, however, for on 16 October, one day before resigning his office, the Minister did present the public with a comprehensive financial reform programme.[24]

The plan, a rather extensive document, does not differ essentially from the provisional programme which Schumpeter had announced more than six months earlier. Again, its focal point is the great capital levy, whose technical complexities are discussed in great detail. Schumpeter is aware of the grave burden which the levy would impose on the Austrian economy, and is prepared to exempt—at least temporarily—all enterprises which continue to employ as many people as before or during the war. More importantly, the plan provides for the temporary exemption from the levy of all persons and enterprises that are capable of putting at the disposal of the government substantial foreign credits. By utilizing the international reputation of its

[23] Der Fall Schumpeter, *Arbeiter-Zeitung*, 10 October 1919.

[24] Der Finanzplan des Staatssekretärs a.D. Dr Schumpeter, *Neue Freie Presse*, 18 October 1919.

citizens and enterprises the Austrian state, so Schumpeter believed, would be able to obtain sufficient foreign credit with which to cover its budget deficit and to stabilize its currency. It is highly questionable, however, whether this method of procuring foreign credit would have yielded positive results in 1919 and the following years. As late as 1925, Walther Federn, the leading Viennese financial writer and editor of the respected *Volkswirt* observed that 'only very few and internationally well known industrial enterprises in Austria have direct access to foreign credit. All others can only obtain it through the services, and with the guarantee, of one of the Vienna banks . . .' (Federn, 1925).

Schumpeter's reform programme contains two further important points: the establishment of a central bank, which must not be allowed to make advances to the government under whatever form or pretext; and the imposition of an indirect tax on the poorer strata of the population, which, according to Schumpeter, 'means nothing else but the extension of the income tax in the downward direction'. The capital levy should be used solely for the liquidation of the war debt; but even so, Schumpeter concedes, the main burden of the war and its tragic outcome would be borne by the 'rentier-class'. It would amount to self-deception, so the author concludes, 'if we did not face frankly the force of this overwhelming fact'.

There are a few passages in Schumpeter's report which are devoted to the problem of socialization. Even if one considers oneself an adherent of socialization, so he argues, one must admit that at the present moment, when the state needs foreign credit, socialization is likely to deter foreign creditors, rather than to attract them. On the other hand, the author does not preclude the possibility that socialized capital will attain creditworthiness in future years through systematic positive work and through real success.

Schumpeter ends his report on the following solemn note:

> the financial program is based on the conviction that we are able to help ourselves. The well-to-do citizens will have to put at the disposal of the state not only the major part of their wealth, but their credit and good name, so that the preservation of our economic order can be assured. The poorer classes must take upon themselves the full sacrifice of indirect taxation, which will enable the state to put lasting order into its finances without resorting to the issue of paper money. To the foreign powers we shall have to prove that we are prepared to help ourselves; only then will they be ready to extend to us their help.

Schumpeter's appeal fell on deaf ears. It soon became known from a report of the Viennese daily *Neue Freie Presse* that he had lost support among the ranks of the Christian Social Party, and that the latter was no longer united behind his financial plan.[25] His resignation was the logical result of his total political isolation. Today, we can only speculate as to why a considerable proportion of the conservative party so suddenly deserted him. It is most likely that his rigorous conception of the capital levy provoked resistance, especially among the rural representatives of the party. This can be inferred from a passage in the above-quoted article.[26] Moreover, his occasional flirtation with the idea of socialism may have cost him the sympathy of some influential conservative politicians.

It is hardly surprising that the *Neue Freie Presse* singled out Otto Bauer as the main adversary of Schumpeter's financial plan. Most certainly Bauer seized upon the programme to get rid of a cabinet colleague with whom he had crossed swords on several vital issues. But, so we may ask today, was Bauer well advised to deprive himself of the cooperation of a man who was the sole and only one among his 'bourgeois' colleagues to have taken up the problem of a capital levy with a great deal of expertise and unequivocally positive intentions? In 1919, so it appears, Bauer did not consider the capital levy, contrary to Schumpeter, a *conditio sine qua non* for the balancing of the budget and the stabilization of the currency. In his essay *The Road to Socialism* he advocated this measure for the sole purpose of compensating the former owners of socialized enterprises. Perhaps the proverbial straw to break the camel's back was Schumpeter's solemn warning, tacked onto his financial programme, to desist from socialization at a moment when the Austrian state needed foreign capital most urgently.

In conclusion we may state that the early withdrawal of the great economist from Austrian politics must be attributed to the fact that one of the dominating political parties considered his ideas too radical, while the other viewed them as too pragmatic, too wilful, and too hostile towards 'Anschluss'.

[25] Der Personenwechsel im Staatsamt für Finanzen, *Neue Freie Presse*, 9 October 1919.

[26] In the above-quoted article there is a reference to the sudden change in attitude towards Schumpeter on the part of Stöckler, the State Secretary for Agriculture.

REFERENCES

Ausch, K. (1968) *Als die Banken fielen*. p. 12. Vienna: Europa Verlag.

Bauer, O. (1923) *Die österreichische Revolution*. Werkausgabe, Vol. 2, 1976, Vienna: Europa Verlag.

Cratz, G. and Schüller, R. (1930) *Der wirtschaftliche Zusammenbruch Österreichs*. Vienna: Edition Hölder, Pickler, Tempsky.

Federn, W. (1919a) *Volkswirt*, 1 March, 373.

Federn, W. (1919b) Die finanzielle Liquidation der Monarchie in Deutsch–Österreichs Finanzen. *Volkswirt*, 31 May, 631ff.

Federn, W. (1919c) Die Währungstrennung und der Wert der Krone. *Volkswirt*, 15 February.

Federn, W. (1925) Die Kreditpolitik der Wiener Banken. *Geldwert und Stabilisierung in ihren Einflüssen auf die soziale Entwicklung in Österreich*, **169**, 69.

Fellner, F. (Ed.) (1954) *Das Politische Tagebuch Josef Redlichs*. Vol. 2, p. 342. Graz, Köln: Verlag Böhlau.

Goldscheid, R. (1976) Staatssozialismus oder Staatskapitalismus. In *Beiträge zur politischen Ökonomie der Staatsfinanzen* (Ed.) Hickel, R. Frankfurt: Edition Sulinkamp.

Goode, Sir William (1920) *Economic Conditions in Central Europe*. Cmd 641, Part II. London: HMSO.

Grünwald, P. (1919) Das Finanzsystem Deutschösterreichs. *Schriften des Vereins für Sozialpolitik*, **158**, 70.

Gulick, C. W. (1948) *Austria from Habsburg to Hitler*. Vol. 1. Beverley: University of California Press.

Hoffmann, R. (1977) Die wirtschaftlichen Grundlagen der britischen Österreichpolitik 1919. *Mitteilungen des österreichischen Staatsarchivs, Sonderdruck*, **30**, 268ff.

Kerschagl, R. (1920) *Die Währungstrennung in den National-Staaten*. Vienna: Manz Verlag.

Kola, R. (1922) *Rückblick ins Gestrige*. p. 247. Vienna: Europa Verlag.

Kreissler, F. (1970) *Von der Revolution zur Annexion*. Vienna: Rikola Verlag.

Mises, L. von (1919) Der Wiedereintritt Deutsch–Österreichs in das Deutsche Reich und die Währungsfrage. *Schriften des Vereins für Sozialpolitik*, **158**, 151ff.

Palla, E. (1920) Ein Jahr Arbeitslosenfürsorge in Österreich. *Nachrichten des Staatsamtes für soziale Verwaltung*, no. 21/22.

Pribram, K. (1921) Die Sozialpolitik im neuen Österreich. *Archiv für Sozialwissenschaft und Sozialpolitik*, **48**, 636.

Rasin, A. (1923) *Die Finanz- und Wirtschaftspolitik der Tschechoslowakei*. p. 151ff. München, Leipzig: Duncker & Humblot.

Schausberger, N. (1978) *Der Griff nach Österreich*. p. 68. Vienna: Verlag Jugend und Volk.

Schumpeter, J. A. (1908) *Das Wesen und der Hauptinhalt der theoretischen Nationalökonomie*. München, Leipzig: Duncker & Humblot.

Schumpeter, J. A. (1912) *Theorie der wirtschaftlichen Entwicklung*. Leipzig: Duncker & Humblot.

Schumpeter, J. A. (1918) *Die Krise des Steuerstaates*. Graz, Leipzig: In *Zeitfragen auf dem Gebiete der Soziologie*. Edition Leuschner & Lube.

Schumpeter, J. A. (1919) Zur Soziologie der Imperialismen. *Archiv für Sozialwissenschaft und Sozialpolitik*, **46**, 1–39.

Schumpeter, J. A. (1921) Sozialistische Möglichkeiten von heute. *Archiv für Sozialwissenschaft und Sozialpolitik*, **48** (part 2), 342.

Strong, D. F. (1939) *Austria, October 1918–March 1919. Transition from Empire to Republic*. New York: Columbia University Press.

Verosta, S. (1976) Josef Schumpeter gegen das Zollbündnis der Donaumonarchie mit Deutschland und gegen die Anschlusspolitik Otto Bauers (1916–1919). *Festschrift für Christian Broda*. Vienna: Europa Verlag.

Index

